POLITICS AND IDEOLOGY
IN THE AGE OF THE CIVIL WAR

Also by Eric Foner:

Free Soil, Free Labor, Free Men:
   The Ideology of the Republican Party
   Before the Civil War   (*1970*)

America's Black Past:
   A Reader in Afro-American History   (*edited, 1970*)

Nat Turner   (*edited, 1971*)

Tom Paine and Revolutionary America   (*1976*)

Politics and Ideology in the Age of the Civil War

ERIC FONER

OXFORD UNIVERSITY PRESS
Oxford   New York   Toronto   Melbourne

For
J. P. S.

Oxford University Press
Oxford   London   Glasgow
New York   Toronto   Melbourne   Wellington
Nairobi   Dar es Salaam   Cape Town
Kuala Lumpur   Singapore   Jakarta   Hong Kong   Tokyo
Delhi   Bombay   Calcutta   Madras   Karachi

First published by Oxford University Press, New York, 1980
First issued as an Oxford University Press paperback, 1981

Library of Congress Cataloging in Publication Data

Foner, Eric.
Politics and ideology in the age of the Civil War.

Includes bibliographical references and index.
1. United States—History—Civil War, 1861–1865—
Causes—Addresses, essays, lectures.   2. Slavery in the
United States—Anti-slavery movements—Addresses,
essays, lectures.   3. Reconstruction—Addresses, essays,
lectures.   I. Title.
E459.F67   973.7'11   80-13024
ISBN 0-19-502781-7
ISBN 0-19-502926-7 pbk.

Printing: 9 8 7 6 5 4 3 2 1

Printed in the United States of America

Contents

I Introduction 3

ORIGINS OF THE CIVIL WAR

II The Causes of the American Civil War: Recent
Interpretations and New Directions 15

III Politics, Ideology, and the Origins
of the American Civil War 34

AMBIGUITIES OF ANTI-SLAVERY

IV Abolitionism and the Labor Movement
in Ante-bellum America 57

V Racial Attitudes of the New York
Free Soilers 77

LAND AND LABOR AFTER THE CIVIL WAR

VI Reconstruction and the Crisis of Free
Labor 97

VII Thaddeus Stevens, Confiscation,
and Reconstruction 128

VIII Class, Ethnicity, and Radicalism
in the Gilded Age: The Land League
and Irish-America 150

Notes 201
Acknowledgments 241
Index 243

POLITICS AND IDEOLOGY
IN THE AGE OF THE CIVIL WAR

·❊{ O N E }❊·

Introduction

For historians of the American Civil War, the 1970s was a troubled decade. The success of *Roots* on television and in bookstores appeared to reflect an enormous popular interest in slavery and emancipation, the issues central to the sectional conflict. But within the discipline of history itself, the situation could not have been bleaker. At a time when the experiences of "ordinary" people became the central concern of historians, the fundamental reference point in the lives of nineteenth-century Americans was all but ignored.

Traditionally, the Civil War framed and provided unity to the inquiries of American historians. Works on slavery and abolition, on intellectual life and economic change, were pursued not simply for their own sake, but to shed light on the causes and consequences of the Civil War. To some extent, these subjects remained vital concerns in the 1970s; indeed, the outstanding body of new literature on the American past probably was that reexamining the South's "peculiar institution." But with few exceptions, it was the social or cultural aspects of slavery which now commanded attention, rather than slavery as a source of political and economic power and a fundamental cause of the Civil War.

The decline of Civil War studies was to some extent self-inflicted, for the subject had by the end of the 1950s reached a conceptual impasse. Discussions of the war's causes had too often resolved into a fruitless metaphysical debate over the problem of inevitability, while their single-minded focus on the sectional conflict had led nineteenth-century historians to ignore other aspects of the period—immigration and the history of women, for example—that bore little apparent relation to the slavery controversy. Those who viewed the Civil War as a great divide in American life often disregarded social and intellectual continuities spanning the decades of the nineteenth century. The study of the Civil War, in other words, was in need of a vigorous infusion of new ideas and approaches. Instead, the Civil War, once at the center stage of historical debate, had, by the end of the 1970s, been relegated to the wings. By 1980, a 500-page volume on historical writing in this country could leave this central concern of earlier generations of historians virtually unmentioned.[1]

The predicament of Civil War historians was more than a reflection of the overall crisis of academic history in the 1970s. It derived from an unprecedented redefinition of historical studies in which a traditional emphasis on institutions and events, politics and ideas, was superseded by a host of "social" concerns. To a large extent, this transformation was a by-product of the ferment of the sixties. Blacks—followed by women, "ethnics," and other groups—looked to history for a "usable past," while traditional political narratives—especially those of the then-dominant "consensus" school—proved unable to explain the reemergence of deep divisions in American life. At the same time, a new technology—the computer—made possible the analysis of vast amounts of quantitative data concerning those Americans who had not produced letters, diaries, speeches, and the other sources historians were accustomed to examining.

New methods, such as quantification, oral history, and demography, and a new purpose—recovering the history of ordinary Americans rather than the elite—defined what came to be called the "new social history." In place of conventional narratives of political and intellectual development, American historians now produced an abundance of works in the various subfields of social investigation: family history, ethnic history, labor history, the histories of sexuality, criminality, and childhood. There were community studies, urban studies, and social mobility studies. Many of these works were inspired not by traditional historical models, but by theories borrowed from allied social sciences. Frequently, they appeared in new journals devoted exclusively to the subdisciplines of social history. As historians intruded into the intimate lives of past generations of Americans, public events and institutions receded into the background. No alternative theory of politics emerged from the ferment within and outside the historical profession. If "the personal is political" was a slogan of the 1960s, "the historical is personal" described much of the historical writing of the seventies.

What was new about the new social history was not simply its innovations in methodology and subject matter, but its high standing within the profession and the insistence with which some of its practitioners pressed its claims. Until the 1960s, social history had been a catch-all for those subjects passed over by more conventional approaches. Often, it was yoked together with intellectual history in the single college course offering departing from a focus on politics. Then, in the seventies, political historians suddenly felt themselves beleaguered, their narrative works never referred to without the mildly patronizing adjective "traditional," their sources deprecated as "impressionistic," their concern with national public issues branded "elitist."

That the new history has broadened—indeed, revolutionized—our understanding of the American experience cannot be doubted. It has delved into realms hitherto all but ignored, and forced all historians to adopt a more critical posture toward their evidence, calling into question broad generalizations based on fragmentary data or the experience of a few eminent individuals. It has reintroduced a sense of complexity to the study of the American past, and destroyed the old "presidential synthesis" in which historical study was organized around the terms of office of elected leaders. American history has been revitalized by an infusion of the new perspectives of blacks, women, labor, and others.

Somehow, however, these advances did not add up to a coherent new vision of the American past. Indeed, what was most striking in the 1970s was the fragmentation of historical scholarship and the larger notion of social process. The broadening of historians' concerns went hand in hand with a narrowing of their vision and the result was often specialized, even trivial, inquiries. American society was divided and subdivided so completely that the ideal of re-creating history as a lived experience seemed more remote than ever. A few books did appear—one thinks of Anthony Wallace's reconstruction of the experience of Rockdale, Pennsylvania, during the industrial revolution—which transcended divisions between the public and private, political and social realms of experience, and saw social classes not in isolation from one another but enmeshed in a complex series of interrelationships. But E. J. Hobsbawm's call, at the beginning of the decade, for a shift from social history to a "history of society" remained largely unfulfilled.[2] One reason for the retreat from Civil War studies may be that events like the Civil War, which affected every facet of American life, are unintelligible if divided into the various subcategories of contemporary historical inquiry.

Older coherent visions of American history, ranging from Turner's frontier thesis to the consensus view of the 1950s, have been shattered, but no new synthesis has emerged to fill the void. Indeed, only a small number of historians continue to believe that a comprehensive view of the American past is possible. Those who do have generally looked beyond American historiography to European Marxist and *Annales* models for an integrated vision. (On the other hand, modernization theory, a home-grown approach, seems, after a brief vogue, to have fallen by the wayside, a victim of its own vagueness and determinism.) Most American historians, however, continue to mistrust theoretical formulations. For many, the need to integrate so many different "histories" has led to a retreat from notions of historical causation altogether. In her study of recent American history textbooks, Frances FitzGerald noted a pervasive confusion as to the causes of historical events. "Problems" appeared and disappeared, events simply happened, with no sense of systematic relationships or underlying causes. Moreover, individual actors seemed to have no discernible effect on the historical process. "There are no human agencies left," wrote FitzGerald, "only abstractions and passive verbs."[3]

The flight from theories of causation underscores the deep strain of empiricism so rooted in American culture, and reinforced among historians by the current vogue of quantification. Indispensable as a tool of historical inquiry, quantitative analysis of statistical data often gained the upper hand in the 1970s, determining the questions to be asked and inspiring an obsession with method at the expense of any larger purpose. Equally significant was the authority of the French *Annales* school. Its emphasis on persistent inherited structures as forces determining historical development rendered the actions of individual men and women all but superfluous.

The influence of the *Annales* school in shaping the agenda of social history could also be detected in the precipitous decline of politics as a subject of inquiry (although this was less pronounced in twentieth-century studies, where the rise of the Presidency remained a central concern and manuscript census data, the raw material of the social historian, are as yet unavailable). When dealt with at all, politics was reduced to a branch of social history—as in the "new political history," which pointedly ignored national issues and explained voting behavior on the basis of ethnocultural affiliations. The British historian G. M. Trevelyan once described social history as "history with the politics left out." Such a definition could hardly encompass the diverse approaches and findings, to say nothing of intentions, of social historians in the 1970s. But it remained apropos in one respect: politics was, indeed, excluded.

So, too, was the history of ideas, especially political ideas. Intellectual history has always occupied a curious status in a society skeptical of non-utilitarian motives and general theorizing. Even in the 1950s and early 1960s, the heyday of intellectual history, many of the genre's most prominent practitioners devoted their works to chronicling the "absence" of ideas in America. Daniel Boorstin celebrated the triumph of indigenous pragmatism over imported theory; Louis Hartz lamented that Americans had never produced an original political idea worthy of note; and Richard Hofstadter perceived anti-intellectualism as a far more potent force than the life of the mind in American culture. In the 1960s, pathbreaking works on American political ideology did appear, especially for the period of the American Revolution. But the dominance of social history in the seventies led to a renewed quest for the social roots of ideas. A salutary counterpoint to an earlier search for a disembodied national character, this strategy was extremely vulnerable to intellectual reductionism. Rather than taking ideas seriously in their own right, many historians sought to study them as either direct reflections of underlying social processes or as inferences from statistically ascertainable data about human behavior. Customs, values, and psychological motivations took the place of ideas in many accounts. Ironically, as a new generation of American Marxist historians was abandoning the mechanistic base-superstructure model for a more dialectical view of the relationship between ideas and social reality, many social historians, when they considered ideas at all, adopted this outmoded framework.

The divorce of social from political and intellectual history had unfortunate consequences for all concerned. For one thing, it remained impossible to fit the findings of social historians into the traditional narrative framework of American history. The failure to consider politics—by which I mean not simply voting returns and legislative alignments, but the ways in which power in civil society is ordered and exercised—and the retreat from the analysis of political ideas deprived social history of the larger context which alone could have imparted to it a broader meaning.

In a sense, the foregoing is by way of explaining why the major concerns of the essays in this collection are subjects eclipsed in recent years: politics and ideology. As my former teacher Richard Hofstadter observed, the best argument for such collections may be the simple one of accessibility—drawing together articles originally published in obscure corners of the academic world into a more readily available and permanent format. But, he went on, such a book also possesses value in illustrating a common cast of mind, for whatever their subject matter, the essays "are at least in their style of thought and their concerns, unified by some underlying intellectual intent . . . a set of related concerns and methods."[4] These essays, written between 1965 and 1980, reflect not simply a common interest in the causes and consequences of the American Civil War, but my ongoing desire to reintegrate the political, social, and intellectual history of that period. Obviously, no single essay or group of essays can fully do this. But I do believe the essays at least illustrate the value of bringing to bear on one another, and on the overall historical process, the insights of the now fragmented disciplines of social, political, economic, and intellectual history. The concerns of the "new" histories have much to contribute to an understanding of American political development in these years. One theme running through several of these essays, in fact, is the interplay of race, class, and political ideology in a society undergoing both a sectional confrontation and an economic revolution. My argument, however, is that the Civil War era cannot be understood unless the way in which power was wielded and conceptualized stands at the forefront of analysis.

American political culture, until well into the nineteenth century, was framed by an ideology of republicanism, a lasting legacy of the American Revolution. The present dissolution of the links between the distinctive realms of public and private experience would have been inconceivable to men and women reared in the republican tradition, for that ideology was grounded in a belief in the interdependence of polity, economy, and society. Republican government, it was thought, could exist only with a certain type of citizenry (virtuous and independent) and a certain kind of society (one characterized by economic equality). Several of the following essays examine a central theme of nineteenth-century development: the contradiction between republican thought and the expansion of capitalist production and market relations which transformed every aspect of American life. The recurrent tension between "virtue and commerce," as J. G. A. Pocock has put it,[5] bore a direct relation to the political debate over slavery and emancipation, posing ideological problems for abolitionism (essay III), and shaping debates over land and labor after the Civil War (essays V–VII). The republican concept of economic independence as the key to personal freedom informed a radical tradition which stretched from Tom Paine and other ideologues of the American Revolution through the labor movement of the 1830s, to the opposition to industrial capitalism expressed so violently during the Gilded Age. The confrontation between this tradition and the complex, interrelated issues of race, class, and ethnicity in American life, and the forging of a comprehensive definition of freedom in a society profoundly divided by slavery, are themes of the essays in this collection. Several trace the historical evolution of the "free labor" ideology which dominated northern society in the Civil War era, a particular expression of republican thought which has been a continuing concern of mine.

Over and above these themes, however, these essays reassert the centrality of the Civil War to the experience of nineteenth-century Americans. For at least half the century, the sectional conflict and its aftermath, or, to put it another way, the institution of slavery and its implications and legacy, dominated American life. This does not mean that it affected every American in the same way, or that issues like immigration and the family were unimportant. It simply means that it increasingly became impossible to think seriously about American society without somehow coming to grips with slavery and the Union. From the standpoint of physical destruction, loss of life, structural changes in the economy, the introduction of new ideas, and the diffusion of enduring sectional passions, the Civil War shaped and altered the lives and consciousness of several historical generations. The sectional controversy spawned the greatest reform movement of the nineteenth century, antislavery, whose legacy affected virtually every subsequent effort to recast American society, even as its triumph—emancipation—strengthened a middle-class culture which saw the end of slavery as a preeminent vindication of its own values. The equivocal legacy of abolition—a theme of several essays—reflects the larger ambiguity of the Civil War and its heritage; the war stood as both a "new birth of freedom" and the wellspring of much that was wrong in Gilded Age America. The "massive, inconvenient reality" of the Civil War, Hofstadter once wrote, posed a serious challenge for earlier consensus historians, for it belied their vision of America as "a land without serious disagreements over fundamental issues."[6] It remains equally true today that a satisfactory portrait of the American experience cannot emerge from an attempt to read the Civil War out of American history.

The age of the Civil War, finally, is the period of our past most relevant to the contemporary concerns of American society. I use the much-abused word "relevant" advisedly. I do not mean by it a one-to-one correlation between our time and the past, nor do I suggest that direct answers to the issues of the present will emerge from the study of the nineteenth century. I mean simply that it is possible to connect history with the present without succumbing to present-mindedness, to respect the integrity, the pastness, of the past while confronting a set of issues as yet unresolved in American life.

The Civil War, after all, raised the decisive questions of our national existence—war and peace, relations between the states and the federal government, the balance between force and consent in generating obedience to authority, and, of course, the pervasive problem of race which still bedevils American society, challenging it to live up to its lofty professed ideals. The themes of race and class, the debates over the meaning of freedom and disadvantage in America, remain controversial. The failure of the first Reconstruction on the rock of intractable racial prejudices and economic inequalities has its parallel in the dissipating of the second in the face of analogous barriers.

Like any political crisis, the Civil War raised timeless moral questions concerning the uses of power and the consequences of human choices—questions of "why," rather than "how," which gave traditional historical studies much of their vitality and which never appear in "social science" history. History teaches few easy lessons, but it should assist us to think creatively about ourselves. By looking again at the age of the Civil War, we may gain insight into the choices facing our own time, and enable history to become, in place of a collection of assorted facts, once again a mode of collective self-education.

ORIGINS
OF THE
CIVIL WAR

⸻❦ T W O ❦⸻

The Causes
of the
American Civil War:
Recent Interpretations
and New Directions

In 1960, as Americans prepared to observe the centennial of the Civil War, one of the foremost historians of that conflict published a brief article entitled, "American Historians and the Causes of the Civil War."[1] Most readers probably expected another survey of the changing course of Civil War interpretation. Instead the author announced that as a subject of serious historical analysis, Civil War causation was "dead."

Looking back over the decade and a half since David Donald wrote, it would appear that he somewhat exaggerated the death of this field of inquiry. In the 1950s, historians were concerned with investigating periods of consensus in America's past. But in the 1960s, as the issues of race and war came to the forefront of national life, earlier times of civil strife in American history attracted renewed attention.

The 1960s, for example, witnessed a renascence of the study of slavery. It is now no longer possible to view the peculiar institution as some kind of accident or aberration, existing out-

Originally published in *Civil War History*, XX (Sept. 1974), 197–214. Reprinted by permission of Kent State University Press.

side the mainstream of national development. Rather, slavery was absolutely central to the American experience, intimately bound up with the settlement of the western hemisphere, the American Revolution, and industrial expansion. It was what defined the Old South and drew southern society along a path of development which set it increasingly apart from the rest of the nation.[2]

At the same time, a striking reversal of interpretations of the abolitionists took place.[3] In fact, there was a paradoxical double reversal. On the one hand the abolitionists, previously castigated as fanatics and agitators, suddenly emerged as the conscience of a sinning nation—much as the Garrisons and Welds had portrayed themselves a century earlier. But simultaneously, a number of writers argued that not only were the friends of the slave not immune from racism, but, far from being truly "radical," they seemed to accept the middle-class values of northern society.[4]

The flood of studies of slavery, abolitionism, and the race issue does not seem, however, to have brought historians much closer to a generally accepted interpretation of the coming of the Civil War than they were in 1960. As the late David Potter pointed out, the irony is that disagreements of interpretation persist in the face of a greatly increased body of historical knowledge.[5] This is partially because the Civil War raised so many still unresolved issues. Perhaps, however, there is another reason. Historians' methodologies and value judgments have changed considerably, but the questions historians have asked of their data have remained relatively static. Like the debate over slavery before the appearance of Stanley Elkins's pathbreaking study in 1959, discussion of the causes of the Civil War continues to be locked into an antiquated interpretive framework. Historians of the Civil War era seem to be in greater need of new models of interpretation and new questions than an additional accumulation of data.

A number of works have appeared, however, in the past fifteen years which have attempted to develop entirely new ways of looking at ante-bellum America and the origins of the Civil War. One of the most striking developments of these years has been the emergence of the "new political historians," who have attempted to recast our understanding of ante-bellum political alignments. They have deemphasized "national" issues like slavery and the tariff, and substituted ethnocultural conflicts between Protestants and Catholics, or between pietistic and ritualistic religious groups, as the major determinants of voting behavior. These works have broadened our understanding of ante-bellum political culture, and demonstrated the inevitable failure of any "monistic interpretation" of political conflict. And they should force historians to abandon whatever economic determinism still persists in the writing of political history. Perhaps most important, they have demonstrated the virtues of viewing voters not as isolated individuals, but as men and women embedded in a complex network of social and cultural relationships.[6]

The "new political history" involves both a new methodology—the statistical analysis of quantitative data—and a distinctive model of historical explanation. The broadening of the methodological tools available to historians can only be applauded, although some writers may at times be guilty of mistaking correlations for causes, and inducing the behavior of individuals from aggregate data. It sometimes seems that the very sophistication of the new methodology has unfortunate effects on these writers' approach to historical data. Not only is undue weight often assigned to historical variables such as ethnicity for which quantifiable data happens to be available, but the definition of basic concepts is reduced to the most easily quantifiable elements. Thus, class is measured by data on occupation and assessed property holdings, culture is reduced to a mixture of ethnicity and religion, and religion is measured purely by church affiliation.[7]

It is in the realm of explanation, and as a contribution to our understanding of the coming of the Civil War, that the "new political history" is most open to criticism. First, while rightly rejecting the economic determinism of progressive historians, the new political historians seem to be in danger of substituting a religious or cultural determinism of their own. Indeed, the interpretive framework of the new school is strikingly similar to that of the progressives. Both pose a sharp distinction between "real" and "unreal" issues, both put thousands of persons in the quasi-conspiratorial position of concealing their real intentions, and both take an extremely limited view of individual motivation. For the "economic man" of the progressives, the new political history has substituted an equally one-dimensional "religious man."

Most important, this new mode of explanation is fundamentally ahistorical; its key variables exist independently of historical context. Religion and ethnicity are generally treated as "unidimensional concepts, without reference to time, place, rate of acculturation, or individual personality." The point is that all historical variables are interrelated, and change as society develops. To take one key variable—religious belief in this case, or an oversimplified version of class for the progressives—and abstract it from its social context and the processes of historical change, is to distort and fracture historical reality.[8]

The arguments of the "new political historians" have profound implications for the question of Civil War causation. Their basic outlook was announced in 1964, in Joel Silbey's influential article, "The Civil War Synthesis," which chided historians for writing the history of the 1850s solely from the vantage point of the slavery issue, ignoring questions, like nativism, which seemed to have little to do with the coming of war. Subsequent writers have agreed with Silbey that a split existed between northern political elites and the mass of voters. The former were, for a variety of reasons, increasingly antisouthern, the latter were "basically unmoved" by the issues of slavery and sectional conflict and were more concerned with so-called "cultural" questions like immigration and temperance.[9]

While often criticizing tiaditional historians for using such "elite sources" as newspapers, speeches, and letters, this new interpretation of ante-bellum politics has its own elitist bias. It assumes that "large portions of the electorate do not have meaningful beliefs,"[10] that only elites are truly issue-oriented. This kind of reasoning, however, can never illuminate the relationship between political leaders and voters in a democratic political culture. Nor can it explain under what circumstances local issues will dominate politics and when national issues will come to the fore, or tell us why Republicans in the late 1850s were constantly trying to play down the issues of temperance and nativism which had supposedly created their party in the first place.[11] The view of the Republican party as the political expression of pietistic Protestantism can hardly encompass a figure like Lincoln, who was southern-born and whose religious beliefs were akin to the deism of that infidel Thomas Paine, whom Lincoln greatly admired.[12] According to the aggregate data, Lincoln should have been a pro-slavery Democrat. At best, he was a historical accident, an ecological fallacy.

But what of the Civil War? Supposedly, when the scientist Laplace described the Newtonian system to Napoleon, the emperor asked, "But where is God in your system?" To which Laplace replied, "I have no need for that hypothesis." Similarly, the "system" of the new political history has no need for the Civil War. Unfortunately, the Civil War did take place. But the new interpretation leaves a yawning gap between political processes and the outbreak of war. Recently, Lee Benson has tried to bridge this gap by arguing that a "small group" of southern conspirators, taking advantage of the "irresponsible character" of the political system, caused the war.[13] To pursue our Enlightenment analogy and paraphrase Voltaire, if Benson's explanation did not exist, we would have to invent it. If only elites cared about the slavery question, we are logically driven back to a neo-revisionist conspiracy theory of the coming of the war. One does not have to assume that great events always have great causes to believe that conspiracy theories are rarely satisfactory as historical explanations.

A second school of historical writing places the coming of the

Civil War within the process political scientists have termed
"modernization." This is as yet an imprecisely defined concept,
but it involves such basic changes in the structure of a society as
rapid economic development, urbanization, industrialization,
the creation of an integrated national economic and political
structure, and generally, the spread of market-oriented capitalist economic relations and of mental attitudes viewing continu-
ous social change as natural and desirable.[14] Within this context, the Civil War becomes the process by which the "modern"
or "modernizing" North integrated the "pre-modern" South
into a national political and economic system. As Raimondo
Luraghi explains, "So, in the nineteenth century, as the industrial revolution was expanding on a worldwide scale, the days
of wrath were coming for a series of agrarian, pre-capitalistic,
'backward' societies throughout the world, from the Italian and
American South down to India."[15] Aside from Luraghi's work,
the modernization framework has not yet been systematically
applied to the coming of the Civil War, although in many respects it is compatible with the work of Eugene Genovese on
the South and with my own discussion of the Republican party
in the 1850s.[16]

As Robert Kelley demonstrates, the ethnocultural and modernization interpretations are not necessarily incompatible. In
his book, *The Transatlantic Persuasion*, the Republicans in
America and the Tories in England become the nationalists,
homogenizers, and cosmopolitans. Intolerant of any social diversity within their societies, they attempted to impose their
values on dissident groups—temperance legislation on the
Irish immigrants, anti-slavery on the South—while the party of
the regional and ethnic minorities (Democrats in America, Liberals in Britain), called for cultural pluralism and local autonomy.[17]

The problem with this analysis is that it views the sectional
conflict primarily as a struggle between local and national institutions. It is significant that in Kelley's stimulating book, the institution of slavery is conspicuous by its absence. But slavery

was what made the South distinct—it was central to the moral, economic, and political antagonisms between the sections.

Nonetheless, this framework has much to offer toward an understanding of the politics of the 1850s. Lincoln's House Divided speech, as J. R. Pole has written, can be viewed as the outlook of a man "who had grasped the essentials of the process of nationalisation that was overtaking the main institutions of American life." Conversely, Stephen A. Douglas's objection to what he termed Lincoln's belief that "there must be uniformity in the local laws and domestic institutions of each and all states of the Union," and his plea for recognition of "diversity and dissimilarity" within the nation, can be read as the cry of all the out-groups and backward areas confronted by the process of modernization in the nineteenth century.[18]

Having said this, I hasten to add that there are certain problems in applying this model to the causes of the Civil War. First, there is the imprecision of the term "modernization." At times, it seems to be used more or less interchangeably with "industrialization," and, in effect, becomes a restatement of the Beardian view of the Civil War as a conflict between industrial and agrarian economies. In this form, the model exaggerates the extent to which northern society itself was as yet fully modernized in the ante-bellum years. Historians, indeed, have not yet produced the studies which will enable us to state with assurance what the class structure of the North was, or how far industrialization had advanced by 1860. Before we can assess the effects of modernization, in other words, we need to know exactly what kind of society was undergoing that process. Ante-bellum northern society may well have been "modern" in some respects. Certainly capitalist economic relations and democratic political procedures prevailed, and according to Richard Brown, the "modern personality" had been dominant since colonial days. But the economy was almost certainly pre-industrial, and the ideals of the yeoman farmer and independent artisan, their belief in the natural right of each individual to the fruits of his labor (which became in the hands of Lincoln so damning an indictment of slavery), still permeated society.[19]

Nevertheless, the modernization model does have two great virtues. First, it enables us to see that what happened in nineteenth-century America was not a unique or local occurrence, but a process which had deep affinities with events in many other areas of the world. Secondly, it demands that political historians place their work in the largest context of the development of American society, for, as Albert Soboul writes, "all studies of political history entail a study of social history."[20] To me, moreover, it suggests a framework for beginning to answer the crucial question raised by David Brion Davis in *The Problem of Slavery in Western Culture*. Why does slavery, which for centuries had been considered a normal part of the social order, suddenly come to be viewed by large numbers of men and women as a totally unacceptable form of labor and social organization? Why, that is, does an anti-slavery movement emerge?

To answer this question, we must place the Civil War in the context of the general abolition of unfree labor systems in the nineteenth century, from slavery in the western hemisphere, to serfdom in Russia and *robot* in the Austrian Empire. Within this context, we need to relate the emergence of the modern anti-slavery movement to two related processes—changes in attitudes toward labor and the condition of laboring classes,[21] and the enormous economic and social transformations of the nineteenth century. Of course, American anti-slavery thought did not emerge full-blown in the 1830s. As C. Vann Woodward has pointed out, patterns of derogatory sectional imagery stretch back into the colonial era. Many New England Federalists employed anti-southern and anti-slavery rhetoric highly suggestive of the Republican assaults of the 1850s. They not only condemned the three-fifths clause of the Constitution and southern domination of the national government, but spoke of the superiority of free labor, the economic stagnation of the South, and the differences in "manners, habits, customs, principles and ways of thinking" between the sections.[22]

The elements of an anti-slavery ideology, therefore, had long been present in America, but a coherent critique of slavery had not. Why could the Federalists not develop one? For one thing, until 1800 they had powerful allies in the South, and after then, the dream of a reunited and triumphant Federalist party never entirely disappeared. Moreover, as several recent writers have emphasized, the Federalist world view centered on a society of order, harmony, and organic unity, one composed of stable and distinctly separated ranks and orders.[23] It was not until this older organic conception of society broke down that a complete anti-slavery ideology could emerge.

We know of course that in the 1820s and 1830s this older vision was thoroughly disrupted, and replaced by one of a society of competing individuals, a vision more in keeping with the requirements of an expanding, market-oriented capitalist society. Why this ideological transformation occurred is not yet, in my opinion, entirely clear. The transportation revolution was a major determinant, but we know too little about the nature of economic change in the ante-bellum era to be able to place this ideological development in its proper social setting. We do know that the ideological transformation had profound effects on the nature of anti-slavery thought. As Rowland Berthoff has observed, "if classes supposedly did not exist, they could not be accepted as constituent institutions of American society; rank or degree was no longer an admissible principle for organizing or even thinking about the social order." That abolitionist thought was utterly individualistic and atomistic has by now become an axiom of historical writing. Historians as diverse in their ideological preconceptions as Stanley Elkins and William Appleman Williams severely chide the abolitionists for viewing slavery not as a functioning institution, embedded in a distinct society, but as a personal sin of the individual master against the individual slave.[24] But it may be that it was only when the ideas of an organic society, and the permanent subordination of any class of men, had been overthrown, that anti-slavery thought could develop in a consistent form. Only a movement that viewed society as a collection of individuals, that viewed freedom as the property of every man, that believed every individual had the right to seek advancement as a unit in competitive society, could condemn slavery as utterly and completely as, in their own ways, abolitionists and Republicans did.[25]

Anti-slavery thus fed on the anti-monopoly, anti-corporate, egalitarian ethos of Jacksonian America. At the same time, as a vision of labor, anti-slavery was curiously ambiguous. Anti-slavery men exalted "free labor," meaning labor working because of incentive instead of coercion, labor with education, skill, the desire for advancement, and also the freedom to move from job to job according to the changing demands of the marketplace.[26] On the other hand, many anti-slavery men were also opponents of union activity, and were closely involved in other reforms—such as the creation of prisons and asylums, temperance, and poor relief (with the ever-present distinction between the deserving and undeserving poor) which to a certain extent can be interpreted as attempts to transform the life style and work habits of labor in an industrializing society.

One could argue that the anti-slavery movement, by glorifying northern society and by isolating slavery as an unacceptable form of labor exploitation, while refusing to condemn the exploitative aspects of "free" labor relations, served to justify the emerging capitalist order of the North. In fact, it is possible that the growing ideological conflict between the sections had the effect of undermining a tradition of radical criticism within northern society.[27] Men like Horace Greeley, highly critical of certain aspects of their society in the 1840s, became more and more uncritical when faced with the need to defend the North against southern assaults. The choices for America came to be defined as free society versus slave society—the idea of alternatives within free society was increasingly lost sight of.[28]

To develop this point further, many anti-slavery men believed in an ideal of human character which emphasized an internalized self-discipline. They condemned slavery as a lack of control over one's own destiny and the fruits of one's labor, but defined freedom as more than a simple lack of restraint. The truly free man, in the eyes of ante-bellum reformers, was one who imposed restraints upon himself. This was also the ideal, as David Rothman shows, of the reformers who constructed the prisons and asylums of this era—to transform the human personality so that the poor, insane, and criminal would internalize a sense of discipline, order, and restraint.[29]

There are parallels between this aim and Lincoln's condemnation in his famous lyceum speech of 1838 of "the increasing disregard for law which pervades the country," of vigilanteeism, mob violence, and those who hoped for the "total annihilation of government." For Lincoln, law, order, and union, commonly accepted and internalized, allowed civilization and progress to exist in America, especially given the highly competitive nature of the society. Or, to quote Theodore Weld, "restraints are the web of civilized society, warp and woof." Of course, on one level, slavery, as some pro-slavery writers argued, solved the problem of disciplining the labor force, but the ideal of the reformers was a society of free (self-governing) individuals. Slavery may have been like an asylum or a school in some respects, but it lacked one essential element of those institutions—release, or graduation. Moreover, it allowed full rein to the very passions which so many northerners desired to see repressed—it encouraged greed, self-indulgence, and all sorts of illicit personal and sexual activities on the part of the masters. When Lincoln in 1861 declared, "plainly, the central idea of secession, is the essence of anarchy," he could have chosen no more damning description.[30]

Thus the anti-slavery movement exalted the character traits demanded by a "modernizing" society while it condemned an institution which impeded that "modernization." Interpreted in this way, the modernization thesis can assimilate some of the insights of the new political history. For example, the ethnoculturalists never deal directly with the relationship between ethnocultural identity and class relations in the setting of a modernizing society. We know how closely related certain ethnic and class patterns were—how, in urban areas, Irish immigrants were overwhelmingly lower-class unskilled laborers, and how, to quote Ronald Formisano, "prosperity and evangelical political character often went together." It is also well known that class and ethnic prejudices were inextricably linked in nativist attacks on Irish immigrants.[31]

If we do expand our notion of culture beyond a relatively narrow definition of ethnicity and religious belief, we may find that "pietists" were much more hospitable to the Protestant work ethic and the economic demands of a modernizing society than were "ritualists" and Catholic immigrants.[32] Is it possible that the resistance of the Irish to "Americanization," rather than simply a desire to maintain cultural identity, was the attempt of a pre-industrial people to resist the hegemony of a modernizing culture, with all that that implied for character structure, work patterns, and life styles? May we view the Democratic party as the representative of the great pre-modern cultures within American society—the white South and the Irish immigrants—and perhaps then better understand why the nativist image of the Irish and the anti-slavery critique of the southern slaveholder stressed the same "undesirable" traits of lack of economic enterprise and self-discipline, and the attack on the Slave Power and Catholic Church denounced corporate monoliths which restricted individual freedom? Was the northern Democratic machine at the local level attuned to the communal, traditionalist behavior of the peasant immigrants, while the intense individualism of the Republicans had little to offer them?

Before we attempt to locate the crusade against slavery within the social history of ante-bellum America, there is a more basic historical question to answer. We still do not understand the social composition of that movement. We do have information about the abolitionist leadership, but also disagreement as to whether abolitionists were a declining elite, using reform as an effort to regain a waning status,[33] or a rising group, challenging older elites, North and South, for social dominance. This latter would seem to be the implication of Leonard Richards's recent study of anti-abolitionist mobs, which concludes that in Utica and Cincinnati, the mobs were composed of members of the pre-industrial upper class of commercial and professional men, while abolitionist membership drew much more heavily on artisans, manufacturers, and tradesmen.[34] Generally, however, to quote David Brion Davis, "little is known of the rank and file members, to say nothing of the passive supporters, of a single reform movement."[35] Historians of reform over the past fifteen years have been much more successful in explicating ideologies than in giving us a clear picture of the movements' social roots.

Without such studies, we have been guilty of accepting an oversimplified version of reform, e.g., the temperance movement was an effort of middle-class Yankees to exert their cultural dominance over immigrant Catholics and the unruly poor. That for many supporters the movement did have his character cannot be doubted, but we need only to read Brian Harrison's study of the English temperance movement to see that our studies have been noticeably one dimensional. Harrison showed that temperance was a cross-class movement which had deep roots in the working class, appealing to aspirations for self-help and social betterment. It was not simply an attempt "to impose middle-class manners on the working class."[36] The same, I suspect, can be said for temperance in this country, and for other reforms, such as the movement for expanded public education, that have been interpreted through the eyes of their middle-class proponents. Historians have often ignored the very different aims of workingmen who supported these reforms. But at present, we know far too little of the extent to which workers, skilled or unskilled, were sympathetic to one phase or another of the anti-slavery movement, or whether anti-slavery workingmen viewed slavery differently than did its middle-class foes. Thus, while Garrison drew a sharp distinction between slavery and the northern system of free labor, how many workingmen were impressed by the *similarities* between the chattel slavery of the South and the "wage slavery" of the North?

Many labor spokesmen were initially hostile to the abolitionists precisely because they believed the Garrisons and Welds were diverting attention from the pressing social problems of the industrializing North. But in the late 1840s and 1850s many workingmen were attracted to free-soilism and the Republican party by the issues of land reform and opposition to the expansion of slavery.[37] To what extent did workingmen oppose the extension of slavery to preserve the safety-valve which, they believed, guaranteed the independence of the northern laborer, and prevented him from being subjected to the degrading discipline of the factory or from being permanently trapped in the status of wage earner? In other words, antislavery could have served as an ideological vehicle for both the proponents of modernization and for those whose objective was to preserve the pre-modern status of the independent artisan.

In a similar vein, many questions remain about the social history of the ante-bellum South. Several recent studies emphasize the "obsession" of the secessionist leadership with internal unity, their fear that slavery was weak and declining in the border area and that the loyalty of the non-slaveholding whites was questionable. The secession of the South on the election of Lincoln, these works argue, was motivated not by paranoia or hysterical fear, but by a realistic assessment that the unity of their society could not survive the open debate on the future of slavery which Republicans seemed determined to stimulate within the slave states.[38]

Before we can assess this interpretation, we must take a new look at the social and economic structure of the Old South. The non-slaveholding whites are probably the least studied of all our social classes. Of course, such an investigation may indeed reveal that the hegemony of the planter class was complete.[39] Or we may find that the loyalty of the non-slaveholders, while

real, was unstable; that, especially in the backwoods areas outside direct planter control, there had developed a culture
which was in many ways hostile to planter rule while, at the
same time, cut off from both the market economy and from effective political power.

Fear of internal disunity can explain the belief of Edmund
Ruffin that a Republican government could accomplish "the
ruin of the South" without a direct assault upon slavery.[40]*
Ruffin was convinced that in the event of civil war, a Southern
victory would ensue, a belief he predicated on the continued
loyalty of the slaves. But if we are to look at the question of internal disunity and its relation to secession, the slaves themselves cannot be ignored. Southerners knew that to exist as a
regional institution within a larger free society, slavery required
a community consensus, voluntary or enforced. Division among
the whites had always been disastrous for discipline of the
slaves. This was why the South had suppressed its own anti-
slavery movement and continually demanded the silencing of
northern abolitionists. Once a Republican administration was
inaugurated, who knew what ideas would circulate in the slave
quarters? Before we can answer these questions, we need to
know more about how the slaves themselves were affected by,
and perceived, the vast changes which took place in the South
in the fifty years preceding secession—the ending of the slave
trade, the rise of the Cotton Kingdom, and the expansion of
slavery southward and westward.

In this connection, one of the most intriguing findings of
Robert Fogel and Stanley Engerman's controversial study of
the economics of slavery is the extent to which the lower level
of the slave system was in the hands of blacks—how slaves were
becoming a larger proportion of the drivers and managers on

---

*Published in the fall of 1860, Ruffin's *Anticipations of the Future* might be considered the first contribution to Civil War historiography. It details the ad-
ministrations of Presidents Abraham Lincoln and William Seward, and the
course of a war in 1867 in which the South wins a glorious military victory,
New York City is destroyed by a mob, and Washington becomes the capital of a
new southern republic.

plantations. This is precisely the class which, in the British West Indies, during the agitation of the years 1816–33, was most strongly influenced by humanitarian anti-slavery ideas and which developed a campaign of non-violent resistance which undermined West Indian slavery in the years immediately preceding emancipation. Of course, the situation in the United States was vastly different from that in the islands, but the experience there, and similar events in the 1880s in Brazil, should remind us again of the dangers of subversive ideas among the slave population, and the reality of southern fears that the very existence of a hostile central government was a threat to the stability of their peculiar institution.[41]

Having previously called on political historians to pay more attention to social history, I would like to conclude by reversing this equation. Of course, our knowledge of the social history of ante-bellum America is still in some ways in its infancy. One of the striking features of the writing of the past fifteen years is the curious disjunction between a growing body of knowledge about nineteenth-century American society, and the reluctance or inability of social historians to relate this information either to the politics of the period or the question of Civil War causation.[42] As one of our most creative social historians, Rowland Berthoff, reminds us, "any basic interpretation of American history will have to account for . . . the coming of the Civil War." And no such interpretation can be complete which does not encompass the course of American political development. "Politics bears critical importance to the history of society, for politics affects the social structure, the economy, and the life of a people."[43]

In other words, the social cleavages that existed in ante-bellum America were bound to be reflected in politics. This was an era when the mass political party galvanized voter participation to an unprecedented degree, and in which politics formed an essential component of American mass culture. Politics became the stage on which the sectional conflict was played out.[44]

Lawrence Stone has identified as an essential prerequisite to any revolution the "polarization into two coherent groups or alliances of what are naturally and normally a series of fractional and shifting tensions and conflicts within a society."[45] For most of the ante-bellum period, the political system served to prevent such a polarization. The existence of national political parties necessitated both the creation of linkages and alliances between elites in various parts of the country, and the conscious suppression of disruptive sectional issues. We can, in fact, view the political history of the coming of the Civil War as an accelerating struggle between the demands of party and those of sectional ideology, in which the latter slowly gained the upper hand. But the triumph was late and never complete. As late as 1860, major political leaders like Stephen A. Douglas hoped to curtail sectional controversy by restoring the political system to its traditional basis, with slavery carefully excluded from partisan debate.

Changes in the political system itself, changes related in ways still obscure to changes in the structure of American society, doomed the old basis of sectional political balance. If the anti-slavery crusade could not have emerged without the transformation of northern society, it could not have entered politics until the instruments of mass democracy had developed. It was no accident that the same decade witnessed the rise of the anti-slavery movement and the height of "Jacksonian democracy." The same institutions which created mass participation in politics also made possible the emergence of the sectional agitator—the radical, North and South, who consciously strove to influence public opinion through speeches, newspapers, lectures, and postal campaigns. This was now an efficacious way both to affect political decision-making and, if Richards is right, to challenge the social and political dominance of older entrenched elites.

Just as the abolitionist assault emerged in the 1830s, so too, spurred by it, did the coherent southern defense of slavery. The process of ideological response and counterresponse, once

set in motion, proved extremely difficult to curtail. In the next
two decades, these sectional ideologies became more and more
sophisticated. As each came to focus on its lowest common de-
nominator, with the widest possible base of support in its society, the political system proved incapable of preventing first the
intrusion, then the triumph of sectional ideology as the organizing principle of political combat.

The Civil War was, at base, a struggle for the future of the
nation. Within the context of modernization, one can agree
with Luraghi that it became part of the process of "building a
modern, centralized nation-state based on a national market,
totally and unopposedly controlled by an industrial capitalistic
class."[46] But is not there a danger here of transposing consequences and causes? It might be more accurate to say that each
side fought to preserve a society it believed was threatened.
Southerners fought to perserve the world the slaveholders
made. As for the North, Lincoln expressed the hopes of his
section, when he defined the Union cause as a struggle to preserve a system in which every man, whatever his station at
birth, could achieve social advancement and economic independence. Lincoln's Union was one of self-made men. The society
he was attempting to preserve was, in this respect, also pre-
modern—the world of the small shop, the independent farm,
and the village artisan. Republicans certainly condemned slavery as an obstacle to national economic development and as a
"relic of barbarism" out of touch with the modern spirit of the
nineteenth century. They exalted the virtues of economic
growth, but only within the context of a familar social order. If
modernization means the growth of large-scale industry, large
cities, and the leviathan state, northerners were no more fighting to create it than were southerners.

Yet modern, total war, against the intentions of those who
fought, was a powerful modernizing force.[47] In the South, the
war experience not only destroyed slavery, but created the opportunity for the two subordinate pre-modern classes, the poor
whites and the slaves, to organize and express their resentment

of planter control. In the North, the war gave a tremendous impetus to the rationalization of capitalist enterprise, the centralization of national institutions, and, in certain industries, mechanization and factory production. The foundations of the industrial capitalist state of the late nineteenth century, so similar in individualist rhetoric yet so different in social reality from Lincoln's America, were to a large extent laid during the Civil War. Here, indeed, is the tragic irony of that conflict. Each side fought to defend a distinct vision of the good society, but each vision was destroyed by the very struggle to preserve it.

⊸❧ THREE ❧⊸

Politics, Ideology, and the Origins of the American Civil War

It has long been an axiom of political science that political parties help to hold together diverse, heterogeneous societies like our own. Since most major parties in American history have tried, in Seymour Lipset's phrase, to "appear as plausible representatives of the whole society," they have been broad coalitions cutting across lines of class, race, religion, and section. And although party competition requires that there be differences between the major parties, these differences usually have not been along sharp ideological lines. In fact, the very diversity of American society has inhibited the formation of ideological parties, for such parties assume the existence of a single line of social division along which a majority of the electorate can be mobilized. In a large, heterogeneous society, such a line rarely exists. There are, therefore, strong reasons why, in a two-party system, a major party—or a party aspiring to become "major"—will eschew ideology, for the statement of a co-

Originally published in *A Nation Divided: Problems and Issues of the Civil War and Reconstruction*, ed., George M. Fredrickson (Minneapolis, 1975), 15–34. Reprinted by permission of Burgess Publishing Company.

herent ideology will set limits to the groups in the electorate to which the party can hope to appeal. Under most circumstances, in other words, the party's role as a carrier of a coherent ideology will conflict with its role as an electoral machine bent on winning the largest possible number of votes.[1]

For much of the seventy years preceding the Civil War, the American political system functioned as a mechanism for relieving social tensions, ordering group conflict, and integrating the society. The existence of national political parties, increasingly focused on the contest for the Presidency, necessitated alliances between political elites in various sections of the country. A recent study of early American politics notes that "political nationalization was far ahead of economic, cultural, and social nationalization"—that is, that the national political system was itself a major bond of union in a diverse, growing society.[2] But as North and South increasingly took different paths of economic and social development and as, from the 1830s onward, antagonistic value systems and ideologies grounded in the question of slavery emerged in these sections, the political system inevitably came under severe disruptive pressures. Because they brought into play basic values and moral judgments, the competing sectional ideologies could not be defused by the normal processes of political compromise, nor could they be contained within the existing inter-sectional political system. Once parties began to reorient themselves on sectional lines, a fundamental necessity of democratic politics— that each party look upon the other as a legitimate alternative government—was destroyed.

When we consider the causes of the sectional conflict, we must ask ourselves not only why civil war came when it did, but why it did not come sooner. How did a divided nation manage to hold itself together for as long as it did? In part, the answer lies in the unifying effects of inter-sectional political parties. On the level of politics, the coming of the Civil War is the story of the intrusion of sectional ideology into the political system, despite the efforts of political leaders of both parties to keep it

out. Once this happened, political competition worked to ex-
acerbate, rather than to solve, social and sectional conflicts. For
as Frank Sorauf has explained:[3]

> The party of extensive ideology develops in and reflects the soci-
> ety in which little consensus prevails on basic social values and in-
> stitutions. It betokens deep social disagreements and conflicts. In-
> deed, the party of ideology that is also a major, competitive party
> accompanies a politics of almost total concern. Since its ideology
> defines political issues as including almost every facet of life, it
> brings to the political system almost every division, every dif-
> ference, every conflict of any importance in society.

"Parties in this country," wrote a conservative northern Whig
in 1855, "heretofore have helped, not delayed, the slow and
difficult growth of a consummated nationality." Rufus Choate
was lamenting the passing of a bygone era, a time when "our
allies were everywhere . . . there were no Alleghenies nor Mississippi rivers in our politics."[4] Party organization and the nature of political conflict had taken on new and unprecedented
forms in the 1850s. It is no accident that the breakup of the last
major inter-sectional party preceded by less than a year the
breakup of the Union or that the final crisis was precipitated
not by any "overt act," but by a presidential election.

From the beginning of national government, of course, differences of opinion over slavery constituted an important obstacle to the formation of a national community. "The great
danger to our general government," as Madison remarked at
the Constitutional Convention, "is the great southern and
northern interests of the continent, being opposed to each
other." "The institution of slavery and its consequences," according to him, was the main "line of discrimination" in convention disputes. As far as slavery was concerned, the Constitution amply fulfilled Lord Acton's dictum that it was an effort to
avoid settling basic questions. Aside from the Atlantic slave
trade, Congress was given no power to regulate slavery in any
way—the framers' main intention seems to have been to place

slavery completely outside the national political arena. The only basis on which a national politics could exist—the avoidance of sectional issues—was thus defined at the outset.[5]

Although the slavery question was never completely excluded from political debate in the 1790s, and there was considerable Federalist grumbling about the three-fifths clause of the Constitution after 1800, the first full demonstration of the political possibilities inherent in a sectional attack on slavery occurred in the Missouri controversy of 1819–21. These debates established a number of precedents which forecast the future course of the slavery extension issue in Congress. Most important was the fact that the issue was able for a time to completely obliterate party lines. In the first votes on slavery in Missouri, virtually every northerner, regardless of party, voted against expansion. It was not surprising, of course, that northern Federalists would try to make political capital out of the issue. What was unexpected was that northern Republicans, many of whom were aggrieved by Virginia's long dominance of the Presidency and by the Monroe administration's tariff and internal improvements policies, would unite with the Federalists. As John Quincy Adams observed, the debate "disclosed a secret: it revealed the basis for a new organization of parties. . . . Here was a new party really formed . . . terrible to the whole Union, but portentously terrible to the South." But the final compromise set another important precedent: enough northern Republicans became convinced that the Federalists were making political gains from the debates and that the Union was seriously endangered to break with the sectional bloc and support a compromise which a majority of northern Congressmen—Republicans and Federalists—opposed. As for the Monroe administration, its semiofficial spokesman, the *National Intelligencer,* pleaded for a return to the policy of avoiding sectional issues, even to the extent of refusing to publish letters which dealt in any way with the subject of slavery.[6]

The Missouri controversy and the election of 1824, in which four candidates contested the Presidency, largely drawing support from their home sections, revealed that in the absence of two-party competition, sectional loyalties would constitute the lines of political division. No one recognized this more clearly than the architect of the second party system, Martin Van Buren. In his well-known letter to Thomas Ritchie of Virginia, Van Buren explained the need for a revival of national two-party politics on precisely this ground: "Party attachment in former times furnished a complete antidote for sectional prejudices by producing counteracting feelings. It was not until that defense had been broken down that the clamor against Southern Influence and African Slavery could be made effectual in the North." Van Buren and many of his generation of politicians had been genuinely frightened by the threats of disunion which echoed through Congress in 1820; they saw national two-party competition as the alternative to sectional conflict and eventual disunion. Ironically, as Richard McCormick has made clear, the creation of the second party system owed as much to sectionalism as to national loyalties. The South, for example, only developed an organized, competitive Whig party in 1835 and 1836 when it became apparent that Jackson, the southern President, had chosen Van Buren, a northerner, as his successor. Once party divisions had emerged, however, they stuck, and by 1840, for one of the very few times in American history, two truly inter-sectional parties, each united behind a single candidate, competed for the Presidency.[7]

The 1830s witnessed a vast expansion of political loyalties and awareness and the creation of party mechanisms to channel voter participation in politics. But the new mass sense of identification with politics had ominous implications for the sectional antagonisms which the party system sought to suppress. The historian of the Missouri Compromise has observed that "if there had been a civil war in 1819–1821 it would have been between the members of Congress, with the rest of the country looking on in amazement." This is only one example of the intellectual and political isolation of Washington from the general populace which James Young has described in *The*

Washington Community.[8] The mass, non-ideological politics of
the Jackson era created the desperately needed link between
governors and governed. But this very link made possible the
emergence of two kinds of sectional agitators: the abolitionists,
who stood outside of politics and hoped to force public
opinion—and through it, politicians—to confront the slavery
issue, and political agitators, who used politics as a way of
heightening sectional self-consciousness and antagonism in the
populace at large.

Because of the rise of mass politics and the emergence of
these sectional agitators, the 1830s was the decade in which
long-standing, latent sectional divisions were suddenly acti-
vated, and previously unrelated patterns of derogatory sectional imagery began to emerge into full-blown sectional ideology. Many of the anti-slavery arguments which gained wide
currency in the 1830s had roots stretching back into the
eighteenth century. The idea that slavery degraded white labor
and retarded economic development, for example, had been
voiced by Benjamin Franklin. After 1800, the Federalists, increasingly localized in New England, had developed a fairly coherent critique, not only of the social and economic effects of
slavery, but of what Harrison Gray Otis called the divergence
of "manners, habits, customs, principles, and ways of thinking"
which separated northerners and southerners. And, during the
Missouri debates, almost every economic, political, and moral
argument against slavery that would be used in the later sectional debate was voiced. In fact, one recurring argument was
not picked up later—the warning of northern Congressmen
that the South faced the danger of slave rebellion if steps were
not taken toward abolition. (As far as I know, only Thaddeus
Stevens of Republican spokesmen in the 1850s would explicitly
use this line of argument.)[9]

The similarity between Federalist attacks on the South and
later abolitionist and Republican arguments, coupled with the
fact that many abolitionists—including Garrison, Phillips, the
Tappans, and others—came from Federalist backgrounds, has

led James Banner to describe abolitionism as "the Massachusetts Federalist ideology come back to life." Yet there was
a long road to be traveled from Harrison Gray Otis to William
H. Seward, just as there was from Thomas Jefferson to George
Fitzhugh. For one thing, the Federalist distrust of democracy,
social competition, and the Jeffersonian cry of "equal rights,"
their commitment to social inequality, hierarchy, tradition, and
order prevented them from pushing their anti-slavery views to
their logical conclusion. And New England Federalists were
inhibited by the requirements of national party organization
and competition from voicing anti-slavery views. In the 1790s,
they maintained close ties with southern Federalists, and after
1800 hope of reviving their strength in the South never completely died. Only a party which embraced social mobility and
competitive individualism, rejected the permanent subordination of any "rank" in society, and was unburdened by a southern wing could develop a fully coherent anti-slavery ideology.[10]

An equally important reason why the Federalists did not develop a consistent sectional ideology was that the South in the
early part of the nineteenth century shared many of the Federalists' reservations about slavery. The growth of an anti-slavery
ideology, in other words, depended in large measure on the
growth of pro-slavery thought, and, by the same token, it was
the abolitionist assault which brought into being the coherent
defense of slavery. The opening years of the 1830s, of course,
were ones of crisis for the South. The emergence of militant
abolitionism, Nat Turner's rebellion, the Virginia debates on
slavery, and the nullification crisis suddenly presented assaults
to the institution of slavery from within and outside the South.
The reaction was the closing of southern society in defense of
slavery, "the most thorough-going repression of free thought,
free speech, and a free press ever witnessed in an American
community." At the same time, southerners increasingly abandoned their previous, highly qualified defenses of slavery and
embarked on the formulation of the pro-slavery argument. By

1837, as is well known, John C. Calhoun could thank the abolitionists on precisely this ground:[11]

> This agitation has produced one happy effect at least; it has com-
> pelled us at the South to look into the nature and character of this
> great institution, and to correct many false impressions that even
> we had entertained in relation to it. Many in the South once be-
> lieved that it was a moral and political evil; that folly and delusion
> are gone; we see it now in its true light, and regard it as the most
> safe and stable basis for free institutions in the world.

The South, of course, was hardly as united as Calhoun asserted. But the progressive rejection of the Jeffersonian tradition, the suppression of civil liberties, and the increasing stri-
dency of the defense of slavery all pushed the South further
and further out of the inter-sectional mainstream, setting it increasingly apart from the rest of the country. Coupled with the
Gag Rule and the mobs which broke up abolitionist presses and
meetings, the growth of pro-slavery thought was vital to a new
anti-slavery formulation which emerged in the late 1830s and
which had been absent from both the Federalist attacks on slavery and the Missouri debates—the idea of the Slave Power. The
Slave Power replaced the three-fifths clause as the symbol of
southern power, and it was a far more sophisticated and complex formulation. Abolitionists could now argue that slavery
was not only morally repugnant, it was incompatible with the
basic democratic values and liberties of white Americans. As
one abolitionist declared, "We commenced the present struggle
to obtain the freedom of the slave; we are compelled to continue it to preserve our own." In other words, a process of
ideological expansion had begun, fed in large measure by the
sequence of response and counterresponse between the competing sectional outlooks.[12] Once this process had begun, it had
an internal dynamic which made it extremely difficult to stop.
This was especially true because of the emergence of agitators
whose avowed purpose was to sharpen sectional conflict, polar-

ize public opinion, and develop sectional ideologies to their logical extremes.

As the 1840s opened, most political leaders still clung to the
traditional basis of politics, but the sectional, ideological political agitators formed growing minorities in each section. In the
South, there was a small group of outright secessionists and a
larger group, led by Calhoun, who were firmly committed to
the Union but who viewed sectional organization and self-de-
fense, not the traditional reliance on inter-sectional political
parties, as the surest means of protecting southern interests
within the Union. In the North, a small radical group gathered
in Congress around John Quincy Adams and Congressmen like
Joshua Giddings, William Slade, and Seth Gates—men who
represented areas of the most intense abolitionist agitation and
whose presence confirmed Garrison's belief that, once public
opinion was aroused on the slavery issue, politicians would
have to follow step. These radicals were determined to force
slavery into every congressional debate. They were continually
frustrated but never suppressed, and the reelection of Giddings in 1842 after his censure and resignation from the House
proved that in some districts party discipline was no longer able
to control the slavery issue.[13]

The northern political agitators, both Congressmen and Liberty party leaders, also performed the function of developing
and popularizing a political rhetoric, especially focused on fear
of the Slave Power, which could be seized upon by traditional
politicians and large masses of voters if slavery ever entered the
center of political conflict.

In the 1840s, this is precisely what happened. As one politician later recalled, "Slavery upon which by common consent no
party issue had been made was then obtruded upon the field of
party action." It is significant that John Tyler and John C.
Calhoun, the two men most responsible for this intrusion, were
political outsiders, men without places in the national party
structure. Both of their careers were blocked by the major parties but might be advanced if tied to the slavery question in the

form of Texas annexation. Once introduced into politics, slavery was there to stay. The Wilmot Proviso, introduced in 1846, had precisely the same effect as the proposal two decades earlier to restrict slavery in Missouri—it completely fractured the major parties along sectional lines. As in 1820, opposition to the expansion of slavery became the way in which a diverse group of northerners expressed their various resentments against a southern-dominated administration. And, as in 1821, a small group of northern Democrats eventually broke with their section, reaffirmed their primary loyalty to the party, and joined with the South to kill the Proviso in 1847. In the same year, enough southerners rejected Calhoun's call for united sectional action to doom his personal and sectional ambitions.[14]

But the slavery extension debates of the 1840s had far greater effects on the political system than the Missouri controversy had had. Within each party, they created a significant group of sectional politicians—men whose careers were linked to the slavery question and who would therefore resist its exclusion from future politics. And in the North, the 1840s witnessed the expansion of sectional political rhetoric—as more and more northerners became familiar with the "aggressions" of the Slave Power and the need to resist them. At the same time, as anti-slavery ideas expanded, unpopular and divisive elements were weeded out, especially the old alliance of anti-slavery with demands for the rights of free blacks. Opposition to slavery was already coming to focus on its lowest common denominators—free soil, opposition to the Slave Power, and the union.[15]

The political system reacted to the intrusion of the slavery question in the traditional ways. At first, it tried to suppress it. This is the meaning of the famous letters opposing the immediate annexation of Texas issued by Clay and Van Buren on the same spring day in 1844, probably after consultation on the subject. It was an agreement that slavery was too explosive a question for either party to try to take partisan advantage of it. The agreement, of course, was torpedoed by the defeat of Van

Buren for the Democratic nomination, a defeat caused in part by the willingness of his Democratic opponents to use the Texas and slavery questions to discredit Van Buren—thereby violating the previously established rules of political conduct. In the North from 1844 onward, both parties, particularly the Whigs, tried to defuse the slavery issue and minimize defection to the Liberty party by adopting anti-southern rhetoric. This tended to prevent defections to third parties, but it had the effect of nurturing and legitimating anti-southern sentiment within the ranks of the major parties themselves. After the 1848 election in which northern Whigs and Democrats vied for title of "free soil" to minimize the impact of the Free Soil party, William H. Seward commented, "Antislavery is at length a respectable element in politics."[16]

Both parties also attempted to devise formulas for compromising the divisive issue. For the Whigs, it was "no territory"—an end to expansion would end the question of the spread of slavery. The Democratic answer, first announced by Vice President Dallas in 1847 and picked up by Lewis Cass, was popular sovereignty or non-intervention: giving to the people of each territory the right to decide on slavery. As has often been pointed out, popular sovereignty was an exceedingly vague and ambiguous doctrine. It was never precisely clear what the powers of a territorial legislature were to be or at what point the question of slavery was to be decided.[17] But politically such ambiguity was essential (and intentional) if popular sovereignty were to serve as a means of settling the slavery issue on the traditional basis—by removing it from national politics and transferring the battleground from Congress to the territories.[18] Popular sovereignty formed one basis of the compromise of 1850, the last attempt of the political system to expel the disease of sectional ideology by finally settling all the points at which slavery and national politics intersected.

That compromise was possible in 1850 was testimony to the resiliency of the political system and the continuing ability of party loyalty to compete with sectional commitments. But the very method of passage revealed how deeply sectional divisions were embedded in party politics. Because only a small group of Congressmen—mostly northwestern Democrats and southern Whigs—were committed to compromise on every issue, the "omnibus" compromise measure could not pass. The compromise had to be enacted serially with the small compromise bloc, led by Stephen A. Douglas of Illinois, aligned with first one sectional bloc, then the other, to pass the individual measures.[19]

His role in the passage of the compromise announced the emergence of Douglas as the last of the great Unionist, compromising politicians, the heir of Clay, Webster, and other spokesmen for the center. And his career, like Webster's, showed that it was no longer possible to win the confidence of both sections with a combination of extreme nationalism and the calculated suppression of the slavery issue in national politics. Like his predecessors, Douglas called for a policy of "entire silence on the slavery question," and throughout the 1850s, as Robert Johannsen has written, his aim was to restore "order and stability to American politics through the agency of a national, conservative Democratic party." Ultimately, Douglas failed—a traditional career for the Union was simply not possible in the 1850s—but it is equally true that in 1860 he was the only presidential candidate to draw significant support in all parts of the country.[20]

It is, of course, highly ironic that it was Douglas's attempt to extend the principle of popular sovereignty to territory already guaranteed to free labor by the Missouri Compromise which finally shattered the second party system. We can date exactly the final collapse of that system—February 15, 1854—the day a caucus of southern Whig Congressmen and Senators decided to support Douglas's Nebraska bill, despite the fact that they could have united with northern Whigs in opposition both to the repeal of the Missouri Compromise and the revival of sectional agitation.[21] But in spite of the sectionalization of politics which occurred after 1854, Douglas continued his attempt to maintain a national basis of party competition. In fact, from one angle of vision, whether politics was to be national or sectional was the basic issue of the Lincoln-Douglas debates of 1858. The Little Giant presented local autonomy—popular sovereignty for states and territories—as the only "national" solution to the slavery question, while Lincoln attempted to destroy this middle ground and force a single, sectional solution on the entire Union. There is a common critique of Douglas's politics, expressed perhaps most persuasively by Allan Nevins, which argues that, as a man with no moral feelings about slavery, Douglas was incapable of recognizing that this moral issue affected millions of northern voters.[22] This, in my opinion, is a serious misunderstanding of Douglas's politics. What he insisted was not that there was no moral question involved in slavery but that it was not the function of the politician to deal in moral judgments. To Lincoln's prediction that the nation could not exist half slave and half free, Douglas replied that it had so existed for seventy years and could continue to do so if northerners stopped trying to impose their own brand of morality upon the South.

Douglas's insistence on the separation of politics and morality was expressed in his oft-quoted statement that—in his role as a politician—he did not care if the people of a territory voted slavery "up or down." As he explained in his Chicago speech of July 1858, just before the opening of the great debates:

> I deny the right of Congress to force a slave-holding state upon an unwilling people. I deny their right to force a free state upon an unwilling people. I deny their right to force a good thing upon a people who are unwilling to receive it. . . . It is no answer to this argument to say that slavery is an evil and hence should not be tolerated. You must allow the people to decide for themselves whether it is a good or an evil.

When Lincoln, therefore, said the real purpose of popular sovereignty was "to educate and mould public opinion, at least northern public opinion, to not care whether slavery is voted down or up," he was, of course, right. For Douglas recognized that moral categories, being essentially uncompromisable, are unassimilable in politics. The only solution to the slavery issue was local autonomy. Whatever a majority of a state or territory wished to do about slavery was right—or at least should not be tampered with by politicians from other areas. To this, Lincoln's only possible reply was the one formulated in the debates—the will of the majority must be tempered by considerations of morality. Slavery was not, he declared, an *"ordinary* matter of domestic concern in the states and territories." Because of its essential immorality, it tainted the entire nation, and its disposition in the territories, and eventually in the entire nation, was a matter of national concern to be decided by a national, not a local, majority. As the debates continued, Lincoln increasingly moved to this moral level of the slavery argument: "Everything that emanates from [Douglas] or his coadjutors, carefully excludes the thought that there is anything wrong with slavery. All their arguments, if you will consider them, will be seen to exclude the thought. . . . If you do admit that it is wrong, Judge Douglas can't logically say that he don't care whether a wrong is voted up or down."[23]

In order to press home the moral argument, moreover, Lincoln had to insist throughout the debates on the basic humanity of the black; while Douglas, by the same token, logically had to define blacks as subhuman, or at least, as the Dred Scott decision had insisted, not part of the American "people" included in the Declaration of Independence and the Constitution. Douglas's view of the black, Lincoln declared, conveyed "no vivid impression that the Negro is a human, and consequently has no idea that there can be any moral question in legislating about him."[24] Of course, the standard of morality which Lincoln felt the nation should adopt regarding slavery and the black was the sectional morality of the Republican party.

By 1860, Douglas's local majoritarianism was no more acceptable to southern political leaders than Lincoln's national and moral majoritarianism. The principle of state rights and minority self-determination had always been the first line of defense

of slavery from northern interference, but southerners now
coupled it with the demand that Congress intervene to establish
and guarantee slavery in the territories. The Lecompton fight
had clearly demonstrated that southerners would no longer be
satisfied with what Douglas hoped the territories would become—free, Democratic states. And the refusal of the Douglas
Democrats to accede to southern demands was the culmination
of a long history of resentment on the part of northern Democrats, stretching back into the 1840s, at the impossible political
dilemma of being caught between increasingly anti-southern
constituency pressure and loyalty to an increasingly pro-
southern national party. For their part, southern Democrats
viewed their northern allies as too weak at home and too
tainted with anti-southernism after the Lecompton battle to be
relied on to protect southern interests any longer.[25]

As for the Republicans, by the late 1850s they had succeeded
in developing a coherent ideology which, despite internal ambiguities and contradictions, incorporated the fundamental values, hopes, and fears of a majority of northerners. As I have
argued elsewhere, it rested on a commitment to the northern
social order, founded on the dignity and opportunities of free
labor, and to social mobility, enterprise, and "progress." It
gloried in the same qualities of northern life—materialism, social fluidity, and the dominance of the self-made man—which
twenty years earlier had been the source of widespread anxiety
and fear in Jacksonian America. And it defined the South as a
backward, stagnant, aristocratic society, totally alien in values
and social order to the middle-class capitalism of the North.[26]

Some elements of the Republican ideology had roots stretching back into the eighteenth century. Others, especially the
Republican emphasis on the threat of the Slave Power, were
relatively new. Northern politics and thought were permeated
by the Slave Power idea in the 1850s. The effect can perhaps
be gauged by a brief look at the career of the leading Republican spokesman of the 1850s, William H. Seward. As a political
child of upstate New York's burned-over district and anti-

masonic crusade, Seward had long believed that the Whig party's main political liability was its image as the spokeman of the wealthy and aristocratic. Firmly committed to egalitarian democracy, Seward had attempted to reorient the New York State Whigs into a reformist, egalitarian party, friendly to immigrants and embracing political and economic democracy, but he was always defeated by the party's downstate conservative wing. In the 1840s, he became convinced that the only way for the party to counteract the Democrats' monopoly of the rhetoric of democracy and equality was for the Whigs to embrace anti-slavery as a party platform.[27]

The Slave Power idea gave the Republicans the anti-aristocratic appeal with which men like Seward had long wished to be associated politically. By fusing older anti-slavery arguments with the idea that slavery posed a threat to northern free labor and democratic values, it enabled the Republicans to tap the egalitarian outlook which lay at the heart of northern society. At the same time, it enabled Republicans to present anti-slavery as an essentially conservative reform, an attempt to reestablish the anti-slavery principles of the founding fathers and rescue the federal government from southern usurpation. And, of course, the Slave Power idea had a far greater appeal to northern self-interest than arguments based on the plight of black slaves in the South. As the black abolitionist Frederick Douglass noted, "The cry of Free Men was raised, not for the extension of liberty to the black man, but for the protection of the liberty of the white."[28]

By the late 1850s, it had become a standard part of Republican rhetoric to accuse the Slave Power of a long series of transgressions against northern rights and liberties and to predict that, unless halted by effective political action, the ultimate aim of the conspiracy—the complete subordination of the national government to slavery and the suppression of northern liberties—would be accomplished. Like other conspiracy theories, the Slave Power idea was a way of ordering and interpreting history, assigning clear causes to otherwise inexplicable events, from the Gag Rule to Bleeding Kansas and the Dred Scott decision. It also provided a convenient symbol through which a host of anxieties about the future could be expressed. At the same time, the notion of a black Republican conspiracy to overthrow slavery and southern society had taken hold in the South. These competing conspiratorial outlooks were reflections, not merely of sectional "paranoia," but of the fact that the nation was every day growing apart and into two societies whose ultimate interests were diametrically opposed. The South's fear of black Republicans, despite its exaggerated rhetoric, was based on the realistic assessment that at the heart of Republican aspirations for the nation's future was the restriction and eventual eradication of slavery. And the Slave Power expressed northerners' conviction, not only that slavery was incompatible with basic democratic values, but that to protect slavery, southerners were determined to control the federal government and use it to foster the expansion of slavery. In summary, the Slave Power idea was the ideological glue of the Republican party—it enabled them to elect in 1860 a man conservative enough to sweep to victory in every northern state, yet radical enough to trigger the secession crisis.

Did the election of Lincoln pose any real danger to the institution of slavery? In my view, it is only possible to argue that it did not if one takes a completely static—and therefore ahistorical—view of the slavery issue. The expansion of slavery was not simply an issue; it was a fact. By 1860, over half the slaves lived in areas outside the original slave states. At the same time, however, the South had become a permanent and shrinking minority within the nation. And in the majority section, antislavery sentiment had expanded at a phenomenal rate. Within one generation, it had moved from the commitment of a small minority of northerners to the motive force behind a victorious party. That sentiment now demanded the exclusion of slavery from the territories. Who could tell what its demands would be in ten or twenty years? The incoming President had often declared his commitment to the "ultimate extinction" of slavery.

In Alton, Illinois, in the heart of the most pro-slavery area of the North, he had condemned Douglas because "he looks to no end of the institution of slavery."[29] A Lincoln administration seemed likely to be only the beginning of a prolonged period of Republican hegemony. And the succession of generally weak, one-term Presidents between 1836 and 1860 did not obscure the great expansion in the potential power of the Presidency which had taken place during the administration of Andrew Jackson. Old Hickory had clearly shown that a strong-willed President, backed by a united political party, had tremendous power to shape the affairs of government and to transform into policy his version of majority will.

What was at stake in 1860, as in the entire sectional conflict, was the character of the nation's future. This was one reason Republicans had placed so much stress on the question of the expansion of slavery. Not only was this the most available issue concerning slavery constitutionally open to them, but it involved the nation's future in the most direct way. In the West, the future was tabula rasa, and the future course of western development would gravely affect the direction of the entire nation. Now that the territorial issue was settled by Lincoln's election, it seemed likely that the slavery controversy would be transferred back into the southern states themselves. Secessionists, as William Freehling has argued, feared that slavery was weak and vulnerable in the border states, even in Virginia.[30] They feared Republican efforts to encourage the formation of Republican organizations in these areas and the renewal of the long-suppressed internal debate on slavery in the South itself. And, lurking behind these anxieties, may have been fear of anti-slavery debate reaching the slave quarters, of an undermining of the masters' authority, and, ultimately, of slave rebellion itself. The slaveholders knew, despite the great economic strength of King Cotton, that the existence of slavery as a local institution in a larger free economy demanded an inter-sectional community consensus, real or enforced. It was this consensus which Lincoln's election seemed to undermine,

which is why the secession convention of South Carolina declared, "Experience has proved that slaveholding states cannot
be safe in subjection to non-slaveholding states."[31]

More than seventy years before the secession crisis, James
Madison had laid down the principles by which a central government and individual and minority liberties could coexist in a
large and heterogeneous Union. The very diversity of interests
in the nation, he argued in the Federalist papers, was the security for the rights of minorities, for it ensured that no one interest would ever gain control of the government.[32] In the
1830s, John C. Calhoun recognized the danger which abolitionism posed to the South—it threatened to rally the North in the
way Madison had said would not happen—in terms of one
commitment hostile to the interests of the minority South.
Moreover, Calhoun recognized, when a majority interest is
organized into an effective political party, it can seize control of
all the branches of government, overturning the system of constitutional checks and balances which supposedly protected minority rights. Only the principle of the concurrent majority—a
veto which each major interest could exercise over policies directly affecting it—could reestablish this constitutional balance.

At the outset of the abolitionist crusade, Calhoun had been
convinced that, while emancipation must be "resisted at all
costs," the South should avoid hasty action until it was "certain
that it is the real object, not by a few, but by a very large portion of the non-slaveholding states." By 1850, Calhoun was convinced that "Every portion of the North entertains views more
or less hostile to slavery." And by 1860, the election returns
demonstrated that this anti-slavery sentiment, contrary to Madison's expectations, had united in an interest capable of electing a President, despite the fact that it had not the slightest
support from the sectional minority. The character of Lincoln's
election, in other words, completely overturned the ground
rules which were supposed to govern American politics. The
South Carolina secession convention expressed secessionists'
reaction when it declared that once the sectional Republican

party, founded on hostility to southern values and interests, took over control of the federal government, "the guarantees of the Constitution will then no longer exist."[33]

Thus the South came face to face with a conflict between its loyalty to the nation and loyalty to the South—that is, to slavery, which, more than anything else, made the South distinct. David Potter has pointed out that the principle of majority rule implies the existence of a coherent, clearly recognizable body of which more than half may be legitimately considered as a majority of the whole. For the South to accept majority rule in 1860, in other words, would have been an affirmation of a common nationality with the North. Certainly, it is true that in terms of ethnicity, language, religion—many of the usual components of nationality—Americans, North and South, were still quite close. On the other hand, one important element, community of interest, was not present. And perhaps most important, the preceding decades had witnessed an escalation of distrust—an erosion of the reciprocal currents of good will so essential for national harmony. "We are not one people," declared the New York *Tribune* in 1855. "We are two peoples. We are a people for Freedom and a people for Slavery. Between the two, conflict is inevitable."[34] We can paraphrase John Adams's famous comment on the American Revolution and apply it to the coming of the Civil War—the separation was complete, in the minds of the people, before the war began. In a sense, the Constitution and national political system had failed in the difficult task of creating a nation—only the Civil War itself would accomplish it.

AMBIGUITIES
OF
ANTI-SLAVERY

-»❦{ F O U R }❦«-

Abolitionism and the Labor Movement in Ante-bellum America

Among the more ironic conjunctures of ante-bellum American history is the fact that the expansion of capitalist labor relations evoked severe criticism from two very different quarters: the pro-slavery ideologues of the South and the labor movement of the North. Standing outside the emerging capitalist economy of the free states (although also providing the raw material essential for its early development), the South gave birth to a group of thinkers who developed a striking critique of northern labor relations. The liberty of the northern wage earner, according to George Fitzhugh, John C. Calhoun, and the others, amounted to little more than the freedom to sell his labor for a fraction of its true value, or to starve. In contrast to the southern slave, who was ostensibly provided for in sickness and old age, and regardless of the vicissitudes of prices and production, the free laborer was the slave of the marketplace, and his condition exceeded in degradation and cruelty that of the chattel

Originally published in *Anti-Slavery, Religion, and Reform: Essays in Memory of Roger Anstey*, eds. Christine Bolt and Seymour Drescher (Folkestone, 1980). Reprinted by permission of William Dawson and Sons, Ltd.

slave. The prevailing ethos of northern society—free competition—inevitably resulted in poverty for the many and riches for
the few.

The somewhat bizarre spectacle of defenders of slavery justi-
fying the peculiar institution in language redolent of a Marxian
class struggle has long fascinated historians, as has the response
of anti-slavery spokesmen to the southern charges.[1] Less attention has been paid to the role of a third participant in the
complex debate over the relative status of labor in North and
South: the northern labor movement. It is well known that
relations between abolitionists and the radical labor leaders
of the North were by no means cordial during the 1830s
and 1840s. But the reasons remain elusive. Nonetheless, the
not-too-close encounter between abolitionism and the labor
movement not only raises important questions about the con-
stituencies and ideological assumptions underpinning each
movement, but also illuminates in a new way that historical
perennial, the relationship between capitalism and slavery.

The emergence of the nation's first labor movement in the
late 1820s and 1830s was, of course, a response to fundamental
changes taking place in the work patterns and authority relationships within traditional artisan production. Labor historians
have made the elements of this transformation familiar: the
emergence of the factory system, the dilution of craft skill, the
imposition of a new labor discipline in traditional craft production, the growing gap between masters and journeymen, and
the increasing stratification of the social order, especially in the
large eastern cities. Workingmen responded to these developments within the context of an ideology dating back to the
Paineite republicanism of the American Revolution. The central ingredients in this ideology were a passionate attachment to
equality (defined not as a leveling of all distinctions, but as the
absence of large inequalities of wealth and influence), belief
that independence—the ability to resist personal or economic
coercion—was an essential attribute of the republican citizenry,
and a commitment to the labor theory of value, along with its

corollary, that labor should receive the full value of its product. The economic changes of the early nineteenth century posed a direct challenge to these traditional ideals. "You are the real producers of all the wealth of the community," declared New York's *Workingman's Advocate*. "Without your labors no class could live. How is it then you are so poor while those who labor not are rich?"[2]

The search for an answer to this question led labor leaders to a wide variety of programs, ranging from Thomas Skidmore's attack on the inheritance of property, to the more typical denunciation of banks, merchants, and "non-producers" in general, for robbing labor of a portion of its product. Whatever the specific programs advocated, however, labor spokesmen agreed that workingmen were faced with a loss of their status both within the crafts and in the republican polity. Conditions of labor both in the new factories of New England and in the artisan workshops of New York and Philadelphia symbolized the decline of the "dignity of labor." The phrase which entered the language of politics in the 1830s to describe the plight and grievances of the labor movement was "wage slavery." A comparison between the status of the northern worker and the southern slave—usually to the detriment of the former— became a standard component of labor rhetoric in these years. In language remarkably similar to the southern critique of northern labor conditions, Seth Luther declared that northern mill workers labored longer each day than southern slaves, and in worse conditions. A New Hampshire labor newspaper asked, "A great cry is raised in the northern states against southern slavery. The sin of slavery may be abominable there, but is it not equally so here? If they have black slaves, have we not white ones? Or how much better is the condition of some of our laborers here at the North, than the slaves of the South?" The famous Coffin handbill distributed in New York City after striking journeyman tailors were convicted of conspiracy declared, "The Freemen of the North are now on a level with the slaves of the South." And the militant female textile workers of

Lowell, Massachusetts, referred to themselves during one strike as the "white slaves" of New England, and their newspaper, the *Voice of Industry,* claimed the women operatives were "in fact nothing more nor less than slaves in every sense of the word."[3]

There is no point in further multiplying quotations to demonstrate that the idea of "wage slavery" played a central role in the rhetoric of the labor movement. Sometimes, "wage slavery" was used more or less as an equivalent for long working hours or for poverty. But the meaning of the metaphor was far broader than this. The phrase evoked the fears so prevalent in the labor movement of the 1830s and 1840s of the erosion of respect for labor, the loss of independence by the craftsman, and the emergence of "European" social conditions and class stratification in republican America. Most importantly, working for wages itself was often perceived as a form of "slavery," an affront to the traditional artisanal ideal of economic and personal independence. As Orestes Brownson explained in his remarkable and influential essay, "The Laboring Classes," it was not simply low wages, but the wage system itself which lay at the root of labor's probelms. The wage system, said Brownson, enabled employers to "retain all the advantages of the slave system without the expense, trouble, and odium of being slave-holders. . . . There must be no class of our fellow men doomed to toil through life as mere workmen at wages." The emergence of a permanent wage-earning class challenged the traditional definition of the social order of republican America.[4]

What was the attitude of those who raised the cry of "wage slavery" toward slavery in the South? It has often been argued that northern workingmen were indifferent or hostile to the anti-slavery crusade, or even pro-slavery. White laborers, it is argued, feared emancipation would unleash a flood of freedmen to compete for northern jobs and further degrade the dignity of labor.[5] Yet it is important to distinguish the labor movement's response to abolitionism, and, indeed, to black competition, from its attitude toward slavery. After all, inherent in the notion of "wage slavery," in the comparison of the status of the northern laborer with the southern slave, was a critique of the peculiar institution as an extreme form of oppression (unless one agreed with Fitzhugh that northern labor should be enslaved for its own benefit, a position not likely to find many adherents in the labor movement). The entire ideology of the labor movement was implicitly hostile to slavery: slavery contradicted the central ideas and values of artisan radicalism—liberty, democracy, equality, independence. The ideological fathers of the movement, Thomas Paine and Robert Owen, were both strongly anti-slavery.

Recent research, moreover, moving away from an earlier definition of abolitionists as representatives of a declining traditional elite, has underscored the central role played by artisans in the urban abolitionist constituency (although not the leadership of the movement). In Lynn, Massachusetts, according to Alan Dawley, shoemakers equated slaveowners with the city's factory magnates as "a set of lordly tyrants." In Utica and Cincinnati, writes Leonard Richards, artisans were represented far more heavily among the abolitionist constituency than in the mobs which broke up abolitionist meetings. And the careful analysis of New York City anti-slavery petitions between 1829 and 1837 by John Jentz reveals that in most cases, artisans were the largest occupational group among the signers. In New York, the only newspaper publicly to defend Nat Turner's rebellion was not an anti-slavery journal, but the *Daily Sentinel,* edited for the Workingman's party by the immigrant English radical George Henry Evans. The radical artisans who met each year in New York to celebrate Tom Paine's birthday often included a toast to the liberators of Haiti in their celebrations, and Evans's *Workingman's Advocate* went so far as to claim, rather implausibly, that "the Government of Haiti approaches nearer to pure Republicanism than any other now in use or on record." Evans did acknowledge in 1831 that the labor movement sometimes neglected the cause of the slave because of its preoccupation with the grievances of northern workers. But he added that he remained committed to the total eradication of slavery in the South.[6]

The year 1831, of course, was also the one in which William Lloyd Garrison commenced publication of *The Liberator,* the point from which historians usually date the emergence of a new, militant, immediatist abolitionist crusade. As is well known, Garrison addressed the condition of northern labor, and the activities of the labor movement, in his very first issue:[7]

> An attempt has been made—it is still making—we regret to say, with considerable success—to inflame the minds of our working classes against the more opulent, and to persuade men that they are contemned and oppressed by a wealthy aristocracy. . . . It is in the highest degree criminal . . . to exasperate our mechanics to deeds of violence, or to array them under a party banner, for it is not true that, at any time, they have been the objects of reproach. Labour is not dishonourable. The industrious artisan, in a government like ours, will always be held in better estimation than the wealthy idler. . . . We are the friends of reform; but this is not reform, which in curing one evil, threatens to inflict a thousand others.

Of course, Garrison's point about the high regard in which labor was held was precisely what the labor movement contended was no longer true. Four weeks after the editorial appeared, Garrison published a response by the labor reformer William West, arguing that there was, in fact, a "very intimate connexion" between abolition and the labor movement, since each was striving to secure "the fruits of their toil" to a class of workingmen. To which Garrison responded with another denunciation, phrased in the extreme language so characteristic of all his writing:[8]

> In a republican government . . . where hereditary distinctions are obsolete . . . where the avenues of wealth, distinction and supremacy are open to all; [society] must, in the nature of things, be full of inequalities. But these can exist without an assumption of rights—without even a semblance of oppression. There is a prevalent opinion, that wealth and aristocracy are indissolubly allied;

and the poor and vulgar are taught to consider the opulent as their natural enemies. Those who inculcate this pernicious doctrine are the worst enemies of the people, and, in grain, the real nobility. . . . It is a miserable characteristic of human nature to look with an envious eye upon those who are more fortunate in their pursuits, or more exalted in their station.

Thus, from the very outset, a failure of communication characterized relations between the two movements. Fifteen years later, the utopian socialist Albert Brisbane called on abolitionists to "include in their movement, a reform of the present wretched organization of labor, called the wage system. It would add to their power by interesting the producing classes . . . and would prepare a better state for the slaves when emancipated, than the servitude to capital, to which they now seem destined."[9] The proposed alliance never did take place, and Garrison's early editorials suggest some of the reasons. It is not precisely that the abolitionists were complacently "middle class" in outlook, a characterization found quite frequently in the recent historical literature. Abolitionists—both Garrisonians and their opponents within the movement—threw themselves with enthusiasm into all sorts of other movements to reform American society, from the abolition of capital punishment to women's rights, temperance, peace, etc. They often criticized the spirit of competition, individualism, and greed so visible in northern life, as the antithesis of Christian brotherhood and love.[10] It will not do to defang the abolitionist crusade: it was indeed a radical impulse, challenging fundamental aspects of American life (and none so deeply embedded as racism). But in its view of economic relations it did speak the language of northern society. Perhaps this is why the movement, so feared at the outset, eventually could become respectable.

In contrast to the labor movement, most abolitionists—as Garrison's early editorials made clear—accepted social inequality as a natural reflection of individual differences in talent, ambition, and diligence, and perceived the interests of capital and labor as existing in harmony rather than conflict. As a result, they were unable to understand, much less sympathize with, the aims of the labor movement or the concept of "wage slavery." Their attitude toward labor was graphicly revealed in a pamphlet published by the New York abolitionist William Jay in the mid-1830s. In the course of a discussion of the benefits of immediate emancipation, Jay sought to answer the perennial question, what would happen to the slave when free:[11]

> He is free, and his own master, and can ask for no more. Yet he is, in fact, for a time, absolutely dependent on his late owner. He can look to no other person for food to eat, clothes to put on, or house to shelter him. . . . [He is required to work], but labor is no longer the badge of his servitude and the consummation of his misery, for it is *voluntary*. For the first time in his life, he is a party to a contract. . . . In the course of time, the value of negro labor, like all other vendible commodities, will be regulated by the supply and demand.

What is particularly noteworthy in this extraordinary argument is, first, Jay's ready acceptance of the condition which caused so much complaint among the labor movement—the treatment of human labor as a "vendible commodity," and second, the rather loose use of the word "voluntary" to describe the labor of an individual who owns nothing and is "absolutely dependent" on his employer. To the labor movement, Jay's description of emancipation would qualify as a classic instance of "wage slavery"; to Jay, it was an economic definition of freedom.

The labor movement, articulating an ideal stretching back to the republican tradition of the American Revolution, equated freedom with ownership of productive property. To the abolitionists, expressing a newer, liberal definition, freedom meant self-ownership—that is, simply not being a slave. It is one of the more tragic ironies of this complex debate that, in the process of attempting to liberate the slave, the abolitionists did so much to promote a new and severely truncated definition of freedom for both blacks and whites. As many historians have observed, the abolitionist conception of both slavery and freedom was profoundly individualistic. Abolitionism understood slavery not as a class relationship, but as a system of arbitrary and illegitimate power exercised by one individual over another. The slaves and, to some extent, northern workers, were not downtrodden classes but suffering individuals, and it was this liberal, individualist definition of personal freedom which not only cut abolitionists off from the labor movement, but, as Gilbert Osofsky argued, prevented them from making a meaningful response to the economic condition of the Irish, despite a principled effort to overcome nativism and reach out for Irish-American support in the 1840s.[12]

The intense individualism of the abolitionists, historians are agreed, derived from the great revivals of the Second Great Awakening, which identified moral progress with each individual's capacity to act as an instrument of God and opened the possibility of conversion for all as the prelude to eliminating sin from society and paving the way for the Second Coming. Religious benevolence was, it seems clear, the primary root of ante-bellum reform.[13] But it was not the only root, and historians' single-minded emphasis on revivalist Protestantism as the origin of immediate abolitionism has tended to obscure the equally sincere anti-slavery convictions of the radical artisans, so many of whom were influenced by Enlightenment deism. Indeed, the tensions between the labor movement and evangelical abolitionism were part of a larger confrontation during the 1830s between evangelicism and the powerful opposition it generated within northern society. As Jentz has shown, the New York Workingman's leaders were intensely hostile to the evangelical campaign, viewing it as an attempt to unite church and state in a campaign for special privileges incompatible with the principles of republicanism. The campaign against the Sunday mails, led by Lewis and Arthur Tappan shortly before their involvement in abolitionism, aroused considerable opposition among free-thinking artisans, and these same radical artisans were estranged from the anti-slavery movement because of the

presence of evangelicals like the Tappans in leadership positions. Nonetheless, when New York's anti-abolitionist riot occurred in 1834, George Henry Evans defended the right of the
Tappan brothers to freedom of speech. Later, he again praised
abolition as a "just and good cause," although he could not
resist the opportunity to add, "many of the Abolitionists are ac-
tuated by a species of fanaticism, and are desirous of freeing
the slaves, more for the purpose of adding them to a religious
sect, than for a love of liberty and justice."[14]

In the eyes of Evans and the radical workingmen for whom
he spoke, moreover, Tappan the intolerant Sabbatarian was
not unrelated to Tappan the wealthy merchant who was one of
the very men helping to transform labor relations at the expense of the laborer. Certainly, the Tappan brothers were not
averse to using their economic power to coerce artisans into
supporting their various causes. In January 1830, a tailor complained that Lewis Tappan approached him with a petition
against the Sunday mails and, when refused, threatened that
the tailor would get no more of the trade of his brother Arthur's mercantile firm. To the tailor, Tappan was a "redoubt-
able champion of Calvinism, illiberalism, etc." To the Tappans,
the "infidelity" of men like Robert Owen and George Henry
Evans was as offensive as their economic views. Indeed, before
leaders of the benevolent empire like the Tappans took control
of New York City's abolition movement, anti-slavery had a reputation for being "largely composed of irreligious men, some of
infidel sentiments."[15] The great revival of the 1830s changed
that, identifying abolitionism with evangelicism and, one pre-
sumes, alienating anti-slavery men like Evans from organized
abolitionism. But, given the large number of artisans who
signed abolitionist petitions, we should not let the evangelicism
of the abolitionist leaders obscure that portion of the anti-
slavery constituency whose roots lay in Enlightenment ra-
tionalism and republican notions of equality and liberty, rather
than in Christian benevolence.

For most of the 1830s and 1840s, relations between the abolition and labor movements remained strained. Open attacks on labor organizations, such as that in the first issue of *The Liberator*, were not, however, typical of abolitionist literature. By the end of the 1830s, abolitionists were making an attempt to appeal to workingmen for support. But, whereas labor leaders tended to see abolition as a diversion from the grievances of northern labor and slavery as simply one example of more pervasive problems in American life, abolitionists considered the labor issue as artificial or secondary. Whatever problems northern labor might have, whatever legitimate grievances it might articulate, were all rooted in the peculiar institution. Slavery, said abolitionist literature, made all labor disreputable and was the cause of the degradation of labor in the North. "American slavery," as one abolitionist resolution put it, "is an evil of such gigantic magnitude, that it must be uprooted and overthrown, before the elevation sought by the laboring classes can be effected." Both abolitionists and labor leaders spoke of the alliance between the Lords of the Loom and Lords of the Lash—the textile manufacturers of New England and slaveowners of the South—but each drew from it a different conclusion. To the labor movement, factory owner and slaveowner were both nonproducers who fattened on the fruits of the labor of others; to the abolitionists what was objectionable in the factory owners was precisely their pro-slavery political stance, not their treatment of their employees.[16]

During the 1840s, a handful of abolitionist spokesmen did attempt to forge an alliance with the labor leaders, moving toward a critique of labor relations in the North. John A. Collins became convinced on an abolitionist trip to England that the condition of the working classes deserved attention from opponents of slavery. Slavery, he concluded, was but a symptom of a deeper problem. "The cause of all causes," the deep underlying root of poverty, war, intemperance, and slavery was private property, "the admitted right of individual ownership in the soil and its products." In 1843, Collins joined the communistic society at Skaneateles in western New York State and the next year began publishing *The Communist*. Still later, this peripatetic reformer returned to the Whig party, convinced that only governmental power could effect social reform. His mercurial career did not exactly generate enthusiasm among his erstwhile abolitionist colleagues. Garrison condemned the Owenite environmentalism which lay behind Collins's utopian experiment, interpreting it to mean that men were not individually responsible for their sins. And Frederick Douglass accused Collins, not without plausibility, of "imposing an additional burden of unpopularity on our cause" when Collins attempted to introduce socialist ideas at abolitionist meetings.[17]

Probably the most prominent abolitionist who attempted to rethink the relation between northern and southern labor conditions was Nathaniel P. Rogers, editor of the *Herald of Freedom*, published in Concord, New Hampshire. (I leave aside here John Brown who was, in this as in everything else, *sui generis* among abolitionists. Brown's career of business failures in the 1830s and 1840s, usually taken by historians as evidence of maladjustment, may have made him rather more skeptical of the virtues of the northern economic order than other abolitionists. Interestingly, the Provisional Constitution Brown drafted to apply to territory he planned to "liberate" in the South included a provision that all property captured from the enemy or produced by the labor of his associates would be held "as the property of the whole" and used "for the common benefit.")[18] Rogers proposed a grand alliance of the producing classes North and South, free and slave, against all exploiters of labor. Living amidst the burgeoning factory system of New Hampshire, Rogers concluded that the abolitionist movement had not only been blind to social conditions in the North, but had directed its appeals to the wrong constituency. "We have got to look to the working people of the North, to sustain and carry on the Anti-Slavery Movement," he announced in 1843. "The people who work and are disrespected here, and who disrespect labor themselves, and disrespect themselves because they labor—have got to abolish slavery. And in order to do this, they must be emancipated themselves first." Rogers soon took to organizing anti-slavery meetings at which the condition of northern workingmen received more attention than the plight of the slave. "Very little time was wasted in talk about floggings and starvings, etc.," he said of one such meeting. "Tyranny here at the North; northern servitude and lack of liberty were our main topics. The working people were admonished of their own bondage and degradation." It is easy to understand why veteran abolitionists might find such meetings disquieting. At one New Hampshire gathering, the *Herald of Freedom* was denounced as an "infidel paper" and members of "the Priesthood," as Rogers called the local clergy, attempted to break up the meeting.

Rogers was unique among abolitionist leaders in his complete rejection of the ethos of technological progress and his acceptance of the idea of conflict between capital and labor. Many abolitonists condemned an excessive spirit of greed in northern society, but most were fascinated by technological change, viewing it, indeed, as yet another evidence of the superiority of the northern social system to that of the slave South. Rogers, however, could write: "The money-built Railroad, like all other labor-saving machinery, makes the rich, richer, and the poor, poorer. . . . Monopoly and capital seize on the labor-saving machine, and wield it to the poor man's destruction." Northern labor, "the slave of Capital," was bought and sold "at auction" as in the South, and the abolitionist movement, Rogers insisted, should demand "Liberty for the New Hampshire day-laborers" as well as for the southern bondsman.[19]

Rogers's position was, to say the least, atypical of the abolition leadership. This was made abundantly clear in a lengthy series of letters and editorials which appeared in *The Liberator* in 1846 and 1847. The issue of September 4, 1846, contained a letter Wendell Phillips had addressed to George Henry Evans, whose quest for a solution to the problems of poverty and inequality had come to focus on land policy. Along with the emigrant Irish radical Thomas Devyr, Horace Greeley, and a few

others, Evans now identified land monopoly as the root cause
of poverty and demanded the free distribution of homesteads
to settlers on the public lands, and a limitation on the amount
of land any individual could own. Land monopoly, which
caused low wages and poverty in the eastern cities, was the underlying reason for the "wages slavery" which, Evans still believed, was "even more destructive of the life, health and hap-
piness than chattel slavery as it exists in our Southern States."
(Moreover, insisted the land reformers in a striking antici-
pation of the debates of the Reconstruction years, the emancipated slave would simply "be subject to the slavery of wages,
to be ground down by the competition in the labor market"—a
view of the post-emancipation situation quite different from
that of William Jay quoted above.) Phillips, while admitting the
validity of some of Evans's criticisms of the concentration of
land ownership, was forced to take exception to the equation
of "wages slavery" with slavery in the South, proposing once
again the abolitionist definition of freedom as self-ownership.
Whereupon Evans responded, "the men robbed of their land
are robbed of themselves most effectually."[20]

This exchange touched off a series of editorials and letters
lasting well into the following year. William West rushed to
Evans's defense, insisting land reformers did not ignore the
plight of the slave. "They do not hate chattel slavery less, but
they hate wages slavery more. Their rallying cry is, 'Down with
all slavery, both chattel and wages.' " Some months later, Garrison accused land reformers of "magnifying mole-hills into
mountains, and reducing mountains to the size of mole-hills" in
comparing labor conditions in the North with slavery. "To say
that it is worse for a man to be free, than to be a slave, worse to
work for whom he pleases, when he pleases, and where he
pleases," was simply ridiculous, Garrison insisted. Moreover, it
was "an abuse of language to talk of the slavery of wages. . . .
The evil in society is not that labor receives wages, but that the
wages given are not generally in proportion to the value of the
labor performed. We cannot see that it is wrong to give or re-

ceive wages." Nothing could have made more clear the gap which separated the social outlook of the abolitionists from that of the labor movement. Garrison, defending capitalist labor relations, viewed the ability to contract for wages as a mark of liberty, and he was wholly unable to appreciate the coercions implicit in the marketplace for labor and the wage relation itself. As the indefatigable William West responded, it seemed "surpassing strange" that Garrison had "lived forty years" and still could believe that the northern laborer possessed complete freedom to work when and for whom he desired.[21]

The debate continued in the pages of *The Liberator* until October 1847, when Edmund Quincy closed it with yet another abolitionist defense of northern labor relations. But, apart from a slight diversion in which one correspondent explained that the rule of Christ on earth required a shift to communal ownership of property, the most revealing contribution came from the pen of Wendell Phillips. Once again denying the applicability of the concept "wage slavery" to northern conditions, Phillips perceptively observed that "many of the errors on this point seem to me to proceed from looking at American questions through European spectacles, and transplanting the eloquent complaints against capital and monopoly, which are well-grounded and well-applied there, to a state of society here, where they have little meaning or application." Phillips was certainly correct that many labor leaders viewed American conditions "through European spectacles." The ferocious attack on the evangelical movement in the 1830s, for example, was seemingly more relevant to the situation in the Old World, where the established churches were bulwarks of the status quo, than the very different religious environment of the United States. But Phillips perhaps failed to appreciate fully the central importance of fear of "Europeanization" as an ideological inspiration of the labor movement. Later in his career, of course, Phillips would himself emerge as an eloquent defender of the rights of labor. But in 1847, his prescription for the grievances of the workingman left little room for social reform or institutional change: "to economy, self-denial, temperance, education and moral and religious character, the laboring class, and every other class in this country, must owe its elevation and improvement."[22]

Perhaps the differences in perception which characterized relations between abolitionists and labor leaders down to the late 1840s are symbolized by the fact that when *The Liberator* in 1847 reprinted an article identifying the condition of northern workers as "white slavery," it did so in its column, "Refuge of Oppression"—a portion of the newspaper reserved for items from the pro-slavery press.[23] Garrison could not free himself from the conviction that, by diverting attention from slavery in the South, the labor movement was, in effect, playing into the hands of the defenders of slavery. Yet at this very moment, changes were taking place within both movements which would transform the relations between labor leaders and anti-slavery. One set of changes involved the emergence of opposition to the expansion of slavery as the central political question of the late 1840s, and the vehicle by which anti-slavery became, for the first time, a truly mass movement in the North. Increasingly, the abolitionists were pushed to the side, while free-soilism took center stage as the most available mode of anti-slavery and anti-southern protest. Evangelical abolitionism, it may be suggested, had done its main work in the 1830s. It had succeeded in shattering the conspiracy of silence surrounding the question of slavery. But because it also generated a powerful opposition within northern society—not only from pro-slavery forces, but from those who could not accept the impulse toward "moral stewardship" which was so integral a part of benevolent reform—evangelicism could not make of abolition a majority sentiment. The more secular, rational, and moderate free-soil position could succeed in a way abolitionism could not.

At the same time, the labor movement, devastated by the depression of 1837–42, was turning toward more individualist and self-help-oriented solutions to the problems of northern workingmen.[24] Evans's own emphasis on the land question, which linked social justice so closely to individual ownership of private property, while seemingly abandoning the cooperative thrust of the labor movement of the 1830s, reflected the change. Evans, as we have seen, still insisted that true freedom required economic independence, but he appeared to be abandoning his critique of the wage system itself. Land reform, not a change in the system of production and labor relations, would solve the problem of urban poverty and offer every workingman the opportunity to achieve economic independence, in the form of a homestead.[25]

Free-soilism was not only the means by which anti-slavery rose to political dominance in the 1850s, but the meeting ground for the two strands of anti-slavery thought which had remained estranged in the 1830s and 1840s. The ideological debate between labor and abolition was solved, in a sense, by the early Republican party, for whom the difference between the condition of labor North and South became a potent political rallying cry. The Republican ideology has been analyzed in detail elsewhere[26]; here I want only to suggest that while the Republicans absorbed much of the moral fervor of the abolitionists—while at the same time making that fervor politically respectable and abandoning the abolitionist demand for equal rights for free blacks—their conception of labor and their definition of freedom had much in common with the themes articulated by the labor movement. In the hands of Abraham Lincoln, the workingman's right to the fruits of his own labor became a devastating critique of the peculiar institution. The Republicans accepted the labor leaders' definition of freedom as resting on economic independence rather than, as the abolitionists had insisted, on self-ownership. To Lincoln, the man who worked for wages all his life was indeed almost as unfree as the southern slave. The anti-slavery of a man like Lincoln (who was personally something of a deist) seemed to connect more directly with the artisan anti-slavery tradition than with evangelical abolition. But like the abolitionists, Lincoln and the Republicans located the threat to the independence of the northern workingman outside northern society. It was not the wage system, but the expansion of slavery, which threatened to destroy the independence of the northern worker, his opportunity to escape from the wage-earning class and own a small farm or shop. For if slavery were allowed to expand into the western territories, the safety-valve of free land for the northern worker and farmer would be eliminated, and northern social conditions would soon come to resemble those of Europe. The Republicans therefore identified themselves with the aspirations of northern labor in a way abolitionists never did, but at the same time, helped turn those aspirations into a critique of the South, not an attack on the northern social order.[27]

It has recently been argued, in quite brilliant fashion, that the abolitionist movement in England helped to crystallize middle-class values and identify them with the interests of society at large. By isolating slavery as an unacceptable form of labor exploitation, abolition implicitly (though usually unintentionally) diverted attention from the exploitation of labor taking place within the emergent factory system. "The anti-slavery movement," in other words, "reflected the needs and values of the emerging capitalist order."[28]

Professor David Brion Davis, who is, of course, responsible for this interpretation, does note, almost in passing, that in the 1790s anti-slavery maintained strong links to the radical artisan societies, who were anything but defenders of "the emerging capitalist order." Yet he gives the impression, perhaps inadvertently, that labor anti-slavery either died out, or was subsumed within an evangelical abolitionism which represented the hegemony of middle-class values in nineteenth-century England. A somewhat similar point has recently been made by Alan Dawley regarding the United States. In his study of the transformation of work in Lynn, Dawley argues that the crusade against slavery diverted attention from the evils of the factory system, stunted the growth of ideas critical of the regime of the factory owners, and, in general, crowded labor radicalism "off the center stage" of political debate. Had it not been for the dominance of the slavery issue in the 1850s and 1860s, Dawley suggests—rather implausibly, I might add—an independent labor party might have emerged in the North. As it was, the Lynn shoemakers joined hands with their employers in a crusade against the South, instead of directing their assault against targets at home. "It is difficult to avoid the conclusion that an entire generation was side-tracked in the 1860s because of the Civil War."[29]

Did the crusade against slavery foreclose the possibility of radical criticism within northern society? Toward the end of the nineteenth century, the great reformer Edward Bellamy made a similar point about Horace Greeley. Greeley, who had been attracted to communitarianism in the 1840s and had authored stinging condemnations of northern labor conditions, by the next decade, as spokesman for the Republican party, was glorifying northern labor relations in contrast to those of the South. "Horace Greeley," wrote Bellamy, "would very possibly have devoted himself to some kind of socialistic agitation had not the slavery agitation come on." Bellamy considered Greeley's change of heart inevitable and necessary: "slavery had to be done away with" before social reform could commence in the North. But others were not so certain. Even during the 1830s and 1840s some labor leaders had accused the abolitionists of being the stalking horses for northern capitalists, seeking to divert attention from the labor issue in the North. One anti-abolitionist pamphlet charged that abolitionists themselves were employers who "bask in the sunshine of wealth obtained by pilfering the mechanic's labor." More typical was the perception of an alliance of abolitionists and capitalists, expressed, for instance, in a poem originally published in England and reprinted in an American labor journal, describing the death of a factory girl from starvation:[30]

That night a chariot passed her
While on the ground she lay,
The daughters of her master
An evening visit pay.
Their tender hearts are sighing
As Negroes' woes are told
While the white slave was dying,
Who earned her father's gold.

Unfortunately, this is not only bad poetry, but bad history. The Lords of the Loom were not interested in hearing about "Negroes' woes." Far from being in some kind of tacit alliance with abolitionists, they were among the most pro-slavery and anti-abolitionist group in the North. This fact, it seems to me, casts a certain doubt on the Davis thesis—at least if one wanted to apply it to America—and the arguments of Dawley. Or, perhaps, it simply points up again the ambiguity of the abolitionist heritage. In the hands of a Garrison, anti-slavery did, indeed, promote the acceptance of the free labor market and the capitalist order of the North. So too did the glorification of the northern social order by the Republicans in the 1850s. But that fact should not lead us to forget the other anti-slavery tradition, that of the early labor movement. Eclipsed by the rise of evangelical reform, sidetracked, perhaps, by the free-labor ethos of the Republican party, the labor-oriented critique which linked slavery to labor conditions in the North rose like a phoenix from the ashes of the Civil War, to inspire the great crusades of the National Labor Union, the Knights of Labor, and even the Irish-American Land League.[31] If anti-slavery promoted the hegemony of middle-class values, it also provided a language of politics, a training in organization, for critics of the emerging order. The anti-slavery crusade was a central terminus, from which tracks ran leading to every significant attempt to reform American society after the Civil War. And the notion of "wage slavery," and the traditional republican definition of freedom it embodied, lived on to help frame the social conflicts of late nineteenth-century America.[32]

Racial Attitudes
of the
New York Free Soilers

In the United States of the mid-nineteenth century, racial prejudice was all but universal. Belief in black inferiority formed
a central tenet of the southern defense of slavery, and in the
North too, many who were undecided on the merits of the
peculiar institution, and even those who disapproved of it, believed that the Negro was by nature destined to occupy a subordinate position in society. After all, until 1780 slavery had existed throughout the country, and it was only in 1818 that
provision had been made for its abolition in every northern
state. And even after slavery had been banished from the
North, that section continued to subject free Negroes to legal
and extra-legal discrimination in almost every phase of their
lives. Though these restrictions were less severe than in the
South, most of the free states denied blacks the right of suffrage, subjected them to segregation in transportation, excluded them from all but menial employment, and barred their
children from the public schools. In the decade of the 1850s,

Originally published in *New York History*, XLVI (Oct. 1965), 311–29. Reprinted
by permission of the New York State Historical Association.

four northern states—Indiana, Iowa, Illinois, and Oregon
—went so far as to pass legislation prohibiting Negroes from
entering their territory. One contemporary black writer could
well complain of the "bitterness, malignity, and cruelty of the
American prejudice against colour." The Free Soiler from Indiana George W. Julian put it more bluntly. "The American
people," he wrote, "are emphatically a *Negro-hating* people."[1]

With anti-black feeling so deep-seated and widespread, it
was inevitable that all political parties would have to cope with
the problem of racial prejudice. From its beginning, the anti-
slavery movement had included social and political equality for
northern Negroes as an essential aspect of its program. But
even the abolitionist Liberty party found that its efforts were
hampered by prejudice within its ranks. In one celebrated incident, a Michigan convention denied two Negro delegates the
right to participate in the nomination of candidates on the
ground that they were not legal voters. And in 1844, the party
nominated for the Vice-Presidency ex-Senator Thomas Morris,
a staunch foe of Negro suffrage. Nonetheless, the party constantly avowed its commitment to "the principles of Equal
Rights," and urged its supporters to combat "any inequality of
rights and privileges . . . on account of color." Almost without
exception, the state and national Liberty platforms included
such resolutions, and throughout the North, the party was an
ardent opponent of political and social discrimination against
the free Negro.[2]

During the decade of the 1840s, great numbers of northerners became opponents of slavery, moved either by the moral
appeals of the abolitionists, fear of the southern Slave Power,
or apprehension that the extension of slavery into the newly
acquired territories would exclude free northern settlers. But
astute observers recognized that many who held these views
had been prevented from embracing anti-slavery because of
the Liberty party's adoption of political and social equality for
blacks as one of its major goals. In order for the political
anti-slavery movement to attract a wide following it would have

to adopt a platform so broad that both the prejudiced and the advocates of equal rights could support it. In other words, it would have to divorce itself from the ideal of equality.

That the Free Soil party would achieve this divorce was perhaps to be expected. For although it was established in 1848 as a coalition of anti-slavery Democrats, Whigs, and Liberty party men, united by their opposition to the extension of slavery, the leading organizers of the party came from the Democracy of New York State, which had long opposed the granting of political rights to black citizens. In New York, where Negro suffrage had been almost wholly a party issue, first the Federalists and then the Whigs had endorsed political equality, while the Democratic-Republicans and later the Jacksonian Democrats, with their close ties to the South, had taken the opposite position. Since Negroes, who until 1821 enjoyed full suffrage rights, tended to vote Federalist, and since the Democratic-Republicans and the Democrats were chiefly supported by those elements of the population that feared Negro competition and wished to make the state unattractive for black immigration, the Democrats had both political and economic reasons for wishing to restrict Negro suffrage. At the Constitutional Convention of 1821, the Democrats, even as they were striving to remove all property qualifications for white voters, succeeded in instituting a $250 property requirement for blacks.[3]

In 1846, when another Constitutional Convention was held, friends and opponents of the Negro again divided along party lines. The Whig party did not formally endorse equal suffrage, doubtless because of the prevailing prejudice, but its views were made known through unofficial sources. The leading Whig journal, Horace Greeley's New York *Tribune,* listed elimination of the property qualification for Negroes among its proposals for constitutional reform, and bewailed the "Colorphobia which prevails so extensively in the ranks of our modern 'Democracy.' "[4] The Liberty party took the same position.[5]

The Democratic press, on the other hand, staunchly opposed

any reduction in the property requirement. The *Morning News,* which espoused the views of the party's loco-foco wing, from which many of the Free Soilers would come, had, in 1845, argued that the annexation of Texas would rid the nation of Negroes by providing a "safety-valve" for their migration to Latin America. Now, it bluntly asserted that the Negro race was inferior to the white, insisted that free Negroes should be allowed no political rights at all, and defended Samuel J. Tilden against the "base charge" of favoring Negro suffrage. William Cullen Bryant's *Evening Post,* soon to become the state's chief Free Soil organ, completely avoided the issue of Negro suffrage in its discussions of constitutional reform, but seemed to agree with other Democratic papers that equal suffrage would dangerously increase Whig power in the state. Though Bryant insisted that free Negroes should be considered citizens, he pointed out that New York's white voters had the right to place limits on that citizenship, if they chose. When the election of delegates to the Convention took place, the Democrats appealed so blatantly to racial prejudice that Greeley later recalled, "we should, in all probability, have carried two-thirds of the Constitutional Convention but for the cries of 'Nigger Party,' 'Amalgamation,' and 'Fried Wool,' etc., which were raised against us."[6]

For some years, the New York Democracy had been divided into two wings, differing on matters of economic policy and federal patronage. At the Convention of 1846, however, both Hunkers and Barnburners stood together to block any extension of Negro suffrage. Thirteen of the Democratic delegates later became prominent Free Soilers, yet none voted in favor of a motion granting equal suffrage to the state's black citizens.[7] Indeed, a majority of these delegates, including Samuel J. Tilden, also opposed a proposal to reduce the property qualification to $100. And when equal suffrage was voted upon as a separate issue in November, it was defeated by a resounding margin: 223,845 to 85,306. St. Lawrence County, in 1848 termed the "banner county" of the Free Soil party, opposed equal suffrage by a two-to-one margin. Years later, Horace Greeley would tell a New York audience how he had stood at a polling place on that rainy election day, peddling ballots for equal suffrage. "I got many Whigs to take them," he recalled, "but not one Democrat."[8]

But the Democracy's unity on the question of Negro rights could not offset its internal divisions on other issues. The party which had enjoyed political hegemony for so many years in the Empire State was disrupted and driven from power by the issue of the Wilmot Proviso. In September 1847, when the State Democratic Convention, controlled by the Hunker faction, tabled a resolution demanding that slavery be excluded from the territory acquired from Mexico, and then denied renomination to the Barnburner Comptroller Azariah C. Flagg, the Barnburners walked out. A month later they met at Herkimer, endorsed the Proviso, and repudiated the Hunker nominees, who were decisively defeated at the polls by the Whigs. The most prominent members of the New York Democracy—John Van Buren, Preston King, Samuel J. Tilden, C. C. Cambreleng, and Flagg—remained aloof from their party in 1848, and organized the Free Soil party.[9]

Although the question of the extension of slavery was the immediate cause of the Barnburner revolt, the bolters did not alter their attitude toward the Negro as a result of their adherence to the Proviso. On the contrary, they made it clear that their support of the Proviso was based as much on repugnance to the prospect of a Negro population, free or slave, in the territories, as on an opposition to the spread of the institution of slavery. Theirs was no moral opposition to the slave system; ex-Congressman Michael Hoffman, for example, a leading Barnburner until his death early in 1848, had sneered at John P. Hale's anti-slavery campaign a few years earlier as "that *Negroism* that shakes the granite hills of New Hampshire." The Barnburners were concerned for the fate of the free white laborer of the North. They had been ardent expansionists and were now determined to prevent the new territories from being

swallowed up by slavery. Free white laborers would never mi-
grate to an area of slavery, both because of their animosity to
the Negro, and because they could not compete with slave
labor.[10]

Over and over the Barnburners reiterated that their interest
was not in the Negro, free or slave, but in the free white laborer. As one Barnburner Congressman put it in 1848:

> I speak not of the condition of the slave. I do not pretend to
> know, nor is it necessary that I should express an opinion in this
> place, whether the effect of slavery is beneficial or injurious to
> him. I am looking to its effect upon the white man, the free white
> man of this territory.[11]

Moreover, when they enumerated the degrading effects of
slavery on the free white worker, the Barnburners invariably
listed association with Negro slaves as most important. They
were worried by the assertions of some southerners, that the
territories provided a "natural outlet" for some of the South's
Negro population, and in order to safeguard the rights of
white labor in the territories, they insisted that slavery, and
therefore the Negro, be excluded. The Barnburners made no
real distinction between the free Negro and the slave, and believed that white labor would be degraded by association with
"the labor of the black race." For them, the terms "free labor"
and "white labor" were interchangeable, as were "black labor"
and "slave labor." Often, the seemingly unnecessary adjective
"black" before the word "slave" testified to an aversion to the
presence of any black men in the territories. "We deem it indispensable," wrote Martin Van Buren (who, in 1821, had been
one of the few Democrats at the Constitutional Convention to
support Negro suffrage) "that black slaves shall be excluded
from the territories." On other occasions, the structure of a
sentence indicated that, in Barnburner rhetoric, white and
slave, and black and free, were perfect antonyms. One pamphlet, for example, spoke of a West settled "exclusively by
white yeomen," as contrasted with the vision of "the same

region given up . . . to a slave population." Thus, the Negro, free or slave, had no place in the Barnburners' image of life in the territories. The Wilmot Proviso, as they saw it, was emphatically "the Laboring White Man's Proviso." [12]

The spokesmen of the Barnburners in Congress reiterated this position. Senator John A. Dix, the Free Soil gubernatorial candidate in 1848, who had made frequent assertions of his belief in Negro inferiority, declared in the Senate that North America was destined to be populated by the white race. In a much publicized speech, he declared that the Negro race was doomed "by the unalterable law of its destiny," to die out within a few generations. The extension of slavery would only diffuse the black race, and prolong its existence. The territories, Dix continued, should be reserved for "the multiplication of the white race . . . the highest in the order of intellectual and physical endowments." Dix's speech was widely circulated and one Barnburner wrote him enthusiastically that it was "the great speech of the present age." Dix also indicated that he opposed the abolition of slavery in the District of Columbia, even though the Free Soil platform called for emancipation there.[13] His attitude toward the Negro and slavery was strikingly different from that of his running mate, the veteran anti-slavery Whig Seth M. Gates, who had voted for James G. Birney, the Liberty party candidate, in 1844. Gates's name was revered by Negroes in both northern and border states as one who hid fugitive slaves in his upstate New York home, and helped them reach Canada.[14]

Even Preston King, the Congressman from St. Lawrence County, who represented the most radical wing of the Barnburners, and who had been denied the Free Soil nomination for governor because of his extreme anti-slavery views, insisted that white labor must not be excluded from the territories, nor subjected to association with "the black labor of slaves." The Northwest Ordinance, he declared, had saved the Northwest from "the evils of slavery and a black population," and any man who opposed a similar proscription for the newly acquired territories, he termed "false and recreant to his race." This did not, of course, alter his hatred of slavery, but surely President Polk's Secretary of War, William L. Marcy, was right when he wrote of John Van Buren and King that, though they would "break up the union" over the Wilmot Proviso, "yet neither . . . care for negroes."[15]

These prejudices were shared by the man whose name had become a symbol of resistance to the extension of slavery, David Wilmot, the Democrat who became leader of the Free Soil party of Pennsylvania. Wilmot, like the Barnburners, did not regard slavery as a moral issue. Although he viewed the institution as a political, economic, and social evil, he was particularly outraged by its degradation of the white race. The Proviso, he explained in Congress, was not motivated by any "squeamish sensitiveness upon the subject of slavery, [or] morbid sympathy for the slave," and he objected strenuously when, as he put it, an attempt was made "to bring odium upon this movement, as one designed especially for the benefit of the black race." Instead, he insisted, "I plead the cause and rights of the free white man." The question was simple—should the territories be reserved for the white laborer, "or shall [they] be given up to the African and his descendants?" Wilmot's answer was emphatic—white labor must not be degraded by association with "the servile labor of the black." Besides, he declared, "the negro race already occupy enough of this fair continent." Speaking at the Herkimer Convention, the Pennsylvanian accepted the phrase "White Man's Proviso" as an accurate description of the measure which bore his name.[16]

Indeed, when Wilmot, a life-long opponent of abolitionism, cautiously held out the hope that in the remote future, the South might voluntarily emancipate its slaves, he stressed that coupled with this should be the "great work . . . [of] the separation of the two races." In addition, Wilmot consistently opposed the granting of political rights to northern Negroes. When a southern Congressman charged that he favored political and social equality between the races, the Pennsylvanian cried out indignantly, "my vote shows no such thing." And when Joshua Giddings proposed that *all* the residents of the District of Columbia vote in a referendum to determine the fate of slavery in the nation's capital, Wilmot was incensed. He found it "highly objectionable," he wrote, "to admit the blacks, bond and free, to vote upon the question."[17]

This blatant prejudice did not go unnoticed in Wilmot's own state. A month after the election of 1848, the *Pennsylvania Freeman*, the Keystone State's abolitionist journal, lashed out at Wilmot after a speech in which he repeated his contrast between "black labor" and "free labor" as if, wrote the *Freeman*, "it were the negro and not slavery which degraded labor." The antislavery organ continued:

> A man of Mr. Wilmot's intelligence and observation ought to know that it matters very little for the honor of labor what is the color of the laborers. Enslaved, his labor is degraded, free, it becomes honorable. Let slavery be abolished and the colored people of the North no longer be identified with an *enslaved* race, and this truth will be seen.

Wilmot's attitude, the *Freeman* conjectured, "seemed the result of an old and unconscious prejudice in his mind."[18]

II

It is not surprising that Negroes and many white anti-slavery men were aware of, and distressed by, these expressions of race bias, even during the organizational period of the Free Soil party. Many looked forward to the party's first national assembly, the Buffalo Convention of August 1848, to determine how widespread prejudice would be in the new party. The fact that Negroes were in attendance at Buffalo, and addressed the Convention, led some to hope that the party would not be marred by anti-Negro feeling. One abolitionist wrote enthusiastically to the Liberty party leader Gerrit Smith, that "men of all political and religious complexions and of all *colors* were called to the platform to address the Convention."[19] Yet the harmony which seemed to prevail at Buffalo was, at best, delusive. Abolitionists did not know that it was only after a bitter argument among the Barnburners, and at the insistence of Martin Van Buren, that they had been invited to the gathering at all. Nor were they cognizant of the behind-the-scenes maneuvering which had been necessary to secure the nomination of the ex-President.[20]

And even in the atmosphere of enthusiasm which animated the delegates, racial prejudice did not subside. Francis W. Bird of Massachusetts was presiding officer of one of the sessions. Years later he told how Barnburner delegates surrounded him, urging him not to give the floor to the black abolitionist Frederick Douglass. "They didn't want a 'nigger' to talk to them," he recalled. "I told them," Bird continued, "we came there for free soil, free speech and free men; and I gave a hint to Mr. Douglass that if he would claim the floor when the gentleman who was then speaking gave it up, he should certainly have it."[21] It is true that Douglass was warmly applauded, and that when he indicated that he did not intend to speak, the delegates seemed disappointed. Yet the Negroes who did speak did not receive a completely cordial reception. One Ohio delegate, for example, complained that he resented "taking his cue from a 'nigger.' "[22]

The platform adopted at Buffalo, written by Salmon P. Chase, the Liberty party leader from Ohio, and the Barnburner Benjamin F. Butler, met with the almost unanimous approval of the Liberty men present.[23] In order to secure the nomination of Van Buren, the Barnburners had had to accept a more radical program than they themselves would have written. Thus, the Buffalo platform not only opposed the extension of slavery, but also advocated homestead legislation, and called upon the federal government to disassociate itself from the institution of slavery. Though it acknowledged that slavery in the states was outside the province of federal power, it did call for abolition in the District of Columbia. "The Liberty platform," exclaimed the Chicago *Western Citizen,* "has been adopted by the Free Soil party and its nominee," and almost without exception, the Liberty press of the country flocked to the new standard. Joshua Leavitt, Liberty party leader from Massachusetts, in a widely publicized remark asserted at Buffalo, "the Liberty party is not dead, but translated," and he later wrote an open letter to the supporters of the Liberty party, urging them to vote for Van Buren. The Liberty presidential candidate, John P. Hale, quickly withdrew his candidacy, and one of his abolitionist constituents wrote him that he could "stand very comfortably" on the Buffalo platform.[24]

But one basic plank of the Liberty platform had been sacrificed. Leavitt could ask rhetorically, "what have we lost? Not one of our principles, not one of our aims, not one of our men," but many Liberty men and many Negroes remembered that James G. Birney had written that "the grant of the Elective Franchise to the colored people" was a primary goal of his party.[25] The "translation" of the Liberty party had only been achieved at the expense of the ideal of equality.

To many black leaders, and to the radical wing of the Liberty party, led by Gerrit Smith, this change could not go unnoticed. When a small Negro newspaper, the *Ram's Horn* of New York City, endorsed Van Buren, Smith wrote a sharp letter of protest. He had thought, he wrote, that it would be unnecessary to explain to black men why they should not support the Free Soilers. It was obvious that Van Buren was making no efforts either to deliver the Negro race from slavery, or to combat racial prejudice. The Free Soil candidate, Smith insisted, differed in no essential respect from the vast majority of his fellow Americans in his "views and treatment of the colored race." In view of these facts, Smith contended, black citizens could not expect any better treatment from a Free Soil government than a Democratic or Whig administration. Negroes, he concluded, should not vote for Free Soilers, who "acquiesce, and even take part, in the proscription and crushing of your race," but should give their suffrage to Smith himself. Smith

was running as a Liberty party candidate, and espoused equal
rights for all men.[26]

Samuel R. Ward, a black abolitionist who had been present
at Buffalo, offered the same advice to the Negro community.
The absence of a plank advocating equal rights in the Buffalo
platform might seem an oversight, he wrote, but actually, "it
has the appearance of studied and deliberate design." Ward
pointed out that the Barnburners had always opposed Negro
suffrage, and argued that the equal rights plank had been in-
tentionally left out of the platform, in order not to conflict with
the "words, deeds and character of the leading men of the Free
Soil party in this state." The Free Soilers of New York, wrote
Ward, were "as ready to rob black men of their rights now as
ever they were . . . Mr. Dix and Mr. Butler we know to be
approvers and fosterers of the bitterest prejudices against
us."[27]

Not all Negro leaders, however, agreed with Ward. Frederick
Douglass, for example, though he himself was a non-voting, or
Garrisonian, abolitionist in 1848, urged those friends of the
slave who did vote to support Van Buren. Many Free Soilers,
he insisted, had changed their attitude toward the Negro, and
the party as a whole should be judged by its deeds, not its
words. Besides, few abolitionists had completely freed themselves from prejudice, and bias in the Free Soil party might be
combatted by Negroes working within the new organization.
Douglass realized that men like Gerrit Smith, who had close
personal relationships with free Negroes, were much more
likely to be egalitarian in their views than men like the upstate
New York Barnburners, who rarely saw a Negro. Another
Negro, in a letter to Douglass's newspaper, the *North Star*,
though admitting that it was "well known" that nine-tenths of
the Barnburners had opposed equal suffrage, and would in all
probability do so again, argued that the absence of an equal
rights plank in the Buffalo platform should not prevent Negroes in other states from supporting the party. This, he continued, was a local, not a national issue, and would therefore be

out of place in a national platform. New York Negroes, however, were advised to think twice before supporting Dix and
the other Barnburners, who had openly proclaimed the white
race's superiority.[28]

Apparently, most of the free Negroes of the North adopted
this line of thinking, for outside New York, where Free Soil
leaders were mostly former Liberty men or Whigs, more favor-
able to Negro rights than the New York Free Soilers, black citizens overwhelmingly supported the new party. In the Empire
State, however, many remembered that the Liberty party, as
late as 1847, had included the "local issue" of equal rights in its
national resolutions, and followed the advice of Ward: vote
"for Smith and Equal Rights."[29]

By 1850, the New York Democracy had been reunited, and
many of the Free Soil leaders, including C. C. Cambreleng,
John Van Buren, and Samuel J. Tilden, remained with their
party through the Civil War. Even those who, like King, were
destined to join the Republican party within a few years, accepted the Compromise of 1850 and expressed the hope that
agitation of the slavery question was at an end.[30] Many of the
Barnburners had joined the Free Soil party with the primary
purpose of restoring the balance of power between the sections
in the Democratic party by demonstrating that General Lewis
Cass could not be elected without the votes of northern Democrats, and some desired to defeat Cass solely to "revenge" the
denial of the Democratic nomination to Van Buren four years
earlier. With Cass defeated, they were ready to regard the
Hunkers, as John Van Buren said, as "enemies in war—in
peace, friends."[31] Those New York Negroes who had supported the ex-President in 1848 resumed their attitude of hostility to the Democratic party. Just before the election of 1849,
a meeting of black citizens in New York City announced its determination to work for the defeat of the "union" Democratic
ticket. Commenting on this, the *National Era,* the only national
journal of the Free Soil party, indicated that it was "not much
surprised at the conduct of the colored people." "We trust," the

Era continued, "that the reunited Democracy of New York henceforth will show that it no longer measures out justice according to complexion."[32]

The New York *Evening Post,* however, rejected this advice. In the campaign of 1848, Bryant's journal, like the rest of the Barnburner organs, had opposed the introduction of "negro labor" into the territories. After the election, the *Post* continued to object to the introduction of slavery into the territories, either "under the form of well subdued slaves, or hoardes of free negroes," and it protested vigorously when a southern paper proposed that some of the "dense free black population" of the South be sent to New Mexico and California. Bryant did favor the repeal of some discriminatory laws in the North, but he argued that the free states were an "uncongenial clime" for Negroes, and hoped that the races might be permanently separated. Though the *Post* opposed compulsory colonization, it praised the Colonization Society and the Anti-Slavery Society for "contemplating, in different ways, the good of the African race," and said it hoped that both would achieve their objectives.[33]

In addition, the *Post,* which, even after the reunion of the New York Democracy, continued to consider itself a "free soil" journal, bluntly asserted that the white race was superior to the Negro. In urging black citizens to emigrate to some tropical region, it argued that "unequal laws and inveterate social prejudices" made the elevation of the free Negro impossible in this country. Yet it was sure to suggest that the inveterate prejudices were not entirely unfounded. The Negro was, to be sure, unequal to the white man, for in his new home he would have to "take those primary lessons in civilization which his race has never yet mastered." The two races, associate editor John Bigelow (one of the few Barnburners to support equal suffrage in 1846) wrote, could not prosper together, for "the superior intelligence and advantages of the whites" would prevent the Negroes from acquiring self-reliance and independence. Finally, in 1853, the *Post* published a series of articles which perhaps best characterized its position on race and slavery. The series, a "scientific" study of the Negro race, concluded that although the Negro was by nature indolent, mentally inferior, and "hardly capable of elevating himself to the height of civilization," he was a man, and slavery was "an abuse of superior mental endowment." In this manner, the *Post* was able to combine an unrelenting racial prejudice with an anti-slavery position.[34]

III

In assessing the racial attitudes of the Free Soil party of New York, it must be remembered that the Barnburners were less prejudiced in their outlook than their Hunker opponents. Thus, although the New York counties which Van Buren carried in 1848 had, two years earlier, opposed equal suffrage by 16,668 to 10,166, this ratio (1.6 to 1) was much smaller than the state-wide margin of 2.7 to 1. On the other hand, the counties carried by Cass voted against removing the property qualification for black citizens by 8,597 to 2,540, or 3.6 to 1, far greater than the overall margin. After all, the Barnburners, despite their reservations, were able to participate in the Buffalo Convention alongside Negro delegates, while the prospect of an integrated convention filled the Hunkers with horror. As a Boston Free Soil newspaper put it, "there is no hatred so infernal as the hatred of a Northern Hunker towards the blacks."[35]

Moreover, the rather blatant prejudice of the Free Soilers of Democratic extraction was by no means representative of the views of the entire party. Indeed, the *National Era*, in June 1848, sharply criticized the Barnburners' prejudice. "Studiously placing their opposition to the extension of slavery on the ground of abhorrence of 'black slaves,' rather than the despotism that imbrutes them" it charged, many Barnburners were "apparently fearful of having their Anti-Slavery position attributed to generous convictions of the brotherhood of the

Human Race." "We distrust these men," the *Era* added. And in Pennsylvania, the leading Free Soil newspaper, the Philadelphia *Republic*, openly differed with the views of David Wilmot by denouncing racial prejudice and calling the restriction of suffrage to white citizens a disgrace to the state.[36]

It is thus an oversimplification to equate Free Soil with an aversion to the presence of Negroes in the territories, as some historians have done.[37] The Free Soil party, or, as it was later called, the Free Democracy, was a political party with no truly national organization, only one national newspaper (the *National Era*), and only a handful of recognized spokesmen in Washington. Most of its work was done by the various state parties, some of which died out soon after the election of 1848, some of which survived until 1854, and all of which were completely autonomous. In most of the states outside New York, the Free Soilers came from a tradition of support for Negro rights, and the party, though by no means free from prejudice, sincerely strove to combat discrimination.[38]

But the main organizational impulse in 1848 had come from the Barnburners of New York, and it was inevitable that the Buffalo Free Soil platform would reflect their views. And so for the first time, an anti-slavery political party disregarded the issue of equal rights for free Negroes in its national platform. "The old negro-hating colonizationist of '33 would almost have accepted the present Free Soil platform," complained the *Pennsylvania Freeman,* and it was right.[39] The party's platform was so broad that it could gain the support of those who opposed slavery in order to prevent Negroes from fleeing North and those who desired to keep the territories free from the presence of the Negro slave, as well as the veteran anti-slavery men with their moral abhorrence of the institution, and northerners worried by the great influence of the Slave Power in the federal government. The Free Soil party numbered in its ranks the most vulgar racists and the most determined supporters of Negro rights, as well as all shades of opinion between these extremes. It was the only anti-slavery position that could accomplish this because the question of Negro rights, potentially such a divisive issue, was simply avoided in its national platform.

In this sense, the Free Soil party marked a vital turning point in the development of the anti-slavery crusade. It represented anti-slavery in its least radical form, and its platform gained a popularity which no other could have achieved. Southerners realized that the very fact that the sage old politician from Kinderhook had agreed to run as the party's standard-bearer was proof of its wide support. "Such a man," Calhoun recognized, "would never have consented to be placed in that position unless he was convinced that the North had determined to rally on this great question. . . ." Indeed, some observers believed that Van Buren would have carried the North, had not the free state Whigs and Democrats claimed free soil as their own cause. By the end of 1849, every northern legislature except Iowa's had endorsed the Proviso, and some had even called for abolition in the nation's capital. The effect was summed up by New York's William H. Seward; "Anti-slavery is at length a respectable element in politics."[40]

Even in 1852, when the Barnburners were no longer in the Free Soil party, the ex-Whigs and Liberty men realized that it would be politically inadvisable to call for political and social equality for free Negroes in their national platform.[41] Samuel R. Ward may have been right when he suggested in 1848 that this plank was omitted at Buffalo so as not to offend the Barnburners. But the bulk of the Liberty party and the Free Soilers of Whig background had reacted enthusiastically to the Buffalo platform, even without an equal rights plank, and Free Soil leaders after 1848 realized that to reintroduce a call for equality for the free Negro would cost the party far more support than it would gain. In their short association with the anti-slavery movement the Barnburners thus changed that movement's course decisively. Once the commitment to equal rights had been deleted from the platform of political anti-slavery, it would never again be reinstated.

LAND AND LABOR
AFTER THE
CIVIL WAR

✦ S I X ✦

Reconstruction
and the Crisis
of Free Labor

No period of American history has been the subject of a more thoroughgoing transformation in historical interpretation than Reconstruction, the turbulent era which followed the Civil War. The successive transitions from traditional to revisionist to post-revisionist views of Reconstruction have often been chronicled.[1] More striking, if less frequently noted, is the fact that while an older view of these years as a time of "black supremacy" and rampant misgovernment has long been discredited, no coherent vision of the totality of political and social life has emerged to replace it. Historians have been unable to construct a modern synthesis from the vastly increased body of knowledge and the sensitivity to the politics of race which have been the hallmarks of recent scholarship.

Among the ironies of writing on Reconstruction is that in the desire to jettison the racism of William Dunning and his students—who inaugurated the scholarly study of the period at the turn of this century—their insights have also been abandoned. For, apart from racism, if anything characterized the Dunningites, it was a recognition that Reconstruction was a national phenomenon and could only be understood within a national context. The North, no less than the South, was reconstructed after the Civil War.

At the center of Reconstruction, North and South, stood a transformation of labor relations and the emergence of widespread tension between capital and labor as the principal economic and political problem of the period. The change was more subtle in the North: it involved not the overthrow of an earlier system of labor, but the spread of new forms of industrial organization and labor discipline, and a crisis of the free labor ideology inherited from the pre-war years and based upon the idea of harmony between diverse economic groups. In the South, the abolition of slavery posed the question of labor in a starker form. There, the crucial problem became the one which, over forty years ago, W. E. B. Du Bois identified as the key to Reconstruction: the new status of black labor in the aftermath of emancipation. As William H. Trescot, an unusually far-sighted South Carolina planter, explained to his state's governor late in 1865, "You will find that this question of the control of labor underlies every other question of state interest."[2]

That the transition from slave to free labor involved a revolution in social and racial relations in the South, few contemporaries doubted. "Society has been completely changed by the war," observed former Confederate General Richard Taylor. "The revolution of [1789] did not produce a greater change in the 'Ancien Regime' than has this in our social life." A striking example of the pervasive experience of revolutionary change is afforded in the account of a visit by the great rice planter Louis Manigault to his Savannah River plantation in 1867:

> I imagined myself, for the moment a Planter once more, followed by Overseer and Driver. . . . These were only passing momentary thoughts . . . soon dispelled by the sad reality of affairs. . . . In my conversation with these Negroes, now free, and in beholding them my thoughts turned to other Countries, and I almost imagined myself with Chinese, Malays, or even the Indians in the

interior of the Philippine islands. That mutual and pleasant feeling of Master toward Slave and vice versa is now as a dream of the
past.

Manigault, of course, may have been entirely mistaken as to
how extensively that "mutual and pleasant feeling" had been
shared by his slaves. But it is clear that he perceived himself to
be living in a new and alien world.[3]

The confused early years of Reconstruction become more
comprehensible when we consider the difficulty planters had in
adjusting to their new status as employers, and freedmen in
becoming free laborers. "The former relation has to be un-
learnt by both parties," was how a South Carolina planter put
it. For many planters, the unlearning process was a painful
one. The normal give and take of employer and employee was
difficult to accept; "it seems humiliating," wrote one Georgian,
"to be compelled to bargain and haggle with our servants about
wages." One North Carolina farmer employed a freedman in
the spring of 1865, promising to give him "whatever was right"
when the crop was gathered. Another said he would pay wages
"where I thought them earned, but this must be left to me."
Behavior completely normal in the North, such as a freedman
informing a Georgia farmer he was leaving because "he
thought he could do better," provoked cries of outrage and
charges of ingratitude.[4]

Among white southerners, the all-absorbing question of 1865
and 1866 was, "Will the free Negro work?" For it was an article
of faith among white southerners that the freedmen were in-
herently indolent and would work only under supervision and
coercion by whites. The papers of planters, as well as newspapers and magazines, were filled with complaints of black labor
having become "disorganized and repugnant to work or direction." As one group of Mississippi blacks observed, "Our faults
are daily published by the editors, not a statement will you ever
see in our favor. There is surely some among us that is honest,
truthful and industrious." But to whites, the problem was clear-

cut: as a member of South Carolina's Middleton family put it, "there is no power to make the negroes work and we know that without that they will not work."[5]

In the years following the Civil War, a complex triangular debate was played out among freedmen, northern whites, and southern planters, over the nature of the South's new free labor system. For northerners, the meaning of "free labor" derived from the anti-slavery crusade, at the heart of which stood a critique of slavery dating back at least as far as Adam Smith. Slavery, Smith had insisted (more as an ideological article of faith than on the basis of empirical investigation) was the least efficient, most expensive method of making people work. The reason lay in unalterable facts of human nature. Labor was distasteful, and the only reason men worked productively was to acquire property and satisfy their material wants. Since the slave had no vested interest in the results of his labor, he worked as little as possible. Smith's message had been hammered home by the anti-slavery movement in the years before the Civil War: slavery was costly, inefficient, and unproductive; freedom meant prosperity, efficiency, and material progress.

An elaborate ideology defending the northern system of "free labor" had developed in the two decades before the Civil War. To men like Abraham Lincoln the salient quality of northern society was the ability of the laborer to escape the status of wage earner and rise to petty entrepreneurship and economic independence. Speaking within a republican tradition which defined freedom as resting on ownership of productive property, Lincoln used the term "free labor" to embrace small farmers and petty producers as well as wage laborers. But within this definition a question persisted: why should the independent artisan or farmer work at all, except to satisfy his immediate wants? The answer, once again, derived from the classical paradigm of Adam Smith, as elaborated by his American descendants Henry Carey, E. Pershine Smith, and others. The ever-increasing variety of human wants, desires, and ambitions was, for these writers, the greatest spur to economic progress. It was these "wants" which led northern farmers to produce for the market; indeed, from the northern point of view, participation in the marketplace honed those very qualities that distinguished northern labor from that of the slave—efficiency, productivity, industriousness.[6]

Thus, there was no contradiction, in northern eyes, between the freedom of the laborer and unrelenting personal effort in the marketplace. As General O. O. Howard, head of the Freedmen's Bureau, told a group of blacks in 1865, "he would promise them nothing but their freedom, and freedom means work." Such statements, as well as the coercive labor policies adopted by the Bureau in many localities, have convinced recent scholars that an identity of interests existed between the Bureau and southern planters. Certainly, many Bureau practices seemed designed to serve the needs of the planters, especially the stringent orders of 1865 restricting blacks' freedom of movement and requiring them to sign labor contracts, while withholding relief rations from those who refused. On the other hand, it is difficult to reconcile this recent view of the Bureau with the unrelenting hostility of southern whites to its presence in the South.[7]

The Freedmen's Bureau was not, in reality, the agent of the planters, nor was it precisely the agent of the former slaves. It can best be understood as the agent of the northern free labor ideology itself; its main concern was to put into operation a viable free labor system in the South. To the extent that this meant putting freedmen back to work on plantations, the Bureau's interests coincided with those of the planters. To the extent that the Bureau demanded for the freedmen the rights to which northern laborers were accustomed, it meant an alliance with the blacks. The issue was how the freedmen should be induced to work. Northerners looked to the market itself to provide the incentive, for it was participation in the marketplace which would make self-disciplined free laborers of the blacks, as well as generating a harmony of interests between capital and labor and allowing for social mobility, as, ostensibly, existed in the North. The northern preference for a system in which skilled and educated men worked voluntarily to satisfy ever-expanding wants, generating an endless spiral of prosperity for both capital and labor, was strikingly articulated by the Maine-born Georgia Bureau agent, John E. Bryant: [8]

> Formerly, you were obliged to work or submit to punishment, now you must be induced to work, not compelled to do it. . . . You will be better laborers if educated. Men do not naturally love work, they are induced to work from necessity or interest. That man who has the most wants will usually labor with the greatest industry unless those wants are supplied without labor. The more intelligent men are the more wants they have, hence it is for the interest of all that the laborers shall be educated.

Although Bryant, like so many other Army and Bureau agents in 1865, issued stringent regulations against black "idleness and vagrancy," he essentially viewed the problem of southern economic readjustment through the lens of labor, rather than race. The same psychology that governed white labor, applied to blacks: "*No* man loves work naturally. . . . Why does the *white man* labor? That he may acquire property and the means of purchasing the comforts and luxuries of life. The *colored man* will labor for the same reason."[9]

Spokesmen for the free labor ideology like Bryant viewed the contract system inaugurated by the Freedmen's Bureau in 1865 not as a permanent framework for the southern economy, but as a transitional arrangement, a way of reestablishing agricultural production until cash became readily available and a bona fide free labor system could emerge. General Robert K. Scott, head of the Bureau in South Carolina, explained rather cavalierly to Governor James L. Orr that the state could not hope to escape "the fixed principles which govern [free labor] all over the world." "To the establishment of these principles," he added, "the Bureau is committed." Even Wager Swayne, considered one of the most pro-planter state Bureau chiefs, believed the contract system was "only excusable as a transient." Eventually, as in the North, the natural internal mechanisms of the labor market would regulate employment: "This is more and better than all laws."[10]

Men like Swayne and Scott, however, quickly became convinced that the planters did not comprehend the first principles of free labor. Scott found in 1866 that their idea of a contract was one "that would give the land owner an absolute control over the freedman as though he was his slave." Northern visitors to the South reached the same conclusion. Whitelaw Reid found planters "have no sort of conception of free labor. They do not comprehend any law for controlling laborers, save the law of force." Carl Schurz, one of the most articulate spokesmen for the free labor ideology before the war, concluded that white southerners were unable to accept the cardinal principles that "the only incentive to faithful labor is self-interest," and that a labor contract must be "a free transaction in which neither coercion nor protection is necessary."[11]

Northern and southern perceptions of "free labor" did indeed differ. Planters did not believe that freedmen could ever achieve the internal self-discipline necessary for self-directed labor. The free labor ideology, they insisted, ignored "the characteristic indolence of the negro, which will ever be manifested and indulged in a condition of freedom." It was pointless, therefore, to speak of white and black labor in the same breath: the black was *sui generis,* and you must argue for him upon his own characteristics." Only legal and physical compulsion could maintain the discipline and availability of plantation labor, in the face of the collapse of the planters' authority and the "indolence" of the laborers. "Our little sovereignties and Feudal arrangements are all levelled to the ground," bemoaned one South Carolina planter. As a result, planters turned to the state to provide the labor discipline which they could no longer command as individuals. "A new labor system," declared a New Orleans newspaper in 1865, must be "prescribed and enforced by the state." Hence, the southern legislatures of 1865–66 enacted a series of vagrancy laws, apprenticeship systems, criminal penalties for breach of contract, and all the other coercive measures of the Black Codes, in an effort to control the black labor force. As one Georgian explained, despite the general conviction that "the negro will not work. . . . we can control by wise laws."[12]

The differences in outlook which divided northern and southern whites were strikingly expressed by a southern planter who told a northern visitor, "all we want, is that our Yankee rulers should give us the same privileges with regard to the control of labor which they themselves have." When informed that northern workers were not legally obligated to sign yearly contracts, and that there were no criminal penalties for leaving one's employment, he was incredulous: "How can you get work out of a man unless you *compel* him in some way?" This very question as Joyce Appleby has observed, haunted seventeenth- and eighteenth-century English economic theorists: how could individual freedom and the need for labor be reconciled, especially if it were assumed that men naturally desired to avoid labor? The answer was to posit a labor force imbued with economic rationality, that is, the willingness to subordinate itself to the incentives of the marketplace. "The acceptance of the idea of universal economic rationality," according to Appleby, "was the key step in the triumph of modern liberalism."[13]

"Modern liberalism," however, had implications the leaders of southern society could not accept. The ideological underpinning of economic liberalism is freedom of choice among equals, however much free contract and equality may in fact diverge. By the time of the Civil War, the symbiotic relationship between political and economic liberty had become an article of faith in the North. "Everything which secures freedom and equality of rights at the South," a Republican newspaper stated in 1865, "tends directly to the benefit of trade."[14] And, it might have added, vice versa. As Smith had argued, the market was egalitarian. It freed men from dependent relationships and paternalist obligations, and threatened traditional ruling classes with its guarantee of perpetual social and economic change. By breaking down traditional economic privileges, it fostered the idea of equality.[15]

Yet planter spokesmen did not want a laboring force, black or white, with such ideas. The central premise of the free labor ideology—the opportunity for social mobility for the laborer—was anathema to planters, who could not conceive of either a plantation economy or their own social privileges surviving if freedmen were able to move up the social scale. "You must begin at the bottom of the ladder and climb up," General Howard informed a black New Orleans audience in 1865, but at least he offered the opportunity to climb. A Natchez newspaper at the same time was informing its readers, "the true station of the negro is that of a servant. The wants and state of our country demand that he should remain a servant." A delegate to the Texas Constitutional Convention of 1866 agreed: the freedmen must remain "hewers of wood and drawers of water." As for white labor, there was a concerted, though unsuccessful effort to attract immigrants to the South during Reconstruction. Pamphlets appeared singing the praises of "the thrifty German, the versatile Italian, the sober Englishman, the sturdy sons of Erin," in contrast to blacks who did not understand "the moral obligations of a contract." Yet others noted that such immigrants might bring with them unwanted ideas. "Servants of this description may please some tastes," said a southern newspaper in 1867, "but the majority of our people would probably prefer the sort we have, who neither feel nor profess equality with their employer."[16]

Nor could white southerners accept the other half of the free labor equation—market-oriented rationality on the part of their laborers. In the recent work of "cliometricians" investigating post-bellum southern history, the freedmen emerge from slavery as, to use their terminology, rational, market-oriented profit-maximizers.[17] It is difficult, however, to accept the idea that slavery produced workers socialized to the discipline of capitalist wage labor. The slave's standard of consumption, and his experience with the marketplace, was, of necessity, very limited. The logic of ever-greater effort to meet ever-expanding needs (what capitalist society calls "ambition") had no meaning for him. As one planter complained, freedmen did not respond to the marketplace incentives to steady labor: "released from the discipline of slavery, unappreciative of the value of money, and but little desirous of comfort, his efforts are capricious."[18]

Here, indeed, lies the ultimate meaning of the innumerable complaints about the freedman's work habits—so reminiscent, it might be noted, of labor "problems" in the Third World today. Why did so many whites constantly claim that blacks were lazy and idle? The tendency of historians has been to deny the accuracy of such complaints, attributing them to simple racism. Doubtless, there is justification for this response, but it does not go to the heart of the matter. Consider two examples of such complaints. The first is from a Maryland newspaper in 1864, just after emancipation in that state: "The ambition of the negro, as a race, when left to his own volition, does not rise above the meagre necessaries of life. . . . One fruitful source of idleness has been the ability to possess themselves of a hut and a few acres of land, thereby enabling them to preserve the semblance of a means of living." The second is a remark by the North Carolina planter and political leader Kemp P. Battle in 1866: "Want of ambition will be the devil of the race, I think. Some of my most sensible men say they have no other desire than to cultivate their own land in grain and raise bacon."[19]

On the face of it, a desire to cultivate one's own land in food crops does not appear to warrant the charge of "want of ambition." The term "indolence," it appears, encompassed not simply blacks unwilling to work at all, but those who preferred to work for themselves. The same plantation blacks arraigned for idleness spent considerable time and effort on their own garden plots and, as is well known, it was the universal desire of the freedmen to own their own plots of land. What one Mississippi white called the freedman's "wild notions of right and freedom" were actually very traditional in republican America. Blacks believed, according to another Mississippi planter, "that if they are hirelings they will still be slaves." Whether in withdrawing from churches dominated by whites, refusing to work under drivers and overseers, or in their ubiquitous desire for forty acres and a mule, blacks made clear that, for them, freedom meant independence from white control. "Their great desire," wrote a Georgia planter, "seems to be to get away from all overseers, to hire or purchase land, and work for themselves." From the freedmen's point of view, an Alabama Bureau agent reported, this would "complete their emancipation."[20]

The vast majority of freedmen, of course, were compelled by necessity to labor on the plantations, but they too appeared to respond only imperfectly to the incentives and demands of the marketplace. Many freedmen did seek the highest wages available, whether this meant moving to states like Texas and Arkansas where labor was scarce and wages high, or seeking employment in railroad construction crews, turpentine mills, and lumber companies. Others, however, seemed to value things like freedom of movement off the plantations and personal autonomy more than pecuniary rewards. "Let any man offer them some little thing of no real benefit to them, but which looks like a little more freedom," Georgia's Howell Cobb observed, "and they catch at it with alacrity." And a Mississippi Bureau agent reported, "many have said to me they cared not for the pay if they were only treated with kindness and not over worked."[21]

Instead of working harder than they had as slaves, as Adam Smith would have predicted, the freedmen desired to work less, and black women sought to withdraw from field labor altogether. "The women say that they never mean to do any more outdoor work," said a report from Alabama. "White men support their wives and they mean that their husbands shall support them." Those women who did remain in the fields were sometimes even more "undisciplined" than the men. One rice plantation worker told her employer in 1866 on being ordered to complete a task, "she did not know if she would . . . and could 'not work herself to death before her time came.' "[22]

Most distressing of all, many freedmen evinced a strong resistance to growing the "slave crop" cotton. As one Georgia freedman said, "If ole massa want to grow cotton, let him plant it himself." On the Sea Islands, they refused to repair broken cotton gins and displayed more interest in subsisting on garden plots, fishing, and hunting than producing a crop for the marketplace. Freedom, for Sea Island blacks, seemed to mean "no more driver, no more cotton." The South Carolina planter Edward B. Heyward noted the irony of the situation:[23]

> It seems the belief among planters, that negroes *will not plant cotton* but are interested only in *food*. Wouldn't it be curious if by the voluntary act of the emancipated blacks, the New England manufacturers should fail. . . . They are going to worry somebody, and I think it will be their friends the Yankees. They say we can't *eat cotton* and there they stop.

As Heyward suggested, on the question of cotton a community of interest did indeed exist between northern and southern whites interested in the revitalization of the plantation economy. Their great fear was that the freedmen might retreat into self-sufficiency. "The products of these islands are absolutely necessary to supply the wants of the commercial world," wrote a northern investor from St. Helena, South Carolina, in 1865. Two years later another northerner with an eye to southern investments commented on the absolute necessity of reviving an export cotton crop to "pay our debts and get the balance of trade in our favor." To such men, and many others who looked to the post-war South for the investment of war-generated surplus capital, the idea of granting subsistence plots to the freedmen was disastrous. As Willie Lee Rose has shown, the arguments between land reform and cotton production were articulated during the war itself, in the conflict on the Sea Islands between the freedmen and moral reformers like Laura

Towne on the one hand, and representatives of northeastern business like Edward Atkinson and Edward Philbrick, who envisioned a post-war economy in which blacks worked cotton plantations for reasonable wages.

To Atkinson and Philbrick, the Port Royal experiment provided a golden opportunity to prove "that the abandonment of slavery did not mean the abandonment of cotton," that free blacks could raise the crop more efficiently and profitably than as slaves. Cotton was the measure of freedom, for as Philbrick put it, "as a general thing, the amount of cotton planted will always be a pretty sure index to the state of industry of the people." In order to "multiply their simple wants" as a means of stimulating interest in cotton among blacks, Philbrick established plantation stores, placing a variety of new products within the freedmen's reach. His great fear was that they might retreat into self-sufficiency, removing themselves from the disciplines of the marketplace, eliminating them as consumers of northern goods, and enabling them to resist the exploitation of their labor (except by themselves).[24]

Of course, complete self-sufficiency was rarely possible in nineteenth-century America. But the Sea Island experience—where many blacks did acquire small plots of land—as well as scattered evidence from other states, suggests that black landowners and renters preferred to farm much in the manner of ante-bellum upcountry white yeomen, concentrating on food crops as a first priority, and only to a lesser extent on cotton, for ready cash.[25] The pattern persisted into the 1870s, except where rental contracts specifically required, in the words of one, that "all of said land is to be cultivated in cotton." The ambition of the freedmen to own or rent land, therefore, cannot be understood as simply a quest for material accumulation and social mobility; it reflected above all a desire for autonomy from both individual whites, and the impersonal marketplace. And it was this ambition which frightened both southern planters and the Atkinsons and Philbricks.[26]

The experience of labor in other post-emancipation situations was hardly reassuring to such men. Southerners were well aware of the aftermath of emancipation in the West Indies, which appeared to demonstrate that the end of slavery spelled the end of plantation agriculture. Plantations could not be maintained with free labor, wrote a prominent Charlestonian, "the experiments made in Hayti and Jamaica settled that question long ago." On those islands the freedmen had been able to drift off the plantations and take up small farming, and the result had been a catastrophic decline in sugar production. "See what ruin emancipation brought on that paradise of the tropics," observed one southern writer.[27] Comparative studies of emancipation in the West Indies and South America reveal that nearly every plantation society enacted vagrancy, contract, and debt peonage laws in an attempt to keep freedmen on the plantations. But only where land was not available—or another source of unfree labor was—did the plantation survive. Trinidad, with little free land, was a success: "land . . . is owned by the white man and the negro is unable to get possession of a foot of it." So was Guyana, where imported East Indian coolies replaced the blacks on sugar plantations. But not Jamaica, where uninhabited land was available for the freedmen.[28]

The lesson of the West Indies seemed clear: without "some well regulated system of labor . . . devised by the white man . . . the South would soon become a second Haiti." Basically, the problem seemed to be that free people do not like to work on plantations. This was why slavery had been "necessary" in the first place, and why the chimera of white immigration was bound to fail. As a Georgia newspaper observed in 1866, "everybody must know that no white man is going to work as a negro on a large estate, to rise at the sound of a horn and return when the dews are heavy." But the myth that they would persisted for years, as did the reluctance of white immigrants to move South. The Selma *Southern Argus*, one of the most perceptive spokesmen for the planter class, explained the problem: "Our people . . . have vainly expected an impossibility—white immigrants to take the place of the negro as hewers of wood and drawers of water. . . . They want . . . labor to occupy the social position of negroes and to be treated like negroes." Others looked to the Chinese immigrant, who, it was believed, was more manageable than the black. "He is not likely to covet ownership of the soil, and . . . he is not likely to become a politician," commented a Mississippi planter.[29]

In the end, if the plantations were to continue, it would have to be with black labor. This was why white southerners absolutely insisted that blacks not be allowed access to land. Unlike the West Indies, the "availability" of land in the South was a political issue, not a matter determined by geography, for there was an abundance of uncultivated land. Less than a tenth of Louisiana's thirty million acres, for example, were being tilled at the end of Reconstruction.[30] The fear that access to land for blacks would lead to the disintegration of staple production was graphically expressed by an Alabama newspaper, commenting on the Southern Homestead Act of 1866, which offered public land to black farmers:

> The negroes will become possessed of a small freehold, will raise their corn, squashes, pigs and chickens, and will work no more in the cotton, rice and sugar fields. In other words, their labor will become unavailable for those products which the world especially needs. . . . The title of this law ought to have been, "A bill to get rid of the laboring class of the South and make Cuffee a self-supporting nuisance."

Even if relatively few independent black farmers succeeded economically, the result would be disastrous. As a Mississippi planter put it, in that case, "all the others will be dissatisfied with their wages no matter how good they may be and thus our whole labor system is bound to be upset."[31]

Thus, the problem of adjustment from slave to free labor was compounded by racial and class assumptions, ideas about the nature of labor itself, which dictated to white southerners that blacks not be allowed to escape the plantations, and led many northerners to agree that the road to black landownership should lie through patient wage labor—while market values and responses were learned—rather than a sudden "gift" of land.[32] To complicate matters further, the transition to a free labor system took place within the context of an economic transformation which profoundly affected the status of white farmers in the South as well as blacks.

As is well known, the southern states emerged from the war into a pattern of economic underdevelopment and dependency. Whether one views the ante-bellum South as capitalist (Fogel and Engerman), pre-capitalist (Genovese), or capitalist but not bourgeois—whatever that means—(Barrington Moore),[33] it is certain that the Civil War unleashed an expansion of market relations, reflected in both the emancipation of the slaves and the transformation of the status of the white farmer. The extension of transportation into the predominantly white upcountry, the increased use of commercial fertilizer, and the spread of country stores made possible the absorption of the previously subsistence-oriented upcountry into the Cotton Kingdom during and after Reconstruction. A recent article by Grady McWhiney delineates the change in Alabama from a relatively self-sufficient late ante-bellum society in which 70 per cent of white farmers owned their own land, to a colonial economy, forced into a one-crop mould, and a region that could not feed itself. The most significant aspects of the transformation were first, the fastening of endemic poverty upon the entire South and second, the loss of what McWhiney describes as an independent and leisured, if not indeed "lazy" way of life, based on the free ranging of livestock in the ante-bellum years. The debate over fencing laws in the South after the Civil War reflects the controversy engendered by the change from an almost communal view of land, in which all unenclosed property was deemed open to neighbors' livestock, to a more capitalist and individualist conception. Certainly, economic changes were rapidly undermining the traditional idea that ownership of land was a guarantee of personal autonomy.[34]

The transformation of the status of the white farmer provides an indispensable angle of vision on one of the least understood aspects of Reconstruction, southern white Republicanism. For a time, scalawags, as they were called, controlled the politics of Tennessee, Missouri, Arkansas, North Carolina, and to a lesser degree, Georgia and Alabama. Studies of individual states in recent years have moved beyond earlier debates over whether scalawags were pre-war Democrats or Whigs, to an emphasis on ante-bellum hostility to the planter regime, and Unionist disaffection during the Civil War, as the roots of white Republicanism, especially in the mountain areas stretching from West Virginia down into northern Georgia, Alabama, and Mississippi.[35]

But second only to Unionism as an issue in these areas was the question of debt, the vehicle by which thousands of white farmers were trapped into the cycle of tenancy and cotton production in the post-war decades. The mountain and piedmont areas of Mississippi, Alabama, Georgia, and other states had been devastated by a civil war within the Civil War. Property, tools, and livestock had been destroyed, and the result was severe destitution in 1865–67. "Scenes of the Irish famine" were reported in northern Alabama. As small farmers went bankrupt, large numbers fell into tenancy and lost their lands. Others were forced to grow cotton to obtain needed credit. Governor James L. Alcorn reported in 1871 that tenant farming among Mississippi whites had doubled in the previous decade, and by 1880 one-third of the white farmers in the cotton states were tenants.[36]

The issue of debtor relief pervades the early years of Reconstruction; debates over stay laws and homestead exemptions were as intense as those concerning civil rights for blacks. One correspondent of the North Carolina railroad promoter and banker George Swepson reported in 1867, "everything is so demoralized that men have lost all sight of paying debts," adding that the people would surely "defeat the constitution if repudiation is not in." In Georgia, the homestead and debtor relief provisions of the Constitution of 1868 were the "strong card" of the Republican party, "the most serious obstacle" to Democratic attempts to unite the white vote against Reconstruction. In our preoccupation with the racial politics of Reconstruction we may have overlooked the first stirring of class politics within the white community, a politics as yet inchoate and inhibited by racial divisions, but which foreshadowed the great agrarian upheaval two decades later.[37]

Like the Black Codes of 1865–66, the issue of debtor relief illustrates how economics and politics were intertwined during Reconstruction. For blacks, having lost the struggle for land distribution immediately after the Civil War, the political arena offered an opportunity to compensate for their economic weakness. In many respects, of course, the Reconstruction governments betrayed black dreams. Except in South Carolina, and to a lesser extent, Mississippi, Republican regimes did little to fulfill the shattered dream of forty acres and a mule.[38] In less dramatic ways, however, blacks and their white allies used political power to provide a modicum of protection for black laborers. From the beginning of Radical rule, black legislators pressed for laws granting agricultural laborers a first lien on crops, and such measures were enacted by most of the southern states during Reconstruction. The Black Codes were repealed, along with legislation like that enacted by North Carolina Democrats on the eve of Military Reconstruction, granting a double settlement to landlords in legal disputes with tenants and awarding them the right to appropriate a portion of a tenant's crop on suspicion of an intent to leave for other employment. New tax laws shifted the burden of taxation in a progressive direction, reversing the Presidential Reconstruction policy of high poll taxes and low rates on landed property. And legislation made it illegal to discharge plantation workers for political reasons or, at the end of the year, until they had been paid. "Under the laws of most of the Southern States," a planter complained in 1872, "ample protection is afforded to tenants and very little to landlords."[39]

Perhaps even more significant was the emergence during

Reconstruction of local officials, black and white, who actively sympathized with the economic plight of the black laborer. A recent study criticizes South Carolina's black legislators for not using their power "for the social and economic advancement of the black masses." At the local level, however, that was precisely what many Republican officials tried to do. Contract disputes, during Reconstruction, were heard by locally elected trial justices, and planters were bitter in their complaints over the partiality of these officials toward their black constituents. One leading rice planter observed in 1869, "the planter must have entire control of the crop," but that this was impossible in a situation where "the negro magistrate or majesty as they call him tells them that no rice is to be shipped until it is all got out and divided 'according to law.'" Another Carolinian informed Governor Daniel H. Chamberlain that the state's game laws "would be of great benefit . . . but with such trial justices as we now have, they are not enforced," enabling blacks to hunt on white-owned land.[40]

Similar protests were heard in other states. In Mississippi, it was a standing complaint of whites that they could not prevent the theft of seed cotton and livestock on account of the leniency of black magistrates. Alabama's vagrancy law, still on the books in 1870, was "a dead letter, because those who are charged with its enforcement are indebted to the vagrant vote for their offices and emoluments." In Georgia too, black sheriffs refused to enforce vagrancy statutes and at Darien, where the Rev. Tunis G. Campbell had established an enclave of black political power, a plantation agent found himself "powerless to enforce his orders," fearing the local sheriff would arrest him if he attempted to coerce his black laborers.[41]

An understanding of the class constituency of the southern Republican party not only helps us appreciate the intense opposition it generated, but to reconsider the whole question of the "extravagant" taxation and state expenditures during Reconstruction. That there was corruption and misappropriation of funds is undeniable. But, as Howard K. Beale observed forty years ago, "was not a part of the offense of the Radical leaders that they sought to serve the interests of *poor* men?" As Beale suggested, it was not simply the amount of state expenditure, but that it was "money lavishly spent by men who pay no taxes"—as a Mississippi Democrat put it—which aroused hostility. Property-holders blamed the increasing tax burden on the fact that blacks had no vested interest in government economy, since "nine-tenths of the members of the Legislature own no property and pay no taxes." But there was more here than simply a desire of the propertyless to despoil the propertied. State expenditures during Reconstruction reflected an activism common enough in the North in these years, and should perhaps be viewed as a kind of unarticulated Keynesianism, in which deficit spending financed the promotion of economic growth and the creation of an economic and social infrastructure (railroads and schools) while tax policy promoted a modest redistribution of wealth.[42]

"The Republican party is emphatically the poor man's party of the State," declared a black political leader in South Carolina in 1870. "We favor laws to foster and elevate labor . . . we denounce all attempts of capital to control labor by legislation," a Georgia Republican meeting echoed.[43] In terms of its constituency, the Republicans were indeed "the poor man's party" of the South, but in policy, the situation was more ambiguous. The dominant theme in the policies of state Republican leadership was not precisely the elevation of the poor, but economic modernization. A subsidiary theme, articulated primarily by black leaders (although by no means all of them) looked to a more class-conscious program of economic redistribution. The division was analogous to the Civil War debate on the Sea Islands between humanitarian reformers favoring land distribution and northern investors like Atkinson and Philbrick who feared such a policy would prevent the revitalization of staple agriculture. It had also surfaced in the debates in 1867 over whether southern Republicans should endorse the idea of the confiscation of planter lands.

At stake were competing visions of the role of the state in the post-Civil War South. The "modernizers" saw the task of the Radical governments as moving the South as quickly as possible along the economic road marked out by the North, through aid to railroads, industry, and agricultural diversification. They were willing to protect the essential political and economic rights of southern laborers, and harass the planters with heavy taxation, but would generally go no further, although the assumption of their free labor outlook was that their policies would produce a prosperity in which blacks would share. The "redistributionists" were not opposed to economic diversification, but had little interest in grandiose schemes of economic development. Their aim was to use the power of the state to promote land distribution and in other ways directly assist the black and white poor. Generally, party discipline led most Republicans to support such modernizing programs as aid to railroad development, but there were exceptions. The South Carolina Labor Convention of 1869, headed by the state's most prominent black politicians, urged the legislature to withhold the state's credit from railroads, using the money instead to secure land for agricultural laborers. There were also disputes over the exemption of manufacturing corporations from taxation and the repeal of usury laws, measures modernizers believed necessary to attract outside investment, but which others feared would simply raise the tax bill and credit prices for the poor. As for fence laws, demanded by those seeking a more diversified and modern agricultural system, it was widely assumed that "the negroes will defeat any measures" for such legislation, which would deprive landless blacks of the right to graze their livestock on the land of others.[44]

Control of the state, therefore, played a critical role in labor relations during Reconstruction. The point is not that Reconstruction revolutionized the southern economic order—recent research has demonstrated convincingly that it did not.[45] But in seeking seismic changes, historians may have overlooked ones more subtle but significant nonetheless. In some areas, Reconstruction did serve as a shield, protecting black labor from the most exploitative implications of economic relationships, and preventing planters from using the state to bolster their own position. The class conflict between planters and freedmen in this period should be viewed as an anomalous struggle between two weak economic classes, each of which sought to use political power to obtain economic objectives. The result was a stalemate, in which neither side obtained what it wanted. "Capital is powerless and labor demoralized," complained the South Carolina agricultural reformer D. Wyatt Aiken in 1871. What he meant was that, in the absence of Black Codes and vagrancy laws, blacks, though generally landless, were able to utilize the "labor shortage" to improve their economic standing. Like the land question, the labor shortage was a question not simply of numbers, but of power. Labor was scarce, Aiken explained, not primarily because there were fewer workers, but because those who did work were unmanageable: "Though abundant, this labor is virtually scarce because not available, and almost wholly unreliable." "The power to control [black labor]," the *Southern Argus* agreed, "is gone."[46]

Complaints about labor being "perfectly worthless," so prominent in 1865, persisted throughout Reconstruction. "We are the capital," a Mississippi planter declared in 1871, "then let us dictate terms." But virtually every effort to control wages and prevent the "enticement" of workers by others failed, because they were not backed up by the long arm of the law. And although the data are scattered, it does seem that blacks were able to use the "labor shortage" to effect real material gains, especially between 1867 and 1873, when reports from throughout the South spoke of rising wages for agricultural laborers, increasing numbers of blacks able to become renters, and large numbers squatting on uncultivated land, farming "on their own hook." "The struggle," a Texas planter commented, "seems to be who will get the negro at any price."[47]

Southern proponents of agricultural reform were particularly frustrated at their inability to make labor more manageable, for their plans for a more diversified agriculture required a disciplined labor force. They viewed sharecropping—which had developed as a compromise between black desire for autonomy and planter determination not to abandon plantation agriculture—as a particularly inefficient mode of economic organization. A wage system, Ralph I. Middleton believed, was the only way to control plantation labor, but his employees insisted on a share of the crop, and he was compelled to agree. Middleton envied what he considered the labor discipline enjoyed by northern capitalists. "Rice planting cannot be profitable until the plantations are worked up like factories—on *wages*," he insisted. Aiken agreed: "As soon would I think the Lowell manufacturer should share his manufactured calicoes with his operatives, as to approve giving my labour part of the crop." But like Middleton, he had to agree to this "nefarious practice": "I had to yield or lose my labor."[48]

Some agricultural reformers, indeed, advocated the introduction of machinery and a shift to livestock and less labor-intensive crops like hay, corn, and wheat, precisely because they would eliminate the labor shortage. Unlike human beings, the steam plow was "perfectly manageable." Moreover, said a South Carolina newspaper, "machinery . . . cannot vote." From throughout the South came reports that, beginning in 1867, politics was exacerbating the unreliability of labor. Blacks would simply leave plantations without permission to attend political rallies. Once a week, during the summer of 1867, "the negroes from the entire county" quit work and flocked to Waco, Texas, for political rallies. In Alabama, "they stop at any time and go off to Greensboro" for the same purpose.[49]

Obviously, the economic gains achieved by blacks during Reconstruction were more modest than their striking advances in political and civil rights and education. The failure of land distribution ensured that this would be the case. Moreover, another signal failing of the Reconstruction governments, their inability to protect blacks against violence, often had disastrous economic consequences. While Klan violence was most commonly intended to intimidate Republican local leaders and voters, it had economic motivations and consequences as well. Victims were often those blacks who had succeeded economically, or simply resisted white control of their labor. In Demopolis, Alabama, the Klan acted to prevent black renters from gathering their crops. In Georgia, according to a black legislator, "whenever a colored man acquires property and becomes in a measure independent, they take it from him." In South Carolina, a "posse" illegally harassed a plantation, "because it is rented by colored men, and their desire is that such a thing ought not to be."[50]

Even in the absence of violence, the depression that began in 1873 led to a fall in agricultural wages and drove many black renters back into the ranks of sharecroppers and laborers. And planters increasingly learned to use blacks' indebtedness to limit the freedmen's economic leverage. Even in the best of circumstances, Reconstruction would have been an uphill struggle. Every advantage of education, wealth, and prestige were arrayed against these governments. As a freedman told a northern teacher in 1871, "we've no chance—the white people's arms are longer than ours." But as long as Reconstruction survived, so too did the gains blacks did achieve, as well as the possibility of more radical change, a potential which was only closed off completely with Redemption.[51]

In his classic study *Black Reconstruction*, W. E. B. Du Bois referred to the Reconstruction regimes as the rule of the "black proletariat." The terminology is exaggerated, but Du Bois did have a point, for this was how these governments were viewed by their Conservative opponents. Despite all the complaints about corruption, it was the disjunction between property-holding and political power which most alarmed them. The situation in the South, claimed one "Tax-Payers Convention," was entirely "anomalous; it is perhaps without a parallel in the history of civilized communities." The problem, put simply, was the inability of the upper class to exert its traditional influence on state and local government. Reconstruction, this address continued, presented "the unprecedented spectacle of a state in which the Government is arrayed against property."[52]

The complaints of Democratic politicians and Tax-Payers Conventions present a curious amalgam of simple racism, planter elitism, and traditional Jeffersonian country-party ideology, in which corruption, indebtedness, and the decline of republicanism were the inevitable fate of governments controlled by men lacking the virtue and intelligence derived from possession of property. Generally, the racist element was in the ascendant, but at the same time, opposition to Reconstruction generated an elitist rejection of democracy in any form. This was most striking in states like North Carolina, where a large population of white yeomen had long demanded political and social reforms from the state's Whig elite. "Mere *numbers*," ignoring "virtue and property and intelligence," was no proper basis for government, according to Jonathan Worth, the state's Presidential Reconstruction Governor, for it would produce only "agrarianism and anarchy." Universal suffrage, Worth wrote in 1868, "I regard as undermining civilization," and civilization he defined as "the possession and protection of property." It was clear that such remarks did not apply to blacks alone. In 1867, when General Daniel E. Sickles ordered that all taxpayers—instead of only freeholders—be eligible for jury duty, Worth protested to President Johnson: "to say nothing of negroes, juries drawn from the whites only under this order, would not be fit to pass on the rights of their fellow men."[53]

The idea that republican citizenship should rest on the possession of property was, of course, hardly new. Radical carpetbaggers like the Rev. S. S. Ashley, a religious missionary and later superintendent of education in North Carolina, also accepted the idea that "a great landless class will *per force* be lawless and vicious." Like Thaddeus Stevens and George Julian, Ashley believed the solution was to break up the plantations and "secure homesteads to the landless." Southerners, confronting the challenge emancipation posed to traditional republicanism, favored a different approach—keep the freed-men landless and control their votes or exclude them from the political nation. Allen S. Izard, a South Carolina rice planter, agreed with Ashley that landholding would create a feeling of autonomy among blacks, but his conclusion was far different: "that feeling of security and independence has to be eradicated." Men like Izard wanted the best of both worlds: a free labor system which, however, denied the right of the laborers to a free choice in politics. The requirements of the plantation society demanded a revolutionary rethinking of the definition of freedom in republican America. As a Mississippi planter wrote in December 1865:[54]

> Our negroes have a fall, a tall fall ahead of them, in my humble opinion. They will have to learn that freedom and independence are different things. A man may be free and yet not independent.

In South Carolina, where black political power was most pronounced, so too was the assertion by the white upper class that men of property had a right to rule, and willingness to threaten economic reprisals against those who disagreed. Thus, a Democratic address to black citizens, written by Civil War General James Conner, put the issue with admirable candor:

> We have the capital and give employment. We own the lands and require labor to make them productive. . . . You desire to be employed. . . . We know we can do without you. We think you will find it very difficult to do without us. . . . We have the wealth. The houses in which you live are ours; the lands upon which you must labor or starve are ours.

This address, the wife of a planter observed, was "clear and to the point." The problem was that blacks did not respond to such threats. Unexpectedly, perhaps, while the freedmen did not achieve economic autonomy, they did exhibit a remarkable political independence. As Trescot complained, the result of the Civil War and Reconstruction was to destroy utterly "the natural influence of capital on labor, of employer on employee," with the result that "negroes who will trust their white employers in all their personal affairs . . . are entirely beyond advice on all political issues." (Trescot's interchangeable use of the terminology of race and class was not uncommon during Reconstruction—an Alabama opponent of that state's 1867 Constitution asked, "Shall the white man be subordinated to the negro? Shall the property classes be robbed by the no property herd?") It was the remarkable tenacity of black voters in loyalty to the Republican party, despite economic intimidation, which led Democrats increasingly to resort to violence to destroy their political rights. But whatever the method, "the first thing to be done," as Georgia's Democratic leader Benjamin H. Hill explained, "is to secure Home Government for Home Affairs . . . . We must get control of our own labor."[55]

Only with Redemption could the full force of the state's legislative, executive, and judicial authority be mobilized toward the goal of labor control. As C. Vann Woodward has shown, the Redeemers did not immediately disfranchise black voters or impose a legal system of racial segregation. But in the realm of labor relations, there was no delay. "We may hold inviolate every law of the United States," Georgia's Redeemer Governor James M. Smith explained, "and still legislate upon our labor system as to retain our old plantation system." To this end, Redeemer legislatures during the 1870s enacted a series of measures "for the protection of the cotton planters."[56] Some, like severe punishments for burglary and criminal penalties against laborers (but not employers) violating contracts, harked back to the Black Codes of 1865–66. Others, such as the prohibition of the sale of seed cotton between sundown and sunrise and a change in tax laws to benefit planters, had been demanded for years but rejected by Republican lawmakers. Landlords in several states were guaranteed a first lien on crops, and laws and court decisions now defined the sharecropper as a mere employee, with no property right in his share of the crop until division by the landlord.[57]

At the same time, Redeemer legislatures moved to exert control over the all-important local courts which, in the black belt, could still be controlled by black voters. Throughout the South, as an Alabamian explained in 1876, the proper personnel in local courts, "which deal with the practical rights of the people . . . our 'business and lives' " was essential for "confidence . . . in commercial dealing." Or, as a North Carolinian echoed, "it is absolutely necessary . . . that the county funds shall be placed beyond the reach of the large negro majorities" in the eastern part of that state. Responding to such appeals, Alabama and North Carolina Redeemers adopted new constitutions transferring the power to elect justices of the peace from voters to the state legislature. Moreover, local officials like Georgia's Tunis G. Campbell, who had used their authority to protect the rights of black laborers, were driven from office. Campbell himself was jailed on a flimsy charge of illegally arresting a white man. The consequence of Redemption was summed up by a New York business journal at the end of 1877: "This year . . . labor is under control for the first season since the war, and the next year will be more entirely so."[58]

In 1875, as the struggle over Reconstruction entered its final years, John E. Bryant penned an article for the New York *Times*, explaining political alignments in Georgia and the South. After his retirement from the Freedmen's Bureau, Bryant had enjoyed a prominent political career, although he had alienated many Georgia Republicans by aligning himself on occasion with the state's Democrats. But in 1875, his analysis was fully within the free labor tradition. The actions of Georgia's Redeemers, Bryant argued, demonstrated that at the heart of Reconstruction lay the same issue which had caused the Civil War—the struggle between "two systems of labor," one slave and one free. Northerners believed "that the laboring man should be as independent as the capitalist." Southern whites still, in their heart of hearts, felt workers "ought to be slaves."

Although perhaps overstated, Bryant's analysis did underscore once again the centrality of the labor question to the politics of Reconstruction. But on one point, he was out of date. Was it still an article of faith in the North that the laborer should be "as independent as the capitalist?" As one of Bryant's northern friends informed him, while the *Times* article "shows clearly the views of the old ruling class at the South with regard to the labor question," there was "reason to fear that their general view of society and government was substantially shared by a large class in the North."[59]

From his southern vantage point, Bryant was perhaps unaware of the decline of the Radical impulse in the northern Republican party, its shift, as a recent student has noted, toward "a more distinctly antilabor and procorporate stance." Here, in the increasingly divergent social and ideological bases of northern and southern Republicanism, lay a crucial weakness of the Reconstruction governments. They depended for their existence on the support of the federal government and northern public opinion, but their northern allies were now emerging as the party of respectability, the Union, and business. And northern businessmen, especially those interested in investment in the South had, even in the late 1860s, concluded that the policies of Reconstruction governments were inimical to business enterprise. "No one," a New Yorker wrote Governor Orr, "will invest or emigrate, so long as . . . stay laws are made to prevent the collection of debts." Others insisted that so long as ignorant blacks had a dominant voice in southern public affairs, capital would boycott the South. The conclusion was heightened by the effects of the Panic of 1873, for, as Bryant's northern correspondent informed him, "there is a pretty general impression in the country that the financial crisis of 1873 was owing in great part to the paralysis of the South."[60] But there was more to the erosion of support for Reconstruction than a simple matter of dollars and cents, more, too, than the racism which remained so pervasive in northern life. The change in northern attitudes reflected a crisis of the free labor ideology itself. The rapid expansion of industrial capitalism in the post-war years, reflected in the spread of factory production, the beginnings of modern managerial institutions, the expansion of the mining and farming frontiers, the emergence of a powerful trade unionism, and the devastating depression of the 1870s, posed issues which that ideology, with its emphasis on a harmony of interests between capital and labor, proved unable to answer. For one thing, it seemed increasingly difficult to contend that wage labor was simply a temporary stopping point on the road to economic independence. During Reconstruction the coalition which had fought the Civil War dissolved into its component elements, and strands of the free labor ideology were adopted by contending social classes, each for its own purposes. For the middle class, free labor became a stolid liberal orthodoxy, in which individualism, laissez-faire, the defense of private property, and the rule of the "Best Men" defined good government. At the same time, the labor movement, especially after 1873, adopted the free labor outlook as an affirmation of the primacy of the producing classes and a critique of the emerging capitalist order, rather than as a testament to the harmony of all interests in society.[61]

The irony here is indeed striking. With emancipation, the South came face to face with the problem which, according to Edmund Morgan, had generated slavery in the first place—how to preserve social order in the face of a large, propertyless class of laborers. Yet at the same time, the North was also having to face up to this question. After all, 1877 was not only the year of the end of Reconstruction, but of the great railroad strike, the first national strike in American history, and the first to be suppressed by the massive intervention of federal troops. The same administration which withdrew the last federal troops from the South, within a few months sent them against strikers in the North, while the city of Baltimore, which had rioted against the entrance of federal troops on their way to Washington early in 1861, frantically requested the army to restrain the strikers in 1877. "The Southern question," a Charleston newspaper declared, was "dead"—the railroad strike had propelled to the forefront of politics "the question of labor and capital, work and wages."[62]

Sometimes, historical coincidences are revealing, and 1877 is one of those occasions. For if the Civil War proved that America was not unique politically—that it could not always solve its problems by reasoned disputation—the railroad strike shattered an even greater myth, that Americans could have industrialization without the dark satanic mills of Europe and a permanent wage-earning class, could have capitalism without class conflict. So, in the end, Reconstruction came full circle. It began with southerners trying to adjust to the northern system of free labor. It ended with northerners having to accept the reality of conflict between capital and labor—a reality that southerners, white and black alike, had understood all along.

—❧ SEVEN ❧—

Thaddeus Stevens, Confiscation, and Reconstruction

In the history of American politics, Thaddeus Stevens is something of an anomaly. As a self-proclaimed radical, he seemed out of place at the center of a political system which—with the glaring exception of the Civil War—has perennially prided itself on its ability to resolve disputes without resort to extreme measures. Historians have found Stevens a baffling figure, whose unusual complexity of motivations and unique blend of idealism with political opportunism made him almost impossible to categorize. The most perceptive of his contemporaries described him simply as a revolutionary—or at least the closest thing to one imaginable in American politics. To a British observer, he was "the Robespierre, Danton, and Marat of America, all rolled into one." And a leading American newspaper attributed his influence in the 1860s to the nation's having undergone a political and social revolution which "demanded

Originally published in *The Hofstadter Aegis: A Memorial,* eds. Stanley Elkins and Eric McKitrick (New York, 1974). Reprinted by permission of Alfred A. Knopf, Inc.

revolutionary qualities" of its leaders—qualities Stevens seemed to have in abundance.[1]

Only an unparalleled crisis like the Civil War could have brought a man like Stevens to the fore. His personal character-istics—cynicism, courage, imperviousness to criticism or flat-tery, brutal honesty, and willingness to use daring and even outrageous means to achieve his ends—were as necessary in wartime as they seemed inappropriate in peace.[2] And Stevens's combination of genuine idealism with a pragmatism learned in the school of Pennsylvania politics enabled him to recognize and articulate the policies which Union victory required. While Lincoln declared his conviction that the war must not degen-erate into "a violent and remorseless revolutionary struggle," Stevens saw that this was precisely what it must become. From the outset he insisted that only the seemingly draconian mea-sures of freeing and arming the slaves and seizing the property of the leading rebels could produce victory. In Congress, as chairman of the House Committee on Ways and Means, Ste-vens became "the master-spirit of every aggressive movement . . . to overthrow the Rebellion and slavery." By the end of the war he had acquired a national reputation as the radical of rad-icals, and at an age when most men have retired from active pursuits—he was seventy-three in 1865—Stevens embarked on the most important phase of his career.[3]

Any attempt to analyze Stevens's role in Reconstruction is im-mediately confronted with a paradox. Many historians of the period have depicted him as the dictator of the House and the major architect of Reconstruction. Even such hard-headed con-temporary political leaders as James G. Blaine and Justin Mor-rill viewed him as "the animating spirit and unquestioned leader" of the House of Representatives. Stevens was certainly a master of parliamentary tactics. More than once he bullied the House into passing measures by choosing just the right moment to call the previous question, cutting off debate and forcing a vote. His quick tongue and sarcastic wit, moreover, made his colleagues of both parties consciously avoid tangling with him in debate. As one of them remarked, "I would sooner get into difficulty with a porcupine."[4]

And yet if Stevens was a political "dictator," his power was strangely limited. In Pennsylvania he was never able to challenge the Republican kingpins, Simon Cameron and Andrew Curtin, for control of the party machinery; and even in the House, as one puzzled newspaper observed, "no man was oftener outvoted." In addition, as recent research has made clear, the major Reconstruction legislation was the work of no one man or faction but the result of a complex series of legislative compromises and maneuvers in which moderate Senators and Congressmen had as much influence as radicals like Stevens.[5]

Stevens was in fact not a dictator, but neither was he just another Republican politician. In a period of intense political and ideological crisis, his function was to outline a radical position toward which events would force the party to move, and to project the conditions under which change would occur. At a time when every Congress witnessed a high turnover of Representatives, Stevens had a career of service stretching back into the 1850s. He could remind younger colleagues that he had been through the revolution from the beginning, and could speak of the times when southerners like "the mighty Toombs, with his shaggy locks, headed a gang who, with shouts of defiance, rendered this a hell of legislation." Throughout the Civil War, Stevens would stake out a position, confidently predicting that the nation would move leftward and adopt it within a year or two, and usually he was right. As a newspaper in his home district in Pennsylvania declared, "In all the leading questions of the late war, Mr. Stevens has been in advance of his compeers, but the Government has eventually seen the necessity of giving practical effect to his views of the national policy."[6]

Stevens, then, was "a man absolutely convinced, and in a sense rightly, that he and history were for the moment in perfect step." His record of having been proved right by events helps explain why, when Stevens rose to speak, the House fell uncommonly quiet, the galleries quickly filled, Senators often dropped their work to attend, and, as a freshman Congressman commented, "everyone expects something worth hearing."[7] And yet by the very nature of his leadership Stevens was most effective in providing his party with means, rather than ends. During the Civil War, Republicans eventually came to agree with Stevens that freeing and arming the slaves was the only way to achieve the unquestioned goal of Union victory. And during Reconstruction, Stevens would be most successful when his proposals seemed to provide ways of moving toward the party's commonly held goals of Republican ascendancy in the national government, protection of the basic rights of the freedmen, and reorganization of southern governments under the control of genuinely loyal men. Thus as events convinced Republicans that Stevens's proposals, including civil rights and suffrage for the freedmen, a period of military rule in the South, and even the impeachment of the President, were necessary for the achievement of their basic aims, they would follow Stevens—or at least move to the positions he had outlined. But Stevens failed completely in pressing for the confiscation and redistribution of the lands of the leading rebels, because he was unable to convince his party that such a policy was either an essential goal or an acceptable means to other ends.

The issue of confiscation had roots stretching back to the first years of the Civil War, when abolitionists and radical Republicans first linked the goal of landownership for southern blacks with that of emancipation. And as the war progressed, increasing numbers of Republicans were converted to the view that the confiscation of rebel property would be a legitimate war measure. The first Confiscation Act, of August 1861, was directed only against property used in aid of the rebellion, but in 1862 Congress enacted a far more sweeping measure, declaring all property of rebels liable to confiscation. President Lincoln, who strongly opposed widespread confiscation, forced Congress to pass an explanatory resolution, limiting the seizure of land to the lifetime of the owner. Only a handful of Republicans, Stevens among them, voted in opposition. The debates of 1862 indicated that while a majority of Republicans were willing to use confiscation as a war measure and a way of attacking slavery, far fewer envisioned a sweeping revolution of land tenure in the South.[8]

As the war progressed, however, the idea of permanent land confiscation gained wider support. In 1864 and 1865, Stevens and the veteran land reformer George W. Julian led a fight in Congress to repeal the joint resolution of 1862 and authorize the permanent seizure of rebel lands. By the end of the war both Houses, by narrow margins and in votes on different measures, had repealed the 1862 resolution. But no joint measure was ever enacted. The Freedmen's Bureau bill, passed in March 1865, did contain a provision assigning to freedmen and white refugees forty acres of confiscated or abandoned land, although the land was to be rented for three years and there was no promise of permanent ownership. Meanwhile, though the Lincoln administration had left the Confiscation Act of 1862 virtually unenforced, thousands of acres of abandoned land had fallen into government hands, and General Sherman's famous order settling freedmen on such land in South Carolina and Georgia seemed to some to presage a general policy of establishing the blacks on homesteads.[9]

At the outset of Reconstruction, therefore, the Republican party had taken some steps toward Stevens's goal of providing land to the freedmen from the estates of the planter aristocracy. But even in wartime the party had not overcome its inhibitions about such a policy, and once Union victory had been achieved, the notion to many Republicans became unthinkable. For confiscation flew in the face of too many basic tenets of the ideology which had carried the Republicans into the Civil War and which had emerged unchanged, even strengthened, by the war experience.[10] To a party which believed that a free laborer, once accorded equality of opportunity, would rise or fall in the social scale on the strength of his own diligence, frugality, and hard work, confiscation seemed an unwarranted interference with the rights of property and an unacceptable example of special privilege and class legislation.

And yet there were values and aspirations, shared by most Republicans, to which Stevens could and did appeal in an attempt to build a pro-confiscation coalition. Republicans were committed to restricting the power of the planters, protecting the rights of the freedmen, and transforming the South into a democratic (and Republican) society. During the congressional debates of 1865–67 most radical Republicans, and an increasing number of moderates, viewed black suffrage as the most effective means of achieving these goals and of obviating the need for massive federal intervention in the South. Stevens, however, challenged the idea that the impoverished and despised former slaves could immediately become independent voters. As he admitted to the House early in 1866, Stevens did not want Negro suffrage enacted for a few years. If the southern states were readmitted to the Union before the federal Constitution was altered to guarantee black rights and before the freedmen were given the economic wherewithal to establish their independence from economic coercion, the verdict of the Civil War would be undone: "They will give the suffrage to their menials, their house servants, those that they can control, and elect whom they please to make our laws. This is not the kind of suffrage I want."[11]

Stevens thus insisted that it was unrealistic to expect the freedmen to challenge effectively the political dominance of the South's traditional ruling class. John Andrew, the war governor of Massachusetts, who shared Stevens's perception, drew from it the inference that the only stable basis of reunion was an understanding between Republican leaders and "the natural leaders of opinion in the South"—a preview of the policy which would end Reconstruction in 1877. Stevens drew precisely the opposite conclusion. Realizing that emancipation had not destroyed the planter class, whose wealth rested not only on slaveholding but on control of prime black belt lands, he urged that such lands be confiscated.[12] The franchise by itself, he insisted, would not really touch the blacks' basic problems: "homesteads to them are far more valuable than the immediate right of suffrage, though both are their due." Most Republicans would reverse the proposition, as did the radical Congressman James Ashley of Ohio. "If I were a black man," Ashley declared, "with the chains just stricken from my limbs, without home to shelter me or mine, and you should offer me the ballot, or a cabin and forty acres of cotton land, I would take the ballot." Only George Julian, Wendell Phillips, and, occasionally, Benjamin F. Butler and Charles Sumner, stressed the land question, and none did so as consistently and forcefully as Stevens. Phillips, indeed, did not come around to this view until 1866, though when he did, he argued it much in the way Stevens had done:[13] "You cannot govern the South against its educated classes, with their social prestige. If they cannot be hung nor exiled, they must be flanked. . . . Four millions of uneducated negroes, with none of that character which results from position, with none of that weight which comes from one or two generations of recognized manhood, cannot outweigh that element at the South."

Confiscation, for Stevens, thus had two related goals. One was to destroy the power of the planter class; the other, to create a new class of black and white yeomen as the basis of future southern political and social power, and as allies of the Republican middle class of the North. Revolutionary as such a proposal may have been, it could be defended as the corollary of a traditional, widely shared value—the conviction that democratic institutions must rest on an industrious middle class. Stevens had always paid homage to the ideal of the yeoman republic. As he declared in 1850, "the middling classes who own the soil, and work it with their own hands, are the main support of every free government." Stevens's complete lack of racial prejudice was evident in his assumption that distributing land to blacks would make them middle-class yeomen; that their social position, morals, and psychology were the outgrowth of slavery, not of racial inferiority, and could therefore be altered.

But he also recognized that in view of the legacy of slavery and the hostility of southern whites, the traditional American ideal of success through thrift and hard work simply could not apply while the former slaves remained under their present disadvantages. But confiscation, he argued, could achieve a whole panoply of results central to the Republican ethos: [14]

> Nothing is so likely to make a man a good citizen as to make him a freeholder. Nothing will so multiply the productions of the South as to divide it into small farms. Nothing will make men so industrious and moral as to let them feel that they are above want and are the owners of the soil which they till. . . . No people will ever be republican in spirit and practice where a few own immense manors and the masses are landless. Small independent landholders are the support and guardians of republican liberty.

There were other arguments as well as confiscation. For one thing, the seizure of planter lands would be a fitting punishment for the architects of the rebellion, those "who have murdered our brothers, our fathers, and our children." If the lands of the planter class, moreover, were seized and forty acres allotted to each freedman, there would still remain hundreds of millions of acres—90 per cent of the land, in fact—which could be sold to help pay the national debt, reduce taxes, and provide pensions for Union soldiers and reimbursement for loyal citizens whose property had been destroyed during the war (of whom there were many in Stevens's home area of southern Pennsylvania). It would be, moreover, in Wendell Phillips's words, merely "naked justice to the former slave," whose uncompensated labor had cleared and cultivated the southern land and who was certainly entitled to "a share of his inheritance." But Stevens's basic appeal was to the remodeling of southern society: the transformation of an alien, undemocratic, severely stratified social order into a prosperous, democratic, and loyal republic. "The whole fabric of southern society," he declared in 1865, "*must* be changed, and never can it be done if this opportunity is lost." [15]

Stevens seems to have assumed that such a desire was widely shared in the Republican party. And there was certainly some evidence for that assumption. Long before the Civil War, anti-slavery northerners had developed an extensive critique of the southern social order and had declared their wish that the South might be transformed into a society more akin to that of the North and West. And most Republicans in the early years of Reconstruction shared Carl Schurz's view that "a free labor society must be established and built up on the ruins of the slave labor society." But far fewer were prepared to accept confiscation as the means to this end, both because Stevens's plan conflicted with some basic Republican values and because the creation of a black yeoman middle class was not what important elements of the party had in mind for the economic future of the South. Republicans in Boston, New York, and Philadelphia (the ante-bellum centers of the cotton trade), as well as other northerners who hoped to invest in the post-war South, tended to favor the speedy revival of the cotton plantation system, with northern capital and migrants supplanting the former slave-holders. Blacks would remain an essentially propertyless plantation labor force, whose basic legal rights would be recognized but who would hardly be in a position to challenge propertied whites for political and economic dominance. When the New York *Times*, the leading spokesman for this view, spoke of the South's need for a "prosperous yeomanry," it was quick to add, "very many of them will be northerners."[16]

Another group of Republicans, more willing to grant complete legal and political equality to the freedmen, looked to a wider economic transformation of the South, including the creation of a diversified, industrializing economy. But again, the South was to be rebuilt under the auspices of northern capital and settlers. This was the view, for instance, of Horace Greeley's New York *Tribune*, the *Nation*, and spokesmen for Pennsylvania's iron industry. Greeley insisted that what the South needed most was not talk of confiscation, which would paralyze investment and economic development, but an influx of northern capital, settlers, and industrial skills. And Congressman William "Pig Iron" Kelley of Pennsylvania, after touring the South in 1867 and extolling the region's economic resources and latent wealth, concluded, "The South must be regenerated, and we of the North must do it."[17]

Stevens was never able to make confiscation palatable to such Republicans. He feared, indeed, that the quick economic reconstruction of the South under northern auspices was likely to leave the freedmen no better off than under continued planter domination. He may have been influenced by the arguments of George Julian, who in 1864 and 1865 repeatedly pointed to the danger that confiscated and abandoned lands would be swallowed up by northern speculators. In Louisiana, under the direction of General Nathaniel P. Banks, freedmen had been put to work on plantations controlled by such men in "a system of enforced and uncompensated labor." If this was any indication of the economic future of the South, it appeared that "in place of the slaveholding landowner . . . we shall have the grasping monopolist of the North, whose dominion over the freedmen and poor whites will be more galling than slavery itself."[18]

That Stevens was less interested than other Republicans in speedy southern economic development under northern auspices was amply demonstrated during Reconstruction. He fought unsuccessfully in 1866 for a constitutional amendment authorizing an export tax on cotton—hardly the sort of measure investors in southern cotton plantations were likely to support. When Kelley pleaded for aid to a northern-owned railroad, on the ground that railroad development would aid the destitute freedmen of the region, Stevens scoffed: "May I ask my friend how many of these starving people he thinks are stockholders in this road?" And in 1868 he and Julian endorsed a measure, which passed the House but was killed in the Senate, declaring federal land grants to railroads in four southern states forfeited and open to black and white settlers.[19]

Because he was an iron manufacturer and supporter of a protective tariff, many historians have pictured Stevens as a conscious agent of northern capitalism, bent on establishing the North's economic hegemony over the South. But northern business interests did not see it that way. As one Philadelphia businessman complained, after learning of Stevens's opposition to a federal bankruptcy law to aid business in the South, "he seems to oppose any measure that will not benefit the *nigger*."[20]

The combination of ideological and economic obstacles to confiscation became fully apparent after Stevens, in September 1865, outlined his views on Reconstruction in a widely reprinted speech. Only a handful of Republicans endorsed his program, the most cordial reaction being that of an editor who told Stevens that the speech itself had been well received, "with the exception of your extreme views on confiscation. Some object to going as far in that measure as you purpose." Stevens, however, was not the sort to be disheartened by criticism. When Congress convened in December 1865, he introduced and the House quickly passed a resolution directing General O. O. Howard, superintendent of the Freedmen's Bureau, to report how much property under his jurisdiction had been returned to its owners, and "under what pretense of authority." Stevens's purpose was to make plain that President Johnson's lenient pardon and amnesty policies and his insistence that all land which had not been sold be returned to its pardoned owners were leading to wholesale evictions of blacks from abandoned lands on which they had been settled. Howard's reply, which was not ready until April, made the impact of Johnson's policies plain: virtually all the land under Bureau authority had been restored to the former rebels, while the amount in black hands was minuscule.[21]

Even before Howard's report had been received, Stevens introduced a confiscation measure in the House. The occasion was the bill extending the life of the Freedmen's Bureau. Introduced by the moderate Senator Lyman Trumbull, the bill had wide support among Republicans, and Johnson's eventual veto of it would be a decisive step in his break with the party. As drafted by Trumbull, the bill set aside three million acres of public land in the South for homesteading by freedmen and white refugees, affirmed for three years the title of freedmen to the lands set aside for them by General Sherman, and authorized the Bureau to buy lands for resale to blacks. In Stevens's view, none of these provisions was satisfactory. The public domain in the southern states consisted largely of hill and swamp lands, and the impoverished freedmen did not possess the capital necessary to establish homes and farms there, or to buy land from the Bureau. And there was no promise of permanent ownership of the Sherman lands. The bill did not touch the economic power of the planters, nor did it give freedmen access to the black belt land which was the key to the southern economy. When it came to the House, Stevens declared, "I say that this bill is a robbery."

When the Trumbull bill reached the House floor early in February 1886, Stevens proposed a substitute measure, adding "forfeited estates of the enemy" to the land open to settlement, making certain that the land could be purchased by blacks on easy terms, and making permanent their possession of the Sherman lands. When this substitute came to a vote it was overwhelmingly defeated, 126 to 37; Republicans divided 37 in favor, 86 opposed, with 10 abstentions, and many of the House's leading radicals, including Ashley of Ohio and Kelley of Pennsylvania, opposed it.

The tangled complexities of the land question were further illustrated two days after Steven's substitute was rejected and the Freedmen's Bureau bill passed, when the House with virtually unanimous Republican support passed Julian's Southern Homestead Act, opening all public land in the South to settlement and giving blacks and loyal whites preferential treatment until 1867. Republicans were thus quite willing to offer freedmen the same opportunity to acquire land which whites had received under the Homestead Act of 1862; they simply refused to take land from the planters to make farmers of blacks. As Stevens had foreseen, the Julian bill was a dismal failure. The land involved was so inferior, and the freedmen so lacking in capital, that by 1869 only four thousand black families had even attempted to take advantage of the Act, and many of these subsequently lost their land.[22]

These votes of February 1866 posed a dilemma for Stevens. He could have accepted them as defining for all practical purposes the limits to which Republicans were willing to move toward providing blacks with land and reorganizing southern society. As William McFeely has pointed out, the Freedmen's Bureau bill despite its limitations did hold out the possibility of a gradual but far-reaching change in the South's land system. It established federal responsibility for giving blacks access to land, and for assisting them in purchasing it on credit. Because the policy did not involve severe punishment of the planters, a complete upheaval of southern society, or special privilege for the blacks, it commanded wide support in Republican ranks. Had Stevens thrown his weight behind the measure as an acceptable alternative to massive confiscation, it might have become, in effect, official Republican policy on the land question. Yet Stevens's whole experience in the 1860s predisposed him not to accept these votes as a final verdict. The conservative New York *Herald* could exult over his defeat ("thus we see . . . the real strength of the Jacobins in the House"), but Stevens might have retorted that when he first proposed a measure for the use of black troops it had received only thirty votes. He had always been ahead of his party, he once remarked during the war, but "I have never been so far ahead . . . but that the members of the party have overtaken me."[23]

Stevens's strategy was based on the judgment that a prolongation of the national crisis would push the Republican party to the left. The longer the crisis lasted, he thought, the more radical the final settlement was likely to be. Throughout 1866 and 1867, Stevens bided his time on the land question, devoting his energies to the Fourteenth Amendment and Negro suffrage, while trying to delay a final settlement. The leftward drift which Stevens counted on as the dynamic element of the political situation was explained by the *Nation* during the hectic debates of February 1867: "Six years ago, the North would have rejoiced to accept any mild restrictions upon the spread of slavery as a final settlement. Four years ago, it would have accepted peace upon the basis of gradual emancipation. Two years ago, it would have been content with emancipation and equal civil rights for the colored people without the extension of suffrage. One year ago, a slight extension of the suffrage would have satisfied it."[24] Now, in March 1867, the Republicans succeeded in passing the first Reconstruction Act, temporarily forcing the planter class from participation in politics and imposing Negro suffrage on the South. And, just as southern intransigence had swelled the ranks of the Republican party in the 1850s and forced it to embrace emancipation and the arming of the slaves during the Civil War, Stevens could hope that if southern whites again obstructed northern goals, the party would move to an even more radical measure—confiscation. Yet the passage of the Act revealed the weakness of Stevens's strategy. As the *New York Times* had observed in 1866, Stevens's program "presupposes the continuance during peace of a public opinion which acquired force under the excitement and perils of war."[25] Inevitably, however, the impulse for a return to normal, for an end to the crisis, had grown in the Republican party—and Stevens, though unhappy with the new Reconstruction measure, had been powerless to block it. Now, the political initiative in effect passed to southern whites. If they accepted the new situation "in good faith," they could destroy whatever chance Stevens's more radical policies might have had.

Although most historians of Reconstruction have not emphasized the fact, confiscation was very much a live political issue in the spring and summer of 1867. But while the debate was very animated, it soon became clear that the fears aroused by Stevens's proposals far outweighed any attractions the plan contained. When Congress reconvened in March 1867, Stevens, ill and too weak to speak, had a colleague read a long speech and a bill providing forty acres to freedmen from confiscated land.

"To this issue," he announced, "I desire to devote the small remnant of my life." At the same time, Charles Sumner pressed the issue in the Senate, and outside of Congress Benjamin Butler, Wendell Phillips, and the American Anti-Slavery Society endorsed Stevens's proposals.

The moderate majority of Republicans, however, were determined that Congress should embark upon no new Reconstruction experiments until the success or failure of the recently enacted measures had become clear. Stevens's bill was postponed to December, and Sumner's resolutions were handily defeated. William P. Fessenden, perhaps the most powerful Senate Republican, informed Sumner, "This is more than we do for white men." To which Sumner responded, "White men have never been in slavery." The farthest some Republicans would go was a warning to the South. If the recently adopted Reconstruction plan did not achieve satisfactory results, several highly respectable Republican journals declared, confiscation would be the logical next policy. Surprisingly, only the generally conservative Philadelphia *North American,* a self-proclaimed spokesman for the manufacturing interests of Pennsylvania, seemed genuinely sympathetic to confiscation. The key question of Reconstruction, the *North American* announced, was the fate of the "plantation oligarchy," and those who opposed Stevens's proposals "must find some other means of destroying this landed aristocracy." The journal also emphasized that the creation of a yeoman class in the South would greatly benefit northern industry (which in 1867 was suffering from the postwar recession). "Just in proportion as the freedmen rise in the social scale will they consume more of the fabrics we sell to the South. Just in proportion as the South refuses to let them rise . . . do we suffer in our trade." If small farms replaced plantations as the basis of southern agriculture, the South would "buy ten dollars of merchandise off us for every one it now takes."[26]

Despite the discouraging response, Stevens continued to press the land issue. In June, he made public a letter addressed

to the county assessors of southern Pennsylvania, informing
them of his intention to "prosecute the claims for confiscation
at the next session of Congress," and requesting a detailed list
of Civil War losses which might be reimbursed from the pro-
ceeds of confiscated lands. He specifically instructed the assessors to omit his own property from the list, since some opponents charged that his real aim was to secure compensation for
his Caledonia Iron Works, destroyed by the Confederates in
1863. "Feeble as my own powers are," Stevens concluded, "if I
had five years more added to my life, I should not doubt that
this would become an accomplished fact."[27]

By the end of July, the influential Cincinnati *Commercial*
could report the existence of "a considerable number of decided advocates of the confiscation of rebel property" in Republican ranks. By then, however, the opponents of confiscation were marshaling their forces. The sudden prominence of
the confiscation question forced Republicans to take sides, and
most made it clear that Stevens's proposals were incompatible
with their basic beliefs. Respected radical journals like the *Nation* insisted that while possession of property would be emi-
nently desirable for the freedmen, for the government to give
them land would suggest that "there are other ways of securing
comfort or riches than honest work." "No man in America," it
added, "has any right to anything which he has not honestly
earned, or which the lawful owner has not thought proper to
give him." At the same time, more conservative Republicans
denounced Stevens for adding to "the distrust which already
deters capitalists from embarking in [the South's] enterprises."
The New York *Times* printed dispatches from correspondents
in the South, reporting that *"the fear of confiscation"* was paralyz-
ing business. When investors in plantations went to southern
banks for loans, declared a letter from South Carolina, they
were met with the query, "How can you give security against
Thaddeus Stevens?" From Georgia it was reported that gloom
hung over the men of "intelligence, influence, and property,"

because they believed that as long as the confiscation question was agitated, "neither capital nor emigration will flow this way."[28]

Perhaps even more threatening, in the *Times*'s view, was the precedent which might be set by the confiscation of southern property. Others might also warn that the "process of division," once begun in the South, would not be confined there, but it was the *Times* that expressed most clearly the fears felt by northern men of property:

> If Congress is to take cognizance of the claims of labor against capital . . . there can be no decent pretense for confining the task to the slave-holder of the South. It is a question, not of humanity, not of loyalty, but of the fundamental relation of industry to capital; and sooner or later, if begun at the South, it will find its way into the cities of the North. . . . An attempt to justify the confiscation of Southern land under the pretense of doing justice to the freedmen, strikes at the root of all property rights in both sections. It concerns Massachusetts quite as much as Mississippi.[29]

These fears were exaggerated by confiscation's being only one of a series of what the *Nation* called "schemes for interference with property or business" which were agitating the public scene in the spring of 1867. Labor activity seemed to have reached a new peak, with "strikes among the workmen of every kind throughout the country," and demands for federal and state laws to enact the eight-hour day.[30] In June, the radical Senator Ben Wade delivered a widely reported speech in Kansas, declaring that with the slavery issue settled, a new political question—the relations of capital and labor—was about to emerge. "Property," said Wade, "is not equally divided, and a more equal distribution of capital must be wrought out." Though Wade quickly backtracked when his speech aroused a furor in Republican circles, the *Times* insisted that it was now "perfectly clear that we are to have a political party based on the broadest and plainest doctrines of agrarianism. A war on property is to succeed the war on Slavery."[31]

Complicating the political scene—and the confiscation question—still further was the relation between the land issue and the development of the Republican party in the South. Despite black suffrage, most Republicans still envisioned their nascent southern coalition as an alliance of southern merchants, business interests, Whiggish planters, and black voters, with the white propertied elements in control. Republicans, of course, expected most of the newly enfranchised blacks to align with their party, but it was the southern whites who seemed to possess the attributes—"knowledge, character, intelligence, and ability"—necessary for political leadership. The confiscation plan seemed certain to alienate the support of propertied whites, and would create instead a class-oriented party of poor blacks and whites in which a solid black vote would be the controlling element. This fear was succinctly expressed by the *Times:* "Mr. Stevens and General Butler are determined to build up a Southern Party called Republican, on the scheme of confiscation. They expect to get by that bribe the whole negro vote and enough of the white vote to control the Southern States."[32]

In a sense the *Times* was right, although Stevens would hardly have called confiscation a "bribe." He certainly knew, however, that as one newspaper reported in 1867, "these black voters are overwhelmingly in favor of confiscation," and that support for the plan had been growing among white southerners as well. As early as January 1866, Stevens had received letters from southern loyalists endorsing his plans as being the only way to break planter domination. By 1867, such prominent organs of southern Republicanism as the Raleigh *Standard* were speaking in favor of it, and the Philadelphia *Press* reported from Alabama that if confiscation were submitted to a vote in that state, "a majority both of blacks and whites would vote for it." Southern white Republicans seemed to be coming to the realization that if the planters' economic hegemony were not broken, they would eventually "be sure to control the policy of the community." In Stevens's view, moreover, the confiscation plan would allow southern Republicans to transcend the troublesome race issue by uniting freedmen and poor whites on an economic basis. As the Washington *Daily Morning Chronicle*, Stevens's leading newspaper supporter, explained, "the great question of Reconstruction is not a question of race supremacy . . . but . . . is really and truly a question of the rights of labor."[33]

The prospect of the confiscation and redistribution of planter lands, the Boston *Advertiser* reported in June 1867, "has taken possession to a large extent of the mind of the loyal population of the South—the poor whites and land-lack negroes." This was hardly to say, however, that there were not strong Republican elements in the South which opposed such a measure. As each southern state went through the process of organizing a Republican party in the spring of 1867, virtually every convention found itself divided between "confiscation radicals" and more moderate Whiggish elements. The results were not comforting to moderate and conservative northern Republicans. In Alabama the Union League resolved that if former rebels did not accept the new political situation "in good faith," Congress should confiscate their lands. In North Carolina a Republican mass meeting called on Congress to enact Stevens's latest measure. Most disturbing was the situation in Virginia, where black delegates at the state convention almost to a man demanded a confiscation plank. Most white Republicans, led by the venerable John Minor Botts and other one-time Whig Unionists, opposed the plan, but the blacks were supported by certain white radicals such as the Reverend James Hunnicutt, the editor of a Richmond newspaper. In the end, an uneasy compromise was reached, in a resolution threatening confiscation if planters tried to intimidate black voters.[34]

Northern Republicans, including many radicals, were alarmed at the apparent influence of men like Hunnicutt among the freedmen. "Nothing could be more ominous of disaster," declared the Boston *Advertiser*, ". . . than such an array of class against class in the Southern States" as Hunnicutt and others sought. To counteract pro-confiscation influence, three Republican orators, all considered radical in the North, visited the South in the late spring, addressing gatherings of freedmen. Horace Greeley spoke at a large meeting at Richmond's African Church. "I beg you to believe," Greeley told the blacks, "that you are more likely to earn a home than get one by any form of confiscation. . . . Confiscation shrivels and paralyzes the industry of the whole community subjected to its influence." Senator Henry Wilson brought the same message to Virginia and South Carolina, and William D. Kelley also visited the South, praising its potential for economic development and informing the freedmen that "they can have homes of their own by working hard and saving what they earn—not otherwise."[35]

From Washington, Stevens looked on as the gospel of work was brought to the freedmen. Late in April, he denounced Wilson's Virginia speech and warned that "no man should make promises for the party. . . . Who authorized any orator to say that there would be no confiscation?" In May, he reiterated his criticism of the "Republican meteors" pursuing their "erratic . . . course" through the South, and in June he announced his intention of pushing the confiscation plan at the next session of Congress. But by the end of May it had become apparent that Greeley, Wilson, and Kelley were far closer to the mainstream of Republican opinion than was Thaddeus Stevens. Speaker of the House Schuyler Colfax and Senate leader Fessenden publicly supported Wilson against Stevens's criticisms, and a committee of Congressmen charged by the Republican caucus with overseeing political developments in the South declared that the rights of property would not be infringed (although it did piously urge landholders to offer land for sale to blacks at reasonable rates). It was apparent, in short, that whatever southern Republicans desired, the party in the North was hardly prepared to embrace confiscation.[36] Consequently, as the summer progressed, talk of confiscation subsided in southern Republican conventions.[37]

By the end of 1867, the leftward drift which had characterized the Republican party since the beginning of the Civil War
had definitely come to an end. The party suffered a series of
reverses in the state elections of 1867, which many Republican
leaders blamed squarely on Stevens, the radicals, and their "extreme theories." The election returns greatly strengthened the
hand of Republicans like the Ohio banker Henry Cooke and
Boston's liberal industrialist Edward Atkinson, who were determined to "put down" the "ultra infidelic radicals" and "prevent
the creation of an exclusive black man's party [in the South]
and also kill the scheme of confiscation." As the party turned
toward respectability, conservatism, and Grant, it appeared certain that, as an Ohio politician observed, "the Negro will be less
prominent for some time to come."[38]

By August 1868, when he died, Stevens's political influence
was at low ebb. In his characteristically cynical way he had told
an interviewer, "I have no history. My life-long regret is that I
have lived so long and so uselessly." He died aware that
planters were already beginning to use economic intimidation
to counter black voting power and that sharecropping and the
crop lien—a new "system of peonage," as he called it—were
spreading in the black belts, threatening to keep the freedmen
permanently dependent on the planters. Stevens was nonetheless still a formidable figure, venerated by the freedmen and by
millions of other Republicans, and his death produced a public
expression of grief second only to the funeral of Lincoln. It
marked in some ways the end of an era, symbolizing the transition from ideology to political expediency as the guiding force
of the Republican party. Though the Philadelphia *Press* declared, "He dies at the moment when the truths for which he
fought a long and doubtful battle have permanently and almost
universally triumphed," James G. Blaine, one of the rising po-
liticos who would control the party's destinies in the 1870s, saw
it differently. "The death of Stevens," Blaine observed, "is an
emancipation for the Republican party."[39]

Between 1860 and 1868 revolutionary changes had taken

place, changes for which contemporaries gave Stevens more than an average share of the credit. Slavery had been abolished, the freedmen granted civil and political equality, and democratic institutions established in all the southern states. But the final step of the Second American Revolution, the provision of an economic underpinning to the blacks' newly won freedom, had not been taken. The failure of Stevens's campaign for confiscation, his demand that society confront the basic economic questions which the abolition of slavery had entailed, exposed the limitations of the Republican party's middle-class ideology. At the same time, it exposed the vulnerability of Stevens's anomalous position as a radical in politics. Lacking a political base outside the Republican party, Stevens could be successful only so long as his proposals posed no fundamental challenge to the values and interests of the Republican mainstream. Possibly a more flexible man than Stevens, one willing to talk less flamboyantly of punishing traitors, revolutionizing southern society, and destroying social classes, one prepared to accept some form of limited, compensated expropriation of land and its sale on credit, might have achieved more for the cause of black landowning than did Stevens. Probably, however, the very idea of confiscation violated too many of the basic Republican verities for the party ever to become reconciled to it.[40]

Stevens's failure, indeed, revealed the limits to what a bourgeois capitalist culture, even in its most radical phase, will voluntarily yield to radicalism. What is actually most striking about the confiscation debate is the way it prefigured the disillusionment which would soon overtake radical Reconstruction. The same fears aroused by confiscation—special privilege, corruption, black domination, dramatic social upheaval by government fiat, a general undermining of the principles of good government—would shortly come to be associated with Reconstruction itself. The arguments used against Stevens between 1865 and 1867 would eventually justify the entire abandonment of Reconstruction.

EIGHT

Class, Ethnicity, and Radicalism in the Gilded Age: The Land League and Irish-America

On February 2, 1884, Wendell Phillips, the "golden trumpet" of the abolitionist movement and a towering champion of nine-teenth-century reform, died in Boston. In the memorial meet-ings and tributes that followed, Irish-Americans played a prominent part. Organizations ranging from the Wolfe Tone Club of Washington, D.C., to the Ancient Order of Hibernians eulogized Phillips's memory, and the usually secretive Clan na Gael held a special open meeting to laud his principles of "uni-versal liberty and equal rights of all men." Seven years later another veteran of the crusade against slavery, James Redpath, died in New York after being run down by a bus on Broadway. Irish-Americans mourned his passing as well. On the day of his funeral, Irish and American flags flew side by side at Redpath's home.[1]

We are accustomed to thinking of nineteenth-century Irish-Americans as implacably hostile to the major currents of native Protestant reform. Allegedly, abolitionists like Phillips and Red-

Originally published in *Marxist Perspectives*, I (Summer 1978), 6-55. Reprinted by permission of Cliomar Corporation.

path were anathema in the Irish community. Yet, the history of the Irish National Land League, in whose service Phillips and Redpath won the esteem of the Irish community, reveals a conjunction of Irish-America with the Protestant reform tradition. Although the Land League existed for only three years, it introduced thousands of Irish-Americans to modern reform and labor ideologies and helped to transform specifically Irish grievances and traditions into a broader critique of American society in the Gilded Age. The Land League both reflected and helped to shape the traditions of the Irish-American working class, and illuminated the complex interplay of class, ethnicity, and radicalism in industrializing America.

I

Between 1845 and 1889, three million Irish immigrants arrived in the United States, nearly half of whom were "refugees from disaster" fleeing the devastation of the Great Famine. These impoverished agricultural laborers and small farmers brought neither the capital nor skills necessary to acquire a secure place in the rapidly industrializing American economy. Congregating in the great cities of the Northeast, they became the "first genuine American proletariat," working at the low-paying unskilled jobs native-born Americans sought to avoid. The Irish immigrants built America's railroads, performed the work of common laborer, porter, domestic servant, and longshoreman, and inhabited urban ghettos notorious for poverty, crime, and disease. And, although post-Famine migrants came from an Ireland in which capitalist agriculture, literacy, and education were expanding rapidly, they too generally entered the marketplace as unskilled urban laborers. By 1880 the Irish-born population, including both Famine and post-Famine migrants, had risen to over 1.8 million with unskilled labor still the largest single occupation. In New York City 20 per cent of the Irish-born worked as laborers, compared with only 4 per cent of the native population.[2]

"The Irish in America," an English observer wrote in 1880, "are a great floating population of migratory labourers" who "haunt the great cities." Yet, this formulation obscures the large number of Irish-Americans settled in such smaller industrial cities as Fall River, Troy, and Scranton, as well as the increasingly differentiated class structure of the Irish-American community. Beginning as helpers in rolling mills and as laborers in mines and construction, thousands had by this time become plumbers, carpenters, and bricklayers in cities large and small, skilled molders in iron works, and craftsmen and foremen in textile mills. Second-generation Irish-Americans, who by 1880 comprised half the "Irish" community, had rapidly advanced to the status of skilled workmen. In Philadelphia some 30 per cent of the immigrant Irish worked as laborers in 1880, compared with only 15 per cent of those born in the United States of Irish parents. The second generation numbered twice as many as the first as ironworkers, bricklayers, and machinists.[3]

By this time, moreover, a significant middle class had made its appearance. Its most prosperous and respectable members, the "lace curtain" Irish, were mostly merchants and professionals whose offices were located in modern downtown business districts catering to a non-Irish clientele. These "lace curtain" Irish enjoyed less political and social influence in the larger society than economic status. Not fully integrated into the established urban bourgeoisie, they also formed no part of the emerging elite of industrial and finance capitalists. Nevertheless, their lives were far removed from those of their poorer countrymen. Living in non-working-class neighborhoods, they belonged to fraternal organizations limited primarily to persons like themselves. More numerous were the countless saloon keepers and grocers whose enterprises depended on working-class patronage, and the ubiquitous building contractors who required little capital to gain a foothold in business. These petty entrepreneurs often shared the experiences and sympathies of their working-class customers and neighbors. With

its large number of merchants, lawyers, clerks, editors, and political office-holders, New York City was the center of the Irish-
American middle class. The election in 1880 of William R.
Grace as the first Irish Catholic mayor of New York symbolized
the stability of Irish-America, the decline of the virulent nativism of the 1850s, and the success of a visible portion of the
Irish community.

Nevertheless, Irish-America remained overwhelmingly working class. By far the most common form of social advancement—from unskilled to skilled positions—lay within the working class itself. And such advancement was always precarious:
the depression of the 1870s reduced many skilled Irish workers
to the ranks of common labor and filled relief rolls with the un-
employed. Irish-America had come a long way since impoverished laborers fled the Famine, but poverty still stalked the
Irish community. The bitter experience of the 1870s revealed
profound class divisions within Irish-America and helped make
it fertile soil for radical criticism of Gilded Age America.[4]

II

Charles Stewart Parnell, the foremost nationalist leader of late
nineteenth-century Ireland, believed that Irish-Americans were
"even more Irish than the Irish themselves in the true spirit of
patriotism." In America nativism and anti-Catholicism reinforced an ethnic identity nourished by centuries of English rule
and the horrors of the Famine years. "I have met men of the
second generation," said one visitor to America, "sons of Irish
parents, American in voice and appearance, who have never set
foot on Irish soil, with as ardent an affection for Ireland" as
any native-born rebel.[5]

The first organization to tap Irish-American nationalism effectively was the Fenian Brotherhood, organized in 1858 with
distinct but coordinated branches in Ireland and America. A
secret, oath-bound movement devoted to the establishment of
an Irish republic through force of arms, the Fenians organized

an ill-fated "invasion" of Canada in 1866 and then rapidly suc-
cumbed to internal divisions. In the 1870s its successor, the
secret Clan na Gael, organized military units for action in case
England became embroiled in a European war. In Ireland the
Fenians' membership consisted, in the words of a British official, of "the lowest part of the Irish Roman Catholic population—urban craftsmen, shopkeepers' assistants, and agricultural laborers in the countryside." In America too, the Clan na
Gael, numbering perhaps 10,000 at its peak, was recruited almost entirely from the working class, although it did contain a
sprinkling of petty entrepreneurs. By and large the "best class
of Irishmen" held aloof. By 1877 the Clan had succeeded in
raising a considerable sum for its Skirmishing Fund to promote
armed conflict and terrorism in Ireland, but its membership
had declined to the point that the British consul in New York
exulted it was "now only the skeleton of what it once was"—an
assessment with which old Fenian leaders reluctantly agreed.[6]

It is easy to ridicule the Fenian movement. Riddled by British
informers, its few attempts at insurrection were hopelessly mis-
managed. It suffered from constant intrigues among its
leaders, and its obsession with secrecy led it to adopt a code in
which each letter of the alphabet was replaced by the one that
succeeded it, Ireland becoming Jsfmboe, and England, Fohm-
boe. It combined nineteenth-century republicanism with a fan-
tastic rigamarole of passwords, oaths, and initiations which
sometimes seemed to take precedence over its political purposes. The Clan na Gael, equally obsessed with secrecy, nonetheless held an annual fancy-dress ball in Tammany Hall. Yet,
the Fenians raised the first mass nationalist movement in Ireland independent of middle-class leadership and owing nothing to the Catholic Church. A class movement, the Fenians not
only lacked but openly disdained a class program. Most of the
leaders believed that resolution of Ireland's social problems
must await independence.[7]

By 1878 the most far-sighted nationalists had concluded that
the mass of Irishmen and Irish-Americans would never sup-

port a secret organization whose republicanism was devoid of a social program. In October the Fenian exile John Devoy and another leader, Michael Davitt, visiting the United States after his release from prison in Britain, agreed to a policy of supporting the Irish Parliamentary party coupled with a reform of the Irish land system. Here lay the origins of the famous "New Departure"—the attempt to merge Fenianism into a mass, public movement and to bridge the gap separating nationalist leaders from the rural masses.[8]

For Devoy the New Departure did not alter the primacy of the goal of Irish independence. But, as he later recalled, while the politicians debated, "the forces of nature intervened and pushed the agrarian question to the front." Poor weather and massive American agricultural imports produced an agrarian crisis throughout western Europe in the late 1870s. In 1879, after two successive crop failures in Ireland, the prospect of a third revived memories of the Great Famine. That summer, tenants in the West of Ireland organized to demand a reduction of rents. The West, the most backward region of the island, had changed little from a traditional subsistence economy of diminutive holdings and exclusive reliance on the potato. Its tenant farmers displayed an "almost total indifference" to Home Rule: "All their ideas are dominated by the single one of land." Davitt quickly channeled spontaneous protest into a structured organization, the Land League, of which Parnell assumed leadership. By the end of 1879 the League had spread throughout the island, demanding not simply relief for tenants in distress and a halt to evictions, but "the land for the people"—transfer of ownership of the land of Ireland from a few thousand aristocratic families to tenant farmers. Within a year it had over one thousand branches and 200,000 members. "In Ireland," reported Chief Secretary William Forster in 1881, "the Land League is supreme. . . . I am forced to acknowledge that to a great extent the ordinary law is powerless."[9]

Early in 1880 Parnell traveled to America to raise funds and organize American branches. His tour was an unprecedented success. Not only did he arouse unbounded enthusiasm among Irish-Americans, but the non-Irish community welcomed him as well. At every stop he was received by mayors, judges, and prominent businessmen. He became the first foreigner to address the House of Representatives since Louis Kossuth in 1851. The Fenians had been denounced by respectable American opinion, but in Boston and New York substantial Protestant citizens received Parnell into their homes and pledged assistance to the cause of the Irish tenant farmers.

With Parnell called back to Ireland for a general election in March, Davitt continued to tour from New England to California, organizing branches wherever he went. In March 1880 a conference of prominent Irish-Americans founded the American Land League, choosing, perhaps because of factional jealousies, the virtually unknown James McCaffrey of Massachusetts as president. (His only qualification, according to Davitt, was that "he was supposed to be the handsomest man in New England"; he later became president of a college in Argentina.) By September 1881 the Land League had more than 1,500 branches organized in America and, by the fall of 1882, had collected over half a million dollars from American sources.[10]

The Land League was the first nationalist organization to unite the Irish-American community. The land issue had an impact no other could rival. As Devoy explained, commenting on the reception of a group of speakers from Ireland in 1881:

> Perhaps fully seventy-five per cent of that immense throng were men and women born under the dark shadow of landlordism, and not a few were victims of its exterminating operations. Most Irish-American audiences are so, and this explains the readiness with which they grasp the Land Question and the impulse which made them flock to the Land League standard.

Or, as one financial contributor from Michigan explained, he was "red-hot for driving the landlords out of Ireland, as that accursed system was the cause of [my] own emigration."[11]

The wealthy and prominent Irish-Americans, so strikingly absent from the Fenian Brotherhood, found the Land League easier to support, their usual caution outweighed by the respectability conferred on it by Parnell's visit. The founding conference gathered a cross-section of the Irish-American middle class, including twelve merchants, seven lawyers and public officials, and three physicians. The Catholic hierarchy had condemned the Fenians, but bishops and priests played a leading role in the League. Eleven priests attended the founding conference, and priests often played a prominent part in the meetings, rallies, and picnics of the local branches, which often took place at parish churches and schools.[12] In the Land League the three great strands of protest that had emerged in nineteenth-century Ireland finally coalesced: the revolutionary republicanism of the Fenians, the constitutional and parliamentary protest of Daniel O'Connell and Parnell, and the agrarian grievances hitherto expressed in rural secret societies.

Of the various figures associated with the American Land League, none was so controversial as Patrick Ford. Born in Galway in 1837, he had been brought to Boston by his parents at the age of eight. At fifteen he worked as printer's devil on William Lloyd Garrison's *The Liberator,* and at twenty-four edited a short-lived anti-slavery journal in Boston. After serving in the Union army and publishing a Republican newspaper in Charleston during Reconstruction, Ford moved to New York City where he founded the *Irish World* in 1870. By the early 1880s it had become the most important Irish-American newspaper, with a weekly circulation of 35,000.[13]

A small, retiring man who lacked the gift of oratory, Ford, one nationalist recalled, was "probably the only man who ever exercised any considerable influence over the Irish race, who has never made a public speech." His prominence derived from the fact that the *Irish World* had become the voice of the politically conscious Irish-American working class, read, according to Ford, by "every reform advocate in the land." Certainly its influence on the labor movement was considerable. "It

circulates in every city and town in the Republic," said one observer, "and is read not merely by the Irish, but by the 'proletariat' of all nationalities." Its New York offices served as a kind
of headquarters for labor leaders and Irish nationalists, ranging from Samuel Gompers to J. P. McDonnell. Gompers later
recalled that New York's cigarmakers, who paid to have books
and newspapers read aloud as they worked, often listened to
excerpts from Ford's paper. When a Philadelphia labor editor
launched a new newspaper, he declared his ambition was to
create "the paper of the country second only to the *Irish
World*." [14]

From the outset Ford viewed his journal as the voice of the
nationalist, Catholic, and social aspirations of the Irish-
American working class. Its full title reflected the breadth of
his concerns: *The Irish World and Industrial Liberator*. Readers
received a weekly education in the trans-Atlantic radical tradition. Typical issues contained articles on anti-monopoly, land
nationalization, strikes, women's rights, and temperance, as
well as such pieces as "How Labor Is Robbed," and "Value—
What Is It?" Ford declared the French Revolution "one of the
first great victories of labor," and the principles of America in
1776 "the cause of Ireland in 1876." He called Thomas Paine
"an infidel" but praised him as an "advocate of political liberty,"
and one article recounted the life and ideas of the "social
giant," Proudhon.

Employing the traditional language of American radicalism,
Ford insisted that "labor is the one great motive power of production," and blamed the plight of workers on an economic
system in which "non-producers" appropriated most of the
fruits of labor. The same message was conveyed in the regular
articles by John F. Bray and Thomas Devyr, two immigrant
radicals whose long careers illustrated the connection between
the Chartists and the Jacksonian labor movement, and the
labor and land reform movements of the 1870s and 1880s. [15]

Through the *Irish World*, Ford attempted to bridge the gap
that had separated much of the Irish-American community

from the reform tradition. But the heritage with which he wished his readers to identify was abolition. The crusade against slavery had acted as a central terminus from which men and ideas flowed into virtually every effort to change post-bellum society.[16] Ford's own career reflected its influence, and he always regretted that Irish-Americans had adopted "an attitude of seeming hostility to the friends of human freedom." He never tired of singing the praises of his former employer Garrison, and he consistently sought to counteract racial prejudice within the Irish community. "Welcome the colored brother in the Land League," Ford wrote in 1881. "He is a marked example of a defrauded workingman." The history of Reconstruction proved conclusively, he insisted, that "there is no liberty without the soil."[17]

The depression of the 1870s, which propelled Ford into the ranks of the labor-reform movement, convinced him of "The Total Depravity of Our Political and Economic System." The two major parties, he insisted, were hopelessly corrupt and controlled by "a privileged and non-producing class, which [has] for years fattened on labor." Along with extensive coverage of Irish news, the *Irish World* devoted increasing attention to the Greenback-Labor party, which Ford supported in the presidential campaigns of 1876 and 1880. Although no socialist, Ford did call for "a change in our economic system," including such specific measures as the income tax, an eight-hour day, an end to interest on money, the issuance of Federal greenbacks, and the nationalization of the land. Ford was more comfortable lashing out at the emerging industrial order than providing a blueprint for a new society, but he did speak of a future cooperative commonwealth in which the wage system, profit-taking, competition, and the existence of "distinctive classes" would all disappear.[18]

Although the *Irish World*'s litany of demons ranged over the entire capitalist order—encompassing the "new Slave Power" of "railroad thieves," "monopolist kings," bankers, and "stock-gambling millionaires"—Ford viewed land monopoly as "the prime evil" of American life. The *Irish World* reprinted Thomas Spence, Louis Blanc, and, later, Henry George on the evils of private property in land. Week after week Ford reiterated that "the natural gifts of God—land, air, light, and water—are things not to be bought or sold." "Nothing is a man's own property," he insisted, "except it be the result of his labor." The land question assumed decisive importance for urban workers, for "with the land to fall back upon, the worker would have a potential voice in making his bargain both for hours and for wages." In Ireland and America the "land robbers" stood as the foremost social enemy.[19]

Years before the Land League adopted the slogan, "the land for the people" had become the motto of the *Irish World*. The basis of Ford's critique of American society, it explained his dissatisfaction with most Irish nationalists. Too many Fenians, he believed, ignored social issues in their preoccupation with Irish independence. Establishing an Irish republic, however laudable, was not enough: "We have a republic here in America, and here in America, too, we have Pittsburg riots, and Land Grabbers, and Usurers, and slow starvation." To Irish tenant farmers "the right to live like a free man without the accursed shadow of a land thief" was as important as independence from England. The weekly dispatches of "Trans-Atlantic," Ford's European correspondent and a veteran nationalist since the days of O'Connell, condemned all moderate proposals for tenant right and asked, "Is there no man in Ireland advanced enough . . . to call out boldly for *the land to the cultivator?*" According to John Devoy, "Trans-Atlantic"'s articles were "the chief attraction of the paper." Many readers believed him "the apostle of a new and regenerated Ireland."[20]

As land meetings swept the West of Ireland in the summer of 1879, the *Irish World* hailed the "Daybreak in the Irish sky." "Fenianism saw only a green flag," Ford exulted, "but the men of today have discovered that there is such a thing as land." And, he boasted, his paper, more than any other single influence, had spread "the true gospel of the Land Question" in

Ireland. Ford established a "Spread the Light Fund" to finance the free distribution of thousands of copies each week in Ireland.[21]

The *Irish World* brought what one observer called "a vast propaganda to American ideas" to Ireland during the land war. The rapid expansion of literacy since the Famine made possible its wide circulation. In Cork, blacksmiths and shoemakers were said to "gather evenings to read and have it read to them." At one Land League gathering, a voice from the crowd called for three cheers for Ford's newspaper, and many local branches distributed copies "with avidity." "There was scarcely a cabin in the West," William O'Brien later recalled, "to which some relative in America did not despatch a weekly copy of the Irish World. . . . It was as if some vast Irish-American invasion was sweeping the country with new and irresistible principles of Liberty and Democracy."[22]

What made the *Irish World*'s approach to the Land League distinct was that Ford consistently sought to link the land struggle in Ireland with social issues in the United States. And not only in America: at moments he perceived the League as the opening battle in "the war of the great army of the disinherited, in all lands, for their Heaven-willed possessions." When Parnell resorted to the rhetorical device, so familiar among European reformers, of contrasting the egalitarian, democratic United States with aristocratic Ireland, Ford observed that land monopoly was spreading as rapidly in America as in the Old World. Immense land grants to railroads, the spread of bonanza farming in the West, and the monopolization of urban real estate, were threatening the "Europeanization" of American society. The principle "the land for the people" applied in America as in Ireland, for "if an Irish landlord cannot take rent, how can an American landlord?" The *Irish World* suggested that the activities of "heartless speculators and rent-hounds" in America ought to be resisted by a "Tenant League." The land issue in Ireland and social reform in the United States were two dimensions of the same issue.[23]

If the *Irish World* addressed itself to the Irish-American working class, the Boston *Pilot* may be described, in the words of the Irish nationalist T. M. Healy, as "the organ of the wealthier and more cultured portion" of Irish-America. The oldest Catholic newspaper in the country, it had become the official organ of the Archdiocese of Boston in 1876, partially owned by Archbishop John Joseph Williams. A majority of the *Pilot*'s readers were workingmen, but substantial numbers of "priests and prosperous businessmen" were also among its readers.

The *Pilot*'s editor, John Boyle O'Reilly, was "the most distinguished Irishman in America." A poet praised by Whittier, a friend of Phillips and Garrison, and an accepted figure in Boston Brahmin circles, he had been born in County Meath in 1844 and had joined the Fenian movement in the 1860s. Imprisoned in Australia for Fenian activities, he had been rescued and brought to America, where he joined the *Pilot* in 1870. Although he abandoned the Fenians at the behest of Archbishop Williams, he remained a fervent nationalist and became a supporter of the Land League.[24]

Like Patrick Ford, O'Reilly had a bent for reform. Outraged by the poverty of so many Irish-American workers, he often supported strikes. He also criticized the treatment of blacks and Indians, and wrote the poem for the dedication of the Crispus Attucks monument in 1888. Unlike Ford, however, O'Reilly published few articles on labor issues and maintained a much less critical attitude toward American society. He criticized the labor movement for exacerbating social tensions and stressed westward migration rather than social reform as a solution to workingmen's problems. And unlike Ford, he drew a sharp contrast between European society, with its conflict between fixed social classes, and the fluid, egalitarian United States. Wary of violent rhetoric and radical ideas, he made the *Pilot* a far more sedate—indeed a more boring—journal than the *Irish World*.[25]

While Ford castigated both major political parties and often criticized the attitude of the Catholic Church on labor questions, O'Reilly tied the *Pilot* closely to the Democratic party and the Archdiocese of Boston. Ford disdained "the swell mob of Irish 'society' "; O'Reilly published a list of the two hundred wealthiest Boston Irish families. O'Reilly, without doubt a reformer, tempered his ideas for fear of creating dissension within Irish-America. As Arthur Mann suggests, O'Reilly was "uncompromisingly radical as regards England, but moderate with respect to the United States."[26]

A third element in the Land League were the Fenian and Clan na Gael nationalists, for whom the land movement's importance lay only in its ability to stimulate nationalist sentiment in Ireland and undermine British authority. Irish Fenians like Patrick Egan and Thomas Brennan played prominent roles in the Land League from the beginning. But a small group of Irish nationalists, including the Dublin Fenian journal *The Irishman,* opposed the League altogether, fearing establishment of a rival organization competing for funds and influence. "I say it is a pernicious course to put the claims of a class—even though it be so great and influential a class—above the claims of the nation," said one Fenian. "It is not a thing to be wished, by those who love Ireland," declared another, "that class feuds should arise and increase in intensity, so as to dissever those who might be united, and to withdraw to class-disputes the interest which should be concentrated on the National Question."[27]

The most flamboyant critic of the Land League in America was the iconoclastic Fenian exile Jeremiah O'Donovan Rossa, who insisted that only violence could undermine English rule. Rossa's obscure journal, *United Irishman,* published in New York, incited the murder of British officials and the dynamiting of English cities. "The wrongs and injuries of seven centuries of oppression may yet be avenged by the conflagration of London," he wrote. "Liverpool might blaze like another Moscow, or Manchester redden the midnight skies like another Chicago." Particularly intrigued by the possibilities of dynamite, Rossa announced in 1882 that "Professor Mezzroff, the great Russian chemist," would conduct a "school of explosives" in New York City. Such rhetoric thoroughly alarmed British diplomats in America, who forwarded copious extracts from his journal to London, but most Irish-American nationalists considered Rossa a crank. Behind the bombast, however, lay some shrewd political perceptions. Rossa denied that the Land League was a "national movement" at all, since it did not aim at "equal rights on Irish soil for priest and parson, peer and peasant—independent altogether of English government." And he warned that not only would most Irishmen—agricultural and town laborers—not benefit from the land movement, but that making the Irish farmers proprietors of the soil would simply reinforce their traditional conservatism and make it impossible to achieve Irish independence.[28]

Much more influential than Rossa and more representative of Fenian opinion was John Devoy, editor of New York's *Irish Nation* and probably the most important nationalist ideologue on either side of the Atlantic. As one of the fathers of the New Departure, Devoy supported the nationalists' alliance with Parnell and viewed the Land League as an important step toward Irish independence. Participation in the League would help overcome the "isolation from the public life of the country" that had plagued the Irish Fenians for twenty years.

Devoy, who had come to the United States in 1871 after a stint in the French foreign legion and a prison sentence for Fenian activities, was the quintessential political exile. "I respectfully decline the honour of being classed as an 'American,'" he wrote in 1878: American issues were of interest to him only in so far as they served Irish ends. Thanks largely to his efforts, most American members of the Clan na Gael went into the Land League, believing that landlords were "the strongest bulwark of English domination in Ireland."[29]

A final element in Irish-American society taking part in the Land League was the Democratic party, especially New York's Tammany Hall. Tammany's influence rested on its leaders' participation in the daily life of Irish-America: They attended funerals, club meetings, and parties and helped constituents with jobs, rent, and personal problems. Tammany provided a "miniature, private welfare state" for New York City's poor. Boss Tweed, driven from his throne in 1871, was remembered in the popular Irish ballads of the 1870s as an urban Robin Hood, "poverty's best screen," and a friend of the workingman "no matter who may you condemn." Closely linked to the Catholic Church, Tammany made "rich contributions" to parish activities and schools. Tweed's successor, the immensely popular "Honest John" Kelly, was an in-law of New York's Cardinal McCloskey.[30]

The *Irish World* described Tammany Hall as an alliance of "the ten thousand dollar politicians" and "the ninety cents laborers." To which one should add the New York business establishment, for which Tammany performed invaluable services. Kelly helped elect a series of wealthy businessmen mayors of New York and generally opposed political and social radicalism. His house organ, the New York *Star,* claiming a daily circulation of 100,000, did declare its sympathy for "the industrious workingman," but condemned "the so-called labor champions" who set class against class; it insisted that the cause of deteriorating conditions among workers lay not in the economic order per se, but in high taxes and the high tariff enacted during the Civil War. Conveniently, both these measures could be blamed on the Republican party. The *Star* spoke out strongly against such manifestations of independent labor politics as the California Workingmen's party and the Greenback-Labor movement.[31]

Honest John Kelly fully endorsed the Land League movement. Tammany functionaries served on the committee to receive Parnell in 1880, and Kelly set up his own "Tammany Hall Irish Relief Fund" to assist the League. According to one account, the New York delegation to the 1881 Irish National Convention in Chicago was recruited from Tammany's ward clubs. One Fenian leader remarked that in America "societies gotten up in the name of Ireland" were often "used for local or personal politics." But, Tammany's involvement in the Land League simply meant that, as usual, its finger was on the pulse of the Irish community.[32]

John Devoy, though never cordial toward Patrick Ford, acknowledged that the *Irish World* was generally considered "the organ of the movement." Yet, neither in Ireland nor America did the Land League leadership follow policies acceptable to Ford. Parnell, a Protestant revered as the uncrowned king of a Catholic nation and a landlord leading a movement of tenant farmers, steered the Irish Land League on a much more moderate course than the *Irish World* desired. Throughout 1881 Ford urged Parnell to spurn Gladstone's Land Act, which offered concessions in rent and security of tenure to Irish farmers, but the League agreed to "test" the act in the newly created land courts. Long before the ill-fated No-Rent Manifesto was issued at the end of 1881, Ford had called for a rent strike in Ireland, whereas Parnell adopted the policy only as a desperate resort, probably knowing it would fail. The *Irish World* insisted on the common interest of "the Irish serf and the English factory slave" in a struggle against landlordism in both countries, but, with the notable exception of Davitt, the Irish leadership evinced little interest in such an alliance. And throughout the history of the League, while Ford urged Irish leaders not to ignore the claims of landless agricultural laborers, their demands received little real sympathy from their tenant-farmer employers.[33] Although the land movement had begun in the poorest section of the island, its social center of gravity came to rest with the more substantial tenant farmers. Such men had prospered from the rapid spread of capitalist agriculture during the thirty years since the Famine as pasture replaced tillage and the number of farmers on tiny potato plots and of landless agricultural laborers declined sharply. These tenants were determined to preserve their recent economic gains and to win proprietorship of the land from the great landlords. The old agrarian secret societies, in effect primitive trade unions of the poorest agrarian classes, had used threats and violence to regulate rents paid *to* the tenant farmers; the Land League aimed at abolishing rents paid *by* them.[34]

In America, too, the national Land League was tightly controlled by an alliance of nationalists and moderate, respectable representatives of the middle class. O'Reilly, Devoy, and Patrick Collins—"the recognized leader of . . . the Conservative elements in the American League"—were the leading spirits at national conventions. At the January 1881 convention O'Reilly headed the Committee on Resolutions and Collins was elected president.[35] The various elements of the Irish community represented by these three men united against what one conservative called the *Irish World*'s "pernicious doctrines of communism." In Ireland anti-Land League Fenians denounced the *Irish World* for "socialism." In America, Devoy and O'Reilly became alarmed at the spread of Ford's social beliefs. O'Reilly, indeed, suggested at the end of 1881 that the land struggle give way to a renewed agitation for Home Rule, since the issue of social reform would permanently divide both Ireland and Irish-America. An emphasis on Home Rule would win "instant and thorough approval and support" from the two elements of Irish-American life most important to O'Reilly: "the Catholic hierarchy and priests" and "intelligent and conservative men." The Chicago nationalist John Finerty agreed in a letter to Collins: "We do not want to be crusaders for utopian principles."[36]

Even more emphatically, Devoy demanded that the Land League identify its primary purpose:

> Are we men who have undertaken to effect a great and radical change in the tenure of land that will embrace the whole world? . . . Do we propose a great social revolution that will alter the present constitution of human society? . . . Or are we Irishmen struggling for the welfare of our own people?

He answered: "We are fighting for the Irish people and for the Irish people alone." Devoy condemned the "humanitarian cant" of Ford and others: "men who want to use Ireland as a means of working out a social revolution in other countries"

and employ "the Land League in America for American purposes."[37]

In contrast to Ford, the more moderate elements were struck
by the divergence between social conditions in Ireland and
America, not the similarity. The conservative New York *Irish-
American*, the New York counterpart to O'Reilly's Boston *Pilot*,
described the United States as a "land of plenty," peopled by
"free, untrammeled workers," who had no need of the "radical reforms" necessary in Ireland. Landlordism in America,
said the *Irish-American*, was a thing of the past: "It exists no
longer." Here, indeed, was a line of division cutting through
the ideological debates in the American League. Those Ford
called the "conservative element," whatever their disagreements, concurred in one thing: "In their heart of hearts they
do not relish this land question with its logical deductions applicable to America as well as Ireland."[38]

III

Despite Ford's inability to determine Land League policy, the
Irish World's wide circulation on both sides of the Atlantic and
its ability to channel funds to Ireland made it indispensable to
the movement. Although the Land League established a central
treasury overseen by the Rev. Lawrence Walsh of Connecticut,
a majority of local branches forwarded their money to the New
York offices of the *Irish World*. Ford claimed to have sent
$350,000 to Ireland by mid-1882, while receipts for the central
office of Father Walsh, through April of that year, amounted
to $180,000.[39]

Not every dollar forwarded to the *Irish World*, of course,
represented an endorsement of Ford's political principles. The
New York office was simply convenient. For many branches,
however, the destination of funds was a conscious political decision. At one, in Titusville, Pennsylvania, a motion to dispatch
one hundred dollars to the national headquarters failed to receive a second, whereupon the entire body voted for the *Irish*

World. In April 1881, $107 came in from Big Mine Run, Pennsylvania, accompanied by a note: "We recognize in the *Irish World,* the leading light to the great movement which is at present agitating the world," and "admire the stand taken by it against [Patrick] Collins."[40]

The *Irish World's* weekly list of contributions to its Land League Fund provides a profile of Ford's constituency—the grass roots of Irish-American radicalism. "The money that has kept the Land League together," the New York *Times* sneered in 1881, "has come mostly from the day laborers and servant maids of America." Ford agreed that most contributions were from workers. Men of substance, he wrote, were "very scarce at Land League meetings. . . . Fully nineteen-twentieths were poor and unpretentious workingmen." Reports from local branches, at least those associated with the *Irish World,* bear out this judgment. The average contribution listed was less than a dollar. In 1881, for example, 140 members of the Binghamton, New York, branch raised $50; sixty-six workers at the Rhode Island Locomotive Works in Providence, $16.25; and nine "hard-working sons of toil" in Troy, $6.[41]

Significantly, a large number of branches arose at places of work. The *Irish World's* pages in 1880 and 1881 were filled with such contributions as: $270.50 from workers of the Denver and Rio Grande Railroad in southern Colorado; $15.50 from those at the Pawtucket Gas Co., Central Falls, Rhode Island; $314 from those of the Atchison, Topeka and Santa Fe Railroad in New Mexico (to which "Irishmen, Americans and even our Mexican brothers" contributed); and $11 from those in a New York City shoemakers' shop, to "hammer down" landlordism. Pittsburgh's branches were composed overwhelmingly of skilled puddlers and common laborers in the iron and steel works, along with some clerks and saloon keepers, and funds were often collected in the mills. Elsewhere, branches often united workers of different trades in the same vicinity. As the Davitt branch of Chicago reported in 1881, "Our club is composed of men chiefly employed in our South Side Rolling Mill blast furnaces and packing houses." In marked contrast were branches reporting their activities to the Boston *Pilot.* "Our ranks are in the main, sturdy farmers and the substantial business men of the town," said the St. Mary's, Kansas, branch, and a list of officers from Lewiston, Maine, was followed by the statement, "These gentlemen are prominent in business and social circles."[42]

A detailed but incomplete list published by Ford in September 1881 revealed the local sources of funds sent to the *Irish World.* (See table.) New York City and Boston, the centers of Irish-American middle-class respectability, contributed little, most of their money going to Father Walsh. Philadelphia and Chicago, where the middle class was weaker and which lacked the conservative local Irish newspapers and powerful Irish political machines of New York and Boston, sent the largest sums.[43] The center of Ford's constituency, however, lay not in the large eastern and midwestern cities, but in the mining regions of Pennsylvania and the West and in the smaller industrial centers. Here, where Irish workers had taken part in bitter struggles in the 1870s, the *Irish World*'s passion for social change found a fertile soil, and the Land League reflected and helped to shape a developing labor consciousness.

The most remarkable concentration of branches oriented toward the *Irish World* lay in the anthracite coal region of northeastern Pennsylvania, which also included the industrial centers of Scranton and Wilkes-Barre. Five counties accounted for no fewer than forty-seven branches, one-third the number for the state as a whole. This region of closely knit communities had experienced an almost steady deterioration in wages and working conditions since mid-century. A state report of the early 1870s spoke of workers and employers as "completely separated in feeling, habit of thought, purposes, interest and sympathy as if they were separate peoples." Violence wracked labor disputes, culminating in the famous Molly Maguire trials of 1876 and 1877.

A persistent quest for collective organization by anthracite

Funds Collected for Land League via *Irish World,* January 1, 1880—September 13, 1881

Total: $150,434.97

Largest State Totals

Pennsylvania	$16,753.78
New York	12,860.19
Massachusetts	7,401.31
Rhode Island	7,099.01
Illinois	6,322.96
New Jersey	5,989.29
Missouri	5,106.02
Colorado	4,221.05
California	4,109.65

Largest City Totals

		Number of Branches
Philadelphia	$2,008.02	15
Chicago	1,912.20	11
Leadville	1,910.00	1
Troy	1,883.50	8
Albany	1,700.00	3
Providence	1,635.50	9
St. Louis	1,536.00	5
Newark	1,500.00	1
Carbondale, Pa.	1,490.12	5
Scranton	1,410.50	5
Jersey City	1,348.75	8
Fall River	1,274.61	5
New York City	500.00	2
Boston	146.00	2

Pennsylvania Anthracite Region

Carbon County

Mauch Chunk	$50.00	1

Lackawanna County

Archibald	131.00	1
Carbondale	1,490.12	5
Dunmore	390.00	1
Jermyn	228.00	1
Old Forge	14.20	1
Olyphant	30.00	1
Scranton	1,410.50	5
Winton	198.75	1

Luzerne County

Ashley	5.00	1
Drifton	51.10	1
Franklin	34.75	2
Grand Tunnel	60.00	1
Jeddo	80.00	1
Kingston	88.40	1
Milnesville	232.75	1
Mt. Pleasant	36.00	1
Nanticoke	280.00	1
Parsons	200.00	1
Pittston	650.00	3
Plains	40.00	1
Pleasant Valley	32.00	1
Sugar Notch	17.60	1
Wilkes-Barre	200.23	4

Northumberland County

Bear Valley	10.00	1
Mt. Carmel	57.00	1
Shamokin	5.76	1

Schuykill County

Ashland	14.35	1
Big Mine Run	107.09	1
Mahonoy City	90.59	1
New Castle	209.00	1

Western Mining Cities

Bodie, Cal.	$700.00	1
Butte, Mont.	467.10	1
Cherry Creek, Nev.	171.00	1
Eureka, Nev.	476.50	1
Leadville, Col.	1,910.00	1
Tombstone, Ariz.	400.00	1
Virginia City, Nev.	700.00	1

Source: Irish World, Sept. 24, 1881. The list is incomplete since not every branch and contribution listed individually in 1880 and 1881 appears in this accounting.

miners marked the 1870s and 1880s—a quest reflected in the formation of unions, independent political parties, and branches of the Land League, all of which, though predominantly Irish, served to unite miners across ethnic lines. The Irish immigrant John Siney founded the first broadly based anthracite miners' union, the Workingmen's Benevolent Association, in 1869. It crumbled during the "Long Strike" of 1875, which left bitter memories of the "railroad king" Franklin B. Gowan and his "gigantic corporation," the Reading Railroad—an animosity that reappeared when miners of the northern coal fields, joined by the steel workers of Scranton, took part in the national railroad strike of July 1877. Riots wracked such towns as Shamokin, Easton, and Wilkes-Barre, and federal troops occupied the area, breaking the strike in October.[44]

The events of 1877 produced an upsurge of support for the Greenback-Labor party. Three localities chose Greenback-Labor mayors and in 1878 Wilkes-Barre sent Hendrick B. Wright, an old Jacksonian renowned for giving away fresh bread on Christmas Day, to Congress as a Greenbacker. A strong supporter of the Land League, Wright believed "destitution and poverty" were as rife in America as in Ireland and declared there was "quite as much necessity for an American as an Irish Land League." At the same time, the experiences of 1875 and 1877 spurred the growth of the Knights of Labor. Local assemblies flourished in Schuykill, Lackawanna, and Luzerne counties, especially among the Irish miners.[45]

This collective organization and class consciousness nourished the phenomenal growth of the Land League. Throughout the poverty-stricken anthracite region, Irish miners banded together to send funds to Ireland via the *Irish World*. The Carbondale branch raised $1,260 at a fair and reported that more would have been contributed, but "they are working only three days a week in the mines." In Sturmerville the prizes at a Land League picnic illustrated the complex history of the region during the 1870s: a ring, a coal-drilling machine—a highly valuable item for skilled coal miners—and a revolver. Swatara, Pennsylvania, with only seventy-five families, raised $78.53 at a ball, and Mountain Top, a village so small and poor that it could not afford a Catholic church—mass was held only every two months, in the public school—raised ten dollars.[46]

By 1881 the anthracite region was alive with weekly meetings where funds were raised and the radical doctrines of the *Irish World* disseminated. The movement would not end, wrote one miner, "until the Land and its kindred monopolies are destroyed forever throughout the whole world." From Shamokin came seven dollars, in contributions of twenty-five cents, to "rouse the people to a sense of their rights, to a knowledge that the call of the children of God to the things of His creation is equal." The breadth of support indicates that the Land League united skilled miners—virtually independent subcontractors—with the larger number of unskilled mine laborers and helpers they employed. While predominantly Irish, the movement for a time eradicated ethnic divisions. Welsh, English, and Scots joined Land League meetings in Luzerne County, and in Mt. Carmel eastern Europeans, harbingers of the "slav invasion" of the 1880s, "promised to help the Land League cause." The list of contributors from Mt. Carmel— some giving as little as five cents—included, along with such Irish names as Patrick Joyce and James Flynn, Poles and Hungarians like Anthony Pulaski, Ferik Kowerlewski, Jonathan Hunkonkussie, and Anton Ferdodse. "I would like to see the Protestants and the Catholics united in the movement to free Ireland," wrote one Land Leaguer from Mauch Chunk. "Our interests are identical."[47]

The intimate connection between the Land League and the labor movement in the anthracite region is illustrated in the career of Terence V. Powderly. Born in Carbondale in 1849 of Irish-born parents, Powderly had been dismissed and blacklisted from his job as a machinist because of union activities in the early 1870s. In 1874 he joined the fledgling Knights of Labor and became a supporter and local functionary of the Greenback-Labor party. Powderly was elected mayor of Scranton in 1878 and the next year became Grand Master Workman of the Knights. At the same time he served as Finance Chairman for the Clan na Gael and in 1880 became active in Land League affairs.

Elected to the Land League Central Council in 1880, Powderly became a vice president in 1881 and spoke often on "The Irish question viewed from a labor standpoint." For Powderly the land issue was all-important for labor, in both Ireland and America. "The land," he wrote in 1882, "is the question. . . . The soil is the heritage of all men and can neither be bought or sold." At virtually every Knights of Labor convention, Powderly spoke on the land issue, insisting that an end to land monopoly was far more important than a reduction of the hours of labor or an increase in wages. As the *Irish World* observed, Powderly represented "the joining of the Land League and American labor forces."[48]

In the anthracite region the Land League functioned as a kind of surrogate for the Knights of Labor. The Knights' secrecy and oaths alienated the local Catholic clergy, already largely beholden to the coal operators for the land on which their churches were located. Hostility from parish priests impeded the Knights' growth as countless letters to Powderly attested. "All the tyrant operators," wrote one Knight, "could not crush this District Assembly half as fast as the Catholic Church." "The greatest curse to our order seems to me to be the priests," said another. By 1880 the number of Knights' assemblies in the coal region had declined precipitously. Clerical opposition had had its effect, but it also appears that Land League branches virtually took over the functions of the Knights. As Powderly later recalled:

> The Knights of Labor were then working secretly, and, as many members were Irish or sympathizers with the struggle of the Irish people for land reform, they invited me to visit cities and towns throughout the country for the purpose of speaking at Land League meetings. I accepted as many invitations as I could and when the public, or Land League, meeting would be over a secret meeting of the Knights of Labor would follow.

Powderly's activities in the League helped make him one of the most popular Catholic laymen in the country. By the mid-1880s, when he had defused clerical opposition by making the order public, he lectured for Catholic causes, and his portrait was considered a valuable prize at church fairs.[49]

Outside the anthracite region radical Land League branches were concentrated in industrial cities from New England through the middle states into the Old Northwest. Communities like Jersey City, Fall River, Troy, and Providence were high on the list of contributors to the *Irish World* Land League fund, with smaller sums coming from Cohoes and Paterson. These smaller cities were scenes of persistent conflict between capital and labor during the Gilded Age, in which much of the community, including politicians, merchants, and shopkeepers, often sided with the strikers. The Land League emerged from such heavily immigrant, self-consciously working-class communities, in which the labor movement occupied a central place.

One such center of Land League activity was the belt of southern New England textile towns stretching from Fall River, Massachusetts, down to Providence and Pawtucket in Rhode Island. Fall River had become during the 1870s the greatest textile center of America, as well as the city with the largest proportion of immigrants in its population, primarily English, Irish, and French Canadian spinners. In the "great strike" of 1875, about 15,000 weavers, spinners, and carders stayed out for two months, winning broad support among nearby Rhode Island textile workers as well. In 1879 a spinners' strike lasted four months. In 1881 the Massachusetts Bureau of Labor Statistics reported that virtually every worker it interviewed in Fall River complained of overwork, poor housing, tyrannical employers, and the general bitterness between capital and labor. For their part, manufacturers claimed their workmen were "the scum of the English and Irish," apparently laboring under a "hereditary feeling of discontent" and "filled with communistic ideas."

Fall River and Providence, with their receptive audience for the radical doctrines of the *Irish World,* contributed more than $2,900 in 1880 and 1881. The Irish workers interpreted the Land League according to their own recent experiences. At one Fall River meeting a speaker referred to the League as "a great strike" in Ireland, adding, "any man in sympathy with labor must sympathize with the Land League." Then, in words straight from the teachings of Patrick Ford, he went on: "We have the same gigantic evil in this country. The public domain is rapidly passing away into the hands of large corporations and in time the people here will be in no better condition than those of Ireland."[50]

The same symbiotic relationship between class-conscious unionism and Irish national consciousness existed in the West. The third highest urban contribution to the *Irish World* Land League fund came from the booming lead and silver mining center of Leadville, Colorado, which had grown from a collection of log huts and a population of 200 in 1877 to a city of 15,000 three years later. A bitter strike by the miners' union in 1880 was broken by the governor, who proclaimed martial law and sent in troops. Another center of the Land League was Virginia City, Nevada, site of the famous Comstock Lode. Michael Davitt received an enthusiastic reception from the miners in this birthplace of hardrock miners' unionism, but the Irish "bonanza kings" wanted nothing to do with the movement. Other mine union centers like Butte, Bodie, and Cherry Creek contributed substantial sums as well.[51]

In all these communities, a strong sense of solidarity existed among the miners, as well as a radicalism grounded in resentment over the rapid transition from the frontier to industrial civilization and from individual enterprise to absentee corporate ownership of the mines. The same feelings also marked working-class politics in San Francisco, where the Workingmen's party of 1877–78 had blamed a small group of land monopolists for transforming California from an egalitarian to an aristocratic society. When Davitt visited San Francisco in 1880, labor organizations chose the notorious Denis Kearney to welcome him. Kearney stressed that "the same system that has brought such misery to Ireland is being fastened upon us," creating a "double bond of sympathy" between Irish-American workers and the Irish movement. Davitt, who probably shared European reformers' rather sugar-coated image of nineteenth-century American life, confessed he was "astonished" at Kearney's description of California society. Davitt's education progressed when farmers, facing eviction by a California railroad, formed a Land League and asked him to address them on the Irish land system. When he returned home, he told an Irish audience that support for the Land League was growing in California in response to "a system of landlordism growing up there that bore some analogy to the system at home."[52]

Even in New York City, where anti-Ford moderates and nationalists dominated League offices, a strong connection existed between local branches and the labor movement. The relation of Irish and Irish-American issues was all too apparent in a city in which more tenants were evicted annually than in Ireland. Some "Spread the Light Clubs," "consisting of active workingmen," insisted that the principle "the land for the people" be applied in New York as well—that land and homes be owned by the city, not private landlords. Tenant Leagues modeled on the Irish Land League sprang up in New York in the early 1880s. At a meeting to protest evictions, one speaker observed, "he had been thirty years in this country, and now found himself under the same yoke which caused him to flee from Ireland." The New York *Star*, organ of an alarmed Tammany Hall, solemnly insisted that "evictions in New York and evictions in Ireland are not parallel cases," reminding the "large class in the community" who appeared to disagree that "the landlord has rights and feelings" as well as the tenant.[53]

After a temporary setback in Democratic party factional politics, Honest John Kelly suddenly emerged in 1881 as an "antimonopoly" champion. "It is time that the rights of the public be made paramount to those of the corporations," he announced, and for a year or more the *Star* blasted away at railroads, "corporate monopolies," and the "privileged class" in language scarcely less extreme than Patrick Ford's. New York State, Kelly announced, was "governed by the railroads, rich corporations, and great monopolies, who have combined for the purpose of thwarting the popular will and subverting popular rule. . . . Tammany Hall today presents . . . the only rallying point around which the masses may concentrate for the perpetuation of Democratic principles." Conveniently, Tammany directed its assault primarily against such giant national corporations as Standard Oil, rather than the local business community, and it always associated "monopoly" with the Republican party. Did the anti-monopoly crusade mark a radical turn in Honest John Kelley's outlook? More likely, it reflected not only his difficulties in state Democratic politics, but also the Land League's success in spreading radical ideas in the Irish community. Wherever Irish-Americans went, Tammany could not afford to be far behind.[54]

The connection between the Irish movement and New York labor became manifest in January 1882, when 12,000 representatives of the city's unions met at Cooper Union to endorse the No-Rent Manifesto. The meeting was organized by Robert Blissert, who had been born in England of Irish parents and had emigrated after being blacklisted for his role in a London tailors' strike. Active for a time in the First International in New York, he was "one of the oldest Land Leaguers in the city." The January 30 meeting reiterated the connection between Irish and American issues. "The No Rent battle of Ireland," read a banner over the stage, "is the battle of workingmen the world over," and many of the speeches dealt with American rather than Irish conditions. George McNeill, the Massachusetts labor reformer, thought it "amazing to see the children of freemen crowding into the mills in the squalid degradation of pauper laborers." Blissert reminded the audience that "the process of land-stealing" was occurring in America as well as Ireland. And P. J. Maguire of the carpenters cautioned the audience "not to forget their wrongs in this country: . . . the monopoly of the Standard Oil Company," the railroads, and the bonanza farmers. Tammany's *Star*, still in its radical phase, was struck by the atmosphere of the gathering. "There were many thousands of Irishmen in that great assembly," it declared, who had never given "a thought to the similitude of the slave system at home and abroad," but who might begin to think differently because of the rally.[55]

Out of the meeting came New York's Central Labor Union, with Robert Blissert as its architect. At his suggestion the first plank in the CLU declaration of principles affirmed land as "the common property of the people." It immediately supported the strike of Jersey City's Irish-American freight handlers in July 1882. The freight handlers had contributed to the Land League in 1881 and the local branches formed the basis for the swift organization of a union once the strike had begun. Blissert spoke for the strikers in New York and Jersey City. That September, at New York's first Labor Day celebration, he again affirmed, "Labor today declared its right to the soil—to the land—which should belong to everyone in general and no one in particular."[56]

IV

The Land League existed for less than three years; yet, it left an indelible mark on Irish-America. Not only did it reflect and strengthen the growing role of Irish-Americans in the labor movement, but it played a significant part in overcoming the alienation between Irish-Americans and the mostly Protestant native-born reformers. During the 1840s and 1850s the first generation of Irish immigrants tended to stand aloof from the reform movements concerned with women's rights, prohibition, compulsory public education, and, most important, abolition. The galaxy of reforms and their underlying premise—that men could perfect the world—did not impress an immigrant Irish community characterized in its early years by insularity, traditionalism, and anti-intellectualism. Native reformers, for their part, viewed the Irish as a major obstacle to the achievement of reform goals—a view reinforced by their prevalent nativism and middle-class prejudices. Although some abolitionists condemned nativism on principle, Lydia Maria Child spoke for many when she observed in 1870 that the "Roman priesthood wish, and expect, to undermine our free institutions by means of the influence of Catholic voters."[57]

The Irish community was not, in fact, as intractably conservative as often alleged. We know too little about the attitude of Irish-Americans toward the anti-slavery movement to categorize it as uniformly pro-slavery. Some Famine immigrants may well have been among the tens of thousands of Irish who signed the abolitionist petitions circulated by Daniel O'Connell in the 1840s. More important, the Irish brought cultural and political traditions that merged into some expressions of native American radicalism. Many immigrants had sympathized with or taken part in the secret agrarian societies that drew strength from "the general and settled hatred for the law" permeating the Irish countryside. Much agrarian violence never transcended clan and factional feuding, but for some immigrants it represented a radical inheritance which may help explain the swiftness with which the Irish became involved in trade unionism in the United States. In the 1850s the Irish in the great eastern cities gained a reputation for labor militance at a time, significantly, when land reform held a central place in labor ideology.

A wide gap did divide the Irish community from the native reform tradition during the Civil War era, but by the late 1860s it was beginning to narrow. Irish service on the Union side dampened the fires of nativism for a time, and participation in the labor movement, by its very nature, reduced ethnic insularity. The emergence of labor leaders like John Siney of the miners and William McLaughlin of the shoemakers symbolized the new horizons opening before the post-bellum Irish community. Finally, the Fenian movement drew many Irish-Americans into contact with native reformers willing to support the cause of Irish independence. As David Montgomery has argued, Irish-American nationalism provided physically and intellectually a road out of the ghetto.[58]

Yet, the Fenians affected far fewer Irish and Irish-Americans than the Land League. Experience in the Land League first brought the Irish on both sides of the Atlantic into the mainstream of nineteenth-century reform. In Ireland it constituted a stage in the modernization of politics, educating and mobilizing the Irish countryside, and bringing the farmer onto center stage politically for the first time. As a result of the Land League, as one speaker put it, "doctrines hitherto known to be true in halls of learning only, became acceptable in the cabins of Connaught." A conservative newspaper in Dublin complained, "The wild waves of democracy are surging round the shores of Ireland." A new political language, it continued—phrases like "the cause of labor" and "rights of Man"—were now circulating freely throughout Ireland. In place of sporadic, secret, agrarian violence directed against local grievances, farmers were now demanding a thorough reform of the social order. As Davitt declared in 1879, "We do not declare war against individual landlords, not at all; we declare opposition to a system."[59]

In America the Land League caused a reciprocal intellectual reorientation in which Irish-Americans and native radicals each reconsidered their perceptions of the other. Here lies the significance of the identification of men like Wendell Phillips and James Redpath with the land movement, and the affection such men gained among Irish-Americans. Phillips, to be sure, had told the American Anti-Slavery Society as early as 1869 that overcoming the "intense prejudice" against the Irish was the next task confronting reformers. From the League's outset he offered his oratorical services, drawing on the experience and language of the anti-slavery crusade. "I said in the great rebellion, 'Give the negro a vote and forty acres of land,'" he declared in Boston, adding, "Give every Irishman a vote and forty acres of land to stand on." The Land League, Phillips went on, was "the Free Soil Party of Ireland." An active supporter of the labor movement, Phillips added at the same time an attack on "corporate plundering" of land in the United States.[60]

James Redpath, another old abolitionist, hardly seemed a likely candidate to conduct a crusade on behalf of Ireland. As the Scottish-born Redpath said in one speech, he could not remember from his Presbyterian upbringing "a single generous or brotherly expression of regard for the Roman Catholics or for their faith. They were never called Catholics. They were 'Papists' always." When asked, early in 1880, to travel to Ireland as a correspondent for the New York *Tribune,* he held the common view that Irish poverty stemmed from the improvidence of the Irish poor. Once there, Redpath changed his mind. Convinced that the Irish land system was at fault, he perceived the Land League as an extension of the abolitionist movement. In his dispatches to the *Tribune,* in speeches in Ireland, and in more than one hundred addresses throughout America, Redpath reiterated these themes. In language reminiscent of the northern critique of slavery, he insisted that the Irish land system paralyzed industry, encouraged thriftlessness, and stifled economic progress. Irish tenants, as a result, lived in a squalor "more miserable than ever were our southern slaves." For Redpath the landlord-tenant dispute was an "irrepressible conflict," and Michael Davitt "the William Lloyd Garrison of Ireland." His advice to the Irish people recalled Garrison's rhetoric: "Let your war cry be the total and immediate abolition of Irish landlordism." Even the social ostracism of tenants who moved onto land from which others had been evicted (the boycott), stemmed in an ironic way from the abolitionist experience. Boycotting, said Redpath, who had first recommended it, had driven the carpetbaggers out of the South during Reconstruction and could be equally effective against "the renteaters" in Ireland.[61]

To the Irish authorities Redpath was "a rabid republican fanatic," whose "wild harangues have contributed so much during the past fifteen months to stir up hatred of the law." In Ireland he became an instant hero, his name, according to one priest, "a household word in every cabin." Redpath's letters to the *Tribune* won widespread sympathy for the movement among Protestant Americans and especially the inheritors of the anti-slavery mantle.[62]

The Protestant reform tradition itself was undergoing a transformation in these years. By 1880 many reformers had retreated into the genteel elitism of the "Best Men," for whom racism, nativism, and a commitment to the economic status quo had obliterated an earlier passion for social change. The editors of the New York *Tribune,* for example, did not share Redpath's enthusiasm for the Irish movement. Remarkably, many reformers did overcome their hostility to the Irish and identify with the Land League. Abolitionists like Lysander Spooner and former anti-slavery politicians like Francis Bird of Massachusetts endorsed the movement. A mutual reconsideration of long-held stereotypes and prejudices seems to have taken place. When Redpath visited Ireland in 1881, he was accompanied by David R. Locke, editor of the Toledo *Blade* and well known as "Petroleum Nasby." Locke, according to Redpath, was "one of the noblest and most steadfast workers in that great abolition of slavery movement." Because of his anti-slavery past, Locke said, he had come to Ireland "the worst prejudiced man against the Irish cause there was." But his observations led him to support the Land League and abandon those prejudices.[63]

For their part, Irish and Irish-American Land Leaguers adopted the language and idealism of the abolitionist tradition and, in a sense, redressed retroactively their past hostility toward Protestant reform. In Ireland speakers declared that the Land League followed in the footsteps of "that small voice of conscience which smote the slaveholders of the Southern states." In America it was not surprising for a man like Ford to compare the Land League to abolitionism. But it was certainly a departure for Tammany Hall to recall with pride the abolitionism of Daniel O'Connell and the support he purportedly received from "the Catholic Church and people of Ireland." And it was surprising for a speaker at the Land League national convention to recall abolition as a "most brilliant triumph." For the first time, it seemed, Ireland was "in the van of a revolution that is destined to set the world ablaze." "I was brought up to believe that there was an eternal enmity between Saxon and Celt," an Irish-American wrote the *Irish World*, "but . . . now I have none but the kindliest sympathy for the oppressed of all nations and colors."[64]

The Irish land movement, Henry George observed in 1882, "has educated a class of our people who might not for years have been reached by any other influence. . . . It was but natural that in thinking of Ireland thoughts should also be directed to the land monopoly which might be seen in the United States." George himself, more than any other individual, symbolized the link between the Irish land question, Protestant reformers, and labor radicalism. George in these years was attempting to refashion traditional republicanism to meet the immense social problems of the industrial age. "Until a few years ago," he wrote in *Progress and Poverty* (1879), "it was an article of faith with Americans . . . that the poverty of the downtrodden masses of the Old World was due to aristocratic and monarchial institutions." Such a belief had been dispelled by the emergence of "social distress of the same kind" in this country. Private property in land, George insisted, explained the coexistence of progress and poverty, material wealth and ever-increasing squalor:

> From this fundamental injustice flow all the injustices which distort and endanger modern development, which condemn the producer of wealth to poverty and pamper the nonproducer in luxury, which rear the tenement house with the palace . . . and compel us to build prisons as we open new schools.

George's theories merged three long-standing tenets of American radicalism: a safety-valve view of land, a distinction between producers and non-producers, and a labor theory of value. To George, the landlord, the greatest of monopolists and non-producers, contributed nothing to the economy but levied a tax on the earnings of capital and labor alike. "The land question and the labor question" were "but different names for the same thing."[65]

Progress and Poverty became the most widely read economic treatise ever written in this country. Jeremiah Murphey, the Irish-American head of the freight-handlers' union in Jersey City and a leading figure in the Land League, said it had educated countless workingmen in the land issue. George's appeal did not stem from his specific programs. Probably few of his readers understood the intricacies of economic rent or the supposed efficacy of a single tax on land. But, George identified the central problems of the age—the unequal distribution of wealth, the growing squalor in the cities, and the declining status of labor—and offered an apparently plausible solution. His evangelical rhetoric conveyed a passionate attachment to the cause of the poor, rare, to say the least, among economists. "The squalid poverty that festers in the heart of our civilization," he wrote in a typical passage, "the vice and degradation and ravening greed that flow from it, are the results of a treatment of land that ignores the simple law of justice."[66]

The popularity of George among Irish-Americans had even more immediate roots. In 1880 the *Irish World* printed his extended essay on the Irish land question, the basis of the book that appeared the following year. For a time the *Irish World* became George's "organ in reaching the people." Every reader, Ford wrote, should own *Progress and Poverty*, and his office printed and distributed a cheap edition. By early 1881 excerpts were being read aloud at American Land League meetings.

In 1881, having been sent by Ford to Ireland as a special correspondent, George sent back blistering attacks on British rule and on the Irish land system. Arrested, he gained instant popularity among Irish-Americans. George and Ford at this point were working together for what George called "the end we both desire—the radicalization of the movement and the people." This radicalization spelled a commitment to the abolition of the landlord system in Ireland and the mobilization of the American Land League to fight land monopoly and related

social ills. "This fight is also for us," George told a Newark
Land League audience. And in his book on the Irish question,
he urged American branches "to announce this great principle
as of universal application; to give their movement a reference
to America as well as to Ireland." George's writings and
speeches educated both Irish and Irish-Americans in the most
recent and radical doctrines of land reform and social
change.[67]

George embodied one other strain of American radicalism
which, through the Land League, came to influence Irish-
America in the 1880s: the social perfectionism of evangelical
Protestantism. The spirit of evangelicism suffused George's
speeches and writings and supplied much of his language. A
devoutly religious man, he exuded the fervor of the pulpit. His
utopian social vision, as expressed in the conclusion to *Progress
and Poverty,* was ultimately religious: "It is the culmination of
Christianity—the City of God on earth, with its walls of jasper
and its gates of pearl! It is the reign of the Prince of Peace!"
Christianity, George believed, could inspire the reforms
needed to regenerate the world. "But it must be a Christianity
that attacks vested wrongs, not that spurious thing that defends
them." George's writings spurred the emergence of the social
gospel among the Protestant clergy in America and reflected
the wide currency of the language of Christianity among labor
reformers. George McNeill, for example, described labor's
goal, the vaguely defined "cooperative commonwealth," as "the
Golden Rule of Christ" when "the new Pentacost will come."[68]

Historically, such language had been alien to the Catholicism
of Irish-America and often associated with nativism. Before the
1880s the American Catholic Church rarely linked religion to
reform. The clergy generally defined social reform as charity
and moral exhortation to the poor, showing little interest in
economic or social injustice. Only temperance among the galaxy of reform movements engaged the Church's support. The
Knights of Labor and trade unionism met considerable hostility
from the Catholic press and hierarchy.[69]

Radical Irish-Americans had long attempted to create some kind of bond between social radicalism and the Catholicism that for the Irish was not merely a religion, but almost a badge of nationality and culture. Patrick Ford insisted that the *Irish World* sought to "bear aloft the standard of the cross." During the depression of the 1870s, he did criticize the worldliness of the Church and its insensitivity to the plight of the Irish-American poor, singling out Cardinal McCloskey for riding in an elegant carriage through New York City. In 1879 Bishop Gilmour of Cleveland forbade the circulation of the *Irish World* in his diocese, while taking the opportunity to condemn unions and public education. He reminded his parishioners that poverty was no disgrace: "our master was poor." Ford replied that Gilmour's letter only lent credence to Protestant charges that the Church was "the foe of democratic institutions, of liberty of thought, and of education." Yet, when Protestants raised these same issues, Ford passionately defended the Church and reminded his readers of violations of religious liberty by Puritan New Englanders. Ford projected the ideal of America as a multiethnic, multireligious nation. He denounced Protestants who believed that they alone were true Americans, or that this was, in the current phrase, a "Protestant country." Ford envisioned America's future as a pluralistic cooperative commonwealth in which political unity and class harmony coexisted with cultural diversity.[70]

Among the Land League's most significant achievements in America lay in breaching the Church's inertia on social questions and spawning a Catholic counterpart of the Protestant social gospel. The transformation was symbolized by the emergence of Father Edward McGlynn of New York City as a major spokesman for the American Land League. Born in New York City in 1837 of Irish immigrant parents, Father McGlynn spent his first years as a priest as assistant to Father Thomas Farrell of St. Joseph's Church, a strong abolitionist who left money in his will for the establishment of a Catholic church for blacks. In 1866 Father McGlynn became pastor of St. Stephen's, "one of the largest and one of the poorest parishes" in New York City. In 1870 he ran afoul of the hierarchy for an interview with the New York *Sun* in which he defended the public schools as "one of the chief glories of America." While deprecating the use of the Protestant Bible and hymns in public schools, he believed Catholics should send their children there and said he did not intend to establish a parochial school in his parish.[71]

Father McGlynn participated in the American Land League from the outset, but only attracted attention as a speaker during Michael Davitt's visit to New York in June 1882. At a rally for Davitt, organized by the Central Labor Union, Father McGlynn won long and enthusiastic applause for his Catholic version of the social gospel: "The cause of the suffering, martyred poor in Ireland was the cause of true religion. If there seemed to be a divorce between the Church and the masses it was not the fault of the masses." Translating the image of Christ the carpenter, so common in labor circles, into terms closer to the Irish experience, he went on: "Christ himself was but an evicted peasant. . . . He came to preach a gospel of liberty to the slave, of justice to the poor, of paying the full hire to the workman, to teach the humblest, the poorest, the most benighted and enslaved the awful dignity of human nature." Throughout the summer Father McGlynn repeated this message at Land League gatherings. Most striking, he recast the evangelical rhetoric, still offensive to many Catholics, in an Irish-American vein.[72]

However atypical in his opposition to parochial education and the turbulence of his subsequent career, Father McGlynn enunciated a social Catholicism that won support from numerous younger American priests, including such lesser-known supporters of Irish-American labor radicalism as the Rev. Cornelius O'Leary, parish priest of the railroad town, DeSoto, Missouri, and Buffalo's the Rev. Patrick Cronin. During the 1880s, moreover, a powerful "liberal" group emerged in the American Church hierarchy, attempting to reassess the Church's relation to social issues and to break down the isolation of Catholics from contemporary currents of social thought. Men like Archbishop Gibbons of Baltimore, although hardly radicals, supported the Knights of Labor and effectively transmitted their working-class sympathies to Rome.[73]

The career of Father McGlynn illuminates again the conjuncture of Irish and American radicalism in the Land League. Perhaps the most compelling illustration of this conjuncture emerges not from the speeches and writings of the illustrious, but from the resolutions adopted by the Land League of the tiny Pennsylvania mining village of Swatara. Whoever in this town of seventy-five families drew up the three resolutions revealed how Irish hatred of English rule, an insistence on the dignity of labor, belief in religion as an agent of social change, and traditional American republicanism, flowed together and acquired new meaning in the Land League:

1. The present iniquitous landlord system . . . has cursed the Irish people since the final triumph of English rule. . . .
2. It is the obvious design of the Almighty that every individual man should labor, not that one portion of mankind should perform all the drudgery, slave and suffer that the other may revel in luxury.
3. We hold these truths to be self-evident: that land, like air, light, and water, are God-given gifts to His children.[74]

V

The climax of the factional and ideological disputes within the American Land League came in June 1882, during Michael Davitt's visit. Some weeks earlier, Davitt had delivered two speeches in England that caused a sensation in the Irish movement. Abandoning the official Land League program of "peasant proprietary," he adopted George's plan for the nationalization of the land as the true meaning of "the land for the people." Private property in land would be eliminated, with all farmers renting their land from the State and provision being made for access by landless agricultural and urban workers. "It is difficult to see how an increase in the number of those holding private property in land can possibly remedy evils which are so easily traceable to that institution," Davitt argued. However logical, his position flew in the face of the land hunger of the Irish tenant farmers.[75]

By the time Davitt arrived in America, rumors had swept the Land League that he intended to wrest control of the movement from Parnell, that he had been "captured" by Henry George, and that he planned to transform the League into an international alliance of land reformers in Britain, Ireland, and America. The result was a foregone conclusion. Parnell had recently concluded the "Kilmainham Treaty" with Prime Minister Gladstone, agreeing to disband the agrarian agitation and enter into a Parliamentary alliance with the Liberal party; it symbolized his shift to a more conservative nationalism and his determination to retain the good will of a portion of Britain's ruling class. He condemned land nationalization as ill-conceived and not in accord with Land League policy. Other nationalists also feared the effect of Davitt's speeches on moderate opinion. James J. O'Kelly, for instance, considered them " a stupid communistic agitation which would certainly detach from us the most important element among our people both in Ireland and America."

In America the nationalists and moderates who controlled the national Land League united against Davitt and vented their deep-seated hostility to George, Ford, and social radicalism. According to the conservative New York *Irish-American*, Ford and his followers had

> long been striving to identify the national cause of Ireland with those Communistic theories that our people have always repudiated, and to divert the efforts of those who are honestly struggling for the Irish race into those channels of hypo-sublimated revolution by which the liberation, union of all mankind . . . and the "millennium" generally are to be brought about.

The Boston *Pilot* insisted that Davitt had placed himself in "the hands of the Communists," and that men like George "care nothing for Irish nationality. They only want to see their communistic ideas put into practical operation." Tammany's *Star* joined in the denunciations.[76]

The most articulate criticisms of Davitt's new departure came from John Devoy, speaking for the extreme nationalists who snubbed their former comrade when he arrived in America. Behind Davitt's proposals, Devoy discerned the sinister influence of Ford and George, neither, he insisted, truly interested in Irish independence. Ford's intentions, said Devoy, were "not for the benefit of the Irish people, and in his tremendous plans of a universal social reform, Ireland has a very small place indeed." As for George, "Ireland is only a lever with which to stir up England. Then from England the movement is to spread to America, and the American branches of the Land League are to be the centres of the new social revolution."

Despite exaggeration, Devoy had identified the essential division within the American League. For his part, Ford hailed Davitt's speeches as "a return to the old Irish system" of collective ownership of the land, in contrast to "the Norman pattern of individual property." Father McGlynn came to the fore during these weeks by endorsing Davitt's policies. George responded: "If Davitt's trip had no other result, it were well worth this." Finally, the labor element in the Land League rallied to Davitt, and the Central Labor Union held a massive procession of trades in his honor. Banners at the rally praised land nationalization and the No-Rent Manifesto, the Clothing Cutters and Cigar Makers union bands played the Marseillaise, and one placard read, "Is slavery a thing of the past?" The ubiquitous Robert Blissert chaired the meeting, noting that the Irish slogan, "the land for the people," "had found an echo on these shores, and has supplied American workingmen with a watchword for the future."[77]

In his own remarks Davitt referred to the land movement as

"the uprising of the laborers of Ireland against a robbing system of monopoly that has confiscated the fruits of labor." He reiterated support for land nationalization. But by the time he left America, he had abandoned any idea of challenging Parnell. Isolated in Ireland and under fierce assault in America, Davitt agreed to abide by Parnell's decision on land policy. Possibly, Davitt might have taken the leadership in an independent movement of Irish agricultural laborers, who were forming autonomous Labor Leagues in 1882. But he was temperamentally and politically unwilling to challenge Parnell for leadership or to fracture the Irish movement.[78]

Perhaps the significance of the short-lived debate sparked by Davitt's 1882 visit rested less in the issue of land nationalization, which had no real chance of being adopted by the Irish movement, than in its illumination of the gap which divided those Davitt called "Tory nationalists and democratic nationalists." A seemingly subsidiary question surfaced during these weeks to clarify the difference. Davitt intended to spread the land agitation to England and to forge an alliance between the Irish movement and the British working class. His own missing right arm, the result of a childhood accident in a Lancashire factory, symbolized the grievances which could unite the poor of the two countries. Thus, he had chosen England for his land nationalization speeches and insisted that nationalist violence, which alienated all Englishmen, must cease.[79]

After all, anti-landlord sentiment had long been an integral part of both middle-class and working-class English radicalism, in both of which the non-productive landlords, who "toil not, neither do they spin," held pride of place as social villains. The tradition of land reform reached back at least as far as the writings of Thomas Spence and Thomas Paine in the 1790s, and it acquired new urgency as the number of landless urban and rural workers multiplied during the nineteenth century. From Locke to Mill, moreover, English political economy had been "continually engaged in undermining the ideas of justice and social utility" claimed for the British land system. By the second

half of the nineteenth century, glorification of "peasant proprietorship" was common in British economic writings, with English and Irish tenants compared unfavorably with the allegedly
thrifty, energetic, and productive farmers of France, Holland,
and Switzerland, who owned their own land. At mid-century
the Chartists had raised the cry, "the land belongs to the people," while middle-class reformers were demanding abolition of
entail and complex laws of settlement and the establishment of
"free trade in land." By 1882 the agricultural depression of the
late 1870s, the land war in Ireland, and the wide circulation of
the writings of Henry George all propelled the land question to
the forefront of politics. "This question of the land," said one
labor newspaper, "will bring the English and Irish people
together at last."[80]

Davitt's American supporters instantly embraced the vision
of an international radical crusade. Father McGlynn declared
the Irish people must not "hate the depressed, degraded people of England," insisting that "the miners and labourers of England are ground down quite as much as the people of Ireland,
and the poor people of both countries should make common
cause against their oppressors." Robert Blissert agreed, telling a
Land League audience, "There was no fight between the people of England and Ireland. . . . It was simply a struggle between the rich and the poor."

Such views were anathema to conservatives who wished to
see the aims of the land movement narrowly delimited, and to
nationalists like Devoy who could never overcome their hatred
of all things English. The *Irish-American* insisted that no alliance
with "the 'English Democracy' " was possible because of "the responsibility of the English people for the wrongs inflicted on
Ireland." And Devoy wrote, "We firmly believe that when any
awakening does come to the sluggish minds of the English
masses, it will take quite as anti-Irish a turn as in the days of
Cromwell." "Englishmen, whether aristocrats or democrats, are
all the same to us," said Devoy, "—foreigners." To such men,
Davitt's attempt to shatter the chains of historic hatred seemed as

radical as his scheme of land nationalization. Both obstructed a single-minded focus on Irish independence.[81]

By the end of 1882 Irish politics had been transformed. Parnell and the Parliamentary party took control of the land movement, submerging it in the new National League, for which Home Rule was the first demand and land reform—in the guise of peasant proprietorship—a distant second.

Conservatives dominated the American National League, from which Ford and his followers held aloof. "The great body of respectable and dignified Land Leaguers were present," said one account of the opening convention, "attired in black frock coats and beaver hats." The "conservative Parnell platform" of the Irish League was adopted as well, and money poured in from wealthy Irish-Americans. "A reaction has set in," the *Irish World* declared. "The class movement going on in Ireland is the very essence of Toryism." The Land League, Ford announced, no longer existed.[82]

VI

Few histories of the Irish in America contain more than a passing reference to the Land League or to such related subjects as Irish predominance in the Knights of Labor, the social theories of Patrick Ford, or Henry George's campaign for mayor of New York City in 1886. For that matter, few general histories of the Gilded Age mention the Land League or, indeed, the Catholic Church.[83] In the major exception, which has shaped the views of all subsequent students—the work of Thomas N. Brown—Irish-American nationalism emerges as a response to ethnic realities in America. A defensive reaction to nativism and discrimination, its aims were conservative despite occasionally radical rhetoric: namely, to gain a self-respecting place for Irish-Americans in American life. "Mostly," Brown writes, "the Irish wanted to be middle-class and respectable. . . . In the Lace Curtain Irishman the rebel found fulfilment." Almost a century ago the nationalist Alexander Sullivan made a similar judgment, describing the National League as "a positive Americanizing influence" that tamed the wild Irish and taught them the "self-discipline" and "business habits" they never learned in Ireland.[84]

That Irish-American nationalism and, specifically, the Land League in some sense contributed to the assimilation of Irish-Americans is beyond dispute. Yet, the Brown thesis suffers from a fatal narrowness of vision. It views working-class life simply as a transitional stage on the road to bourgeois respectability, and defines assimilation solely as acquisition of middle-class values that enabled the Irish immigrant "to accommodate . . . to an often hostile environment." Or, as William Shannon suggests, Irish-American nationalism helped the Irish enter "the larger American society that was native, Protestant, Anglo-Saxon, and middle-class in its values."

But there was another America—one not "middle-class in its values." During the Gilded Age, class conflict wracked America more fiercely than at any time in our history. The nation experienced a thorough economic revolution and the shocks associated with the development of industrial capitalism spawned massive social discontent, from the great strike of 1877, through the labor upheaval of the 1880s, to the political crisis of the 1890s. Henry George did not exaggerate when he wrote in 1883, "There is a wide-spread consciousness among the masses that there is something radically wrong in the present social organization."[85] The point is that "assimilation" could mean a merger not with the dominant culture and its values, but with a strong emergent oppositional working-class culture. The Land League and the teachings of the *Irish World* helped Americanize a large section of the Irish-American working class. But the American traditions they identified with were those of the abolitionists and Knights of Labor, of Wendell Phillips and Henry George, not those of middle-class complacency. The radical Irish-Americans wished to transform their society even as they became a more integral part of it.

Middle-class values and aspirations did not dominate Irish-

American society as thoroughly as many writers have claimed, and ethnic nationalism did not unite the Irish working and middle classes at the expense of class identification across ethnic lines. The depression of the 1870s and the Land League experience widened the gap between the classes within the Irish community and set the stage for the persistence of Irish-American radicalism during the 1880s and beyond. As one Land Leaguer in Reading, Pennsylvania, wrote to the *Irish World*, enclosing a meager $36 from a League picnic, more would have been collected but:

> The rich Irishmen of Reading do not seem to know of what is going on in Ireland or in America. If they do, the more shame for them. Not one of them ever showed his face at our meetings, or sent a dime to help the cause. Perhaps they have forgotten all about the dear old land in the hoarding of their ill-gotten wealth, which was brought them by the hard labor and hot sweat of others.[86]

Many Irish-Americans saw no contradiction between ethnic nationalism and class consciousness. The inherent tensions between these modes of looking at the world exploded more than once in the ideological struggles between those in the Land League who focused solely on Irish independence and those who sought to forge an alliance with workers in America and England. Yet, national ideas often reinforce class consciousness, and nowhere more so than in a country such as Ireland where the ruling class was of distinct religion and nationality, and in Irish-America where the center of gravity lay so solidly in the working class. In the urban centers of Gilded Age America, class and ethnic differences overlapped: the majority of workers were immigrant and the majority of the middle class, native-born. Thus, many could agree with Terence Powderly that "the American labor movement, and . . . the Irish land movement" were "almost identical."[87]

Long after the demise of the Land League, the radical impulse it embodied continued to affect Irish and Irish-American life. In Ireland, Davitt continued to pursue his dream of a grand alliance of Irish, British, and American workers, helping to organize the Irish Democratic Labor Federation in 1890 and, at the close of his life, supporting such diverse causes as the English Labor party, Indian nationalism, Zionism, and women's rights. Yet, he remained a lonely warrior. The Irish tenant farmers, for whom he had done so much, rejected his social outlook and, when they finally won possession of the land through the Wyndham Land Act of 1903, they retreated into conservatism.

The final settlement of the land issue appears as one of those tricks Ireland so regularly plays on history. Contrary to British hopes and Fenian fears, it did not destroy Irish nationalism, which had taken on a life of its own, independent of specific grievances. Nor did the overthrow of the Irish landlord class provide the lever for social revolution in England, as Marx and others had expected. "I have come to the conclusion," Marx had written in 1870, "that the decisive blow against the English ruling classes . . . cannot be delivered in England but only in Ireland." The overthrow of the Irish aristocracy was "the preliminary condition for the proletarian revolution in England."[88]

Marx, nonetheless, had a point. The English "proletarian revolution" never did take place, but the land issue, reinvigorated by the Irish land war, played havoc with British political life in the 1880s, driving a wedge between upper-class and reform elements in the Liberal party and fueling the socialist revival. Nationalization of the land became an important goal of the Social Democratic Federation founded by H. M. Hyndman in 1881, when land meetings on the Irish model swept the Scottish highlands. "The most active leaven of the present social movement," said one English observer in 1884, "is really the land question." Labor leaders like Kier Hardie found in the writings of Henry George the key to unlocking the secrets of poverty and exploitation and later moved to socialism. Yet, in the end, the British government bought out the Irish landlords, while the British working and middle classes paid the tax bill. Perhaps the most fitting epitaph for the Irish land movement was penned by Patrick Ford in 1903: "The Land war now seems to be coming to a close but whether it is to be a victory or a defeat, or a drawn battle, is something I can't figure out."[89]

In America the causes of Irish nationalism and labor reform remained deeply embedded in the labor movement long after the Land League had ceased to exist. Like the Land League, the labor movement of the 1880s and 1890s brought together Irish nationalists, reformers, and radical intellectuals like Ford and George who had been workers themselves. The labor consciousness that flowered in the 1880s, epitomized by the rapid expansion of the Knights of Labor, owed a great deal to the Ford-George wing of the Land League. Where Irish-Americans predominated, the Knights merged social radicalism and Irish nationalism as effectively as the Land League had done.

The high point of the Knights came in 1886, the year of the Great Upheaval. A large portion of New York City's Irish abandoned Tammany Hall to support Henry George's campaign for mayor, which articulated the principles of the Land League and Central Labor Union. Patrick Ford, Terence Powderly, Father McGlynn, and James Redpath, all Land League veterans, stood behind the George campaign. In 1886, too, the controversy surrounding Father McGlynn reemerged; his participation in George's campaign and subsequent refusal to explain himself in Rome led to his excommunication in 1887. The massive support the "rebel priest" received from his New York parishioners measured the deep impact his brand of social Catholicism had made on the Irish-American poor.[90]

The experience of the Land League, finally, should lead us to reexamine the entire history of the Irish in America, as well as traditional treatments of class relations and ethnic nationalism among other groups. The ideological debates in the League perhaps reflected not only differences of tactics and outlook, but the existence of two overlapping but distinct centers of power, or poles of leadership, within the Irish-

American community. Those who opposed Ford reflected the views of a nexus composed of the Catholic Church, the Democratic party, and the Irish-American middle class. The social dominance of this triple alliance was challenged in the 1880s by the organized social radicalism articulated and institutionalized in the Land League's radical branches and the Knights of Labor. Here were the only organized alternatives to the Tammany-oriented saloon and local clubhouse, as a focus for working-class social life in the Irish-American community. The discussions of political issues, the emphasis on temperance, the reading of the radical labor press, and the very process of union-building across divisions of ethnicity, skill, and craft, all embodied a social ethic that challenged the individualism of the middle class and the cautious social reformism of the Democratic party and Catholic Church.[91]

After 1890 the decline of the Knights, the retreat of Patrick Ford and Henry George from their earlier radicalism, and the continuing transformation of American capitalism combined to direct Irish-American radicalism into new channels. Historians have traditionally viewed Irish-America as becoming increasingly conservative during these years. The growing wealth and power of the Irish middle class, the increasing social importance of the Church, the Democratic party's adoption of labor reform positions on the local level, and the emergence of stable craft unionism, all helped consolidate some of the gains of the 1880s while sapping the strength of radicalism. At the same time, Irish-Americans assumed a prominent place in the labor aristocracy, propelled there by the massive influx of new immigrants. Preempting the best-paying craft and industrial employments, they dominated the American Federation of Labor as it moved toward a cautious program of incremental gains within the capitalist system. At the same time, the land issue appeared increasingly inappropriate as a focus for radical thought as American capitalism entered its modern era.[92]

It will not do, however, simply to update the myth of Irish conservatism by twenty years. Irish-Americans may have played little role in the Socialist party, but they dominated the militant Western Federation of Miners, whose first president, Ed Boyce, was an Irish immigrant. The members of the W.F.M. continued to believe that "our present social system is based upon a fundamental injustice, namely, private ownership of land." The Irish community played a significant part in the anti-imperialist movement of the 1890s and often supported factory legislation, the regulation of business, and other expressions of "urban liberalism" in the early twentieth century. And well into this century, Catholic social activists like Monsignor John A. Ryan, who had first learned of "the agrarian situation in Ireland and industrial problems in the United States" from the *Irish World*, reflected the persistence of the Ford-McGlynn brand of Irish radical thought.[93] Only when American historians have chronicled the evolution of the Irish-American working class, will the ultimate significance of the Land League and the legacy it bequeathed to Irish-America and the society at large be fully revealed.

Notes

I INTRODUCTION

1. Michael Kammen, ed., *The Past Before Us: Contemporary Historical Writing in the United States* (Ithaca, 1980).
2. Anthony Wallace, *Rockdale* (New York, 1978); E. J. Hobsbawm, "From Social History to the History of Society," *Daedalus*, C (Winter 1971), 20–45.
3. Frances FitzGerald, *America Revised: History Schoolbooks in the Twentieth Century* (Boston, 1979), 157–58.
4. Richard Hofstadter, *The Paranoid Style in American Politics* (New York, 1966), vii.
5. J. G. A. Pocock, "Virtue and Commerce in the Eighteenth Century," *Journal of Interdisciplinary History*, III (Jan. 1972), 119–34; Pocock, *The Machiavellian Moment: Florentine Political Thought and the Atlantic Republican Tradition* (Princeton, 1975), ch. 15.
6. Richard Hofstadter, *The Progressive Historians* (New York, 1968), 460–61.

II CAUSES OF THE AMERICAN CIVIL WAR

1. David Donald, "American Historians and the Causes of the Civil War," *South Atlantic Quarterly*, LIX (Summer 1960), 351–55.
2. To cite only a few of the host of works related to this point, David Brion Davis, *The Problem of Slavery in Western Culture* (Ithaca, 1966)

and Edmund S. Morgan, "Slavery and Freedom: The American Paradox," *Journal of American History,* LIX (June 1972), 5–29, stress the centrality of slavery to the American experience. Douglass North, *The Economic Growth of the United States, 1790 to 1860* (New York, 1961), shows how the profits of the cotton trade paid for the economic development of ante-bellum America. Staughton Lynd, *Class Conflict, Slavery, and the United States Constitution* (Indianapolis, 1967), Donald L. Robinson, *Slavery and the Structure of American Politics* (New York, 1971), Richard H. Brown, "The Missouri Crisis, Slavery and the Politics of Jacksonianism," *South Atlantic Quarterly,* LXV (Winter 1966), 55–72, William W. Freehling, *Prelude to Civil War* (New York, 1966), and Eric Foner, *Free Soil, Free Labor, Free Men: The Ideology of the Republican Party Before the Civil War* (New York, 1970) place slavery at the center of politics at various points in ante-bellum history. Eugene D. Genovese, *The Political Economy of Slavery* (New York, 1965), makes clear the centrality of slavery to the society of the Old South.

3. Rather than citing the scores of works on abolitionism, let me simply refer to an admirable historiographical survey: Merton L. Dillon, "The Abolitionists: A Decade of Historiography, 1959–1969," *Journal of Southern History,* XXXV (Nov. 1969), 500–522.

4. On the racism of anti-slavery advocates, see, for example, William H. Pease and Jane H. Pease, "Anti-Slavery Ambivalence: Immediatism, Expediency, Race," *American Quarterly,* XVII (Winter 1965), 682–95; Eric Foner, "Racial Attitudes of the New York Free Soilers" [essay V in this collection]; Eugene H. Berwanger, *The Frontier Against Slavery* (Urbana, 1967); and James H. Rawley, *Race and Politics* (Philadelphia, 1969). For the limitations of abolitionist radicalism, see William Appleman Williams, *The Contours of American History* (London ed., 1961), 254; Aileen Kraditor, *Means and Ends in American Abolitionism* (New York, 1969), 244–53; George F. Fredrickson, *The Black Image in the White Mind* (New York, 1971), 36–37.

5. David Potter, *The South and the Sectional Conflict* (Baton Rouge, 1968), 146.

6. The major works of "new political history" dealing with ante-bellum politics are Lee Benson, *The Concept of Jacksonian Democracy: New York as a Test Case* (Princeton, 1961); Ronald P. Formisano, *The Birth of Mass Political Parties: Michigan 1827–1861* (Princeton, 1971); Paul Kleppner, *The Cross of Culture* (New York, 1970); the essays collected in Frederick C. Luebke, ed., *Ethnic Voters and the Election of Lincoln* (Lincoln, 1971); and Michael F. Holt, *Forging a Majority: The Formation of the Republican Party in Pittsburgh, 1848–1860* (New Haven, 1969). The phrase "monistic interpretation" is quoted from Holt, 125. I should note that obviously not all these writers agree on every interpretation. Holt,

for example, tends to give anti-slavery attitudes more credence as a determinant of voting behavior than do the other writers.

7. Some of these methodological criticisms are raised in Allen G. Bogue, "United States: The 'New Political History,' " *Journal of Contemporary History*, III (Jan. 1968), 22–24; James E. Wright, "The Ethnocultural Model of Voting," *American Behavioral Scientist*, XVI (May–June 1973), 653–74; and James R. Green, "Behavioralism and Class Analysis: A Review Essay on Methodology and Ideology," *Labor History*, XIII (Winter 1972), 89–106. Among other methodological problems is the tendency of some writers to infer the behavior of voters in heterogeneous areas from the actions of those who lived in homogenous ethnic communities, and difficulties created by the use of census data on the number of church seats of each religion in a specified area, as a measure of the breakdown of religious affiliations of that area. There are also simple problems of interpreting data. Formisano, for example, presents a table of the voting of evangelical townships in Michigan in 1860. In eastern Michigan, six of eleven such townships gave Lincoln over 60 per cent of the vote, but Lincoln carried the state with 57 per cent of Michigan's ballots. The table shows that in five of eleven evangelical townships, Lincoln received less than his state-wide percentage. The figures hardly justify the conclusion that evangelical townships voted "strongly Republican" in 1860. Formisano, *Birth of Mass Political Parties*, 312–13.

8. Some of these criticisms are noted in the Wright and Green articles cited above, and in David P. Thelen, review of Kleppner, *Civil War History*, XVII (Mar. 1971), 84–86, and Thelen, review of Formisano, *Civil War History*, XVIII (Dec. 1972), 355–57. The quotation is from Wright, "The Ethnocultural Model of Voting," 664. Wright and Green questions whether these studies are adequately controlled for class and status variables. All three critics question whether class can be adequately measured by looking at units like "farmers" or "workers," or by measuring the wealth of rural and urban precincts without considering the internal class structure of these units.

9. Joel H. Silbey, "The Civil War Synthesis in American Political History," *Civil War History*, X (June 1964), 130–40; Luebke, *Ethnic Voters*, xi.

10. This incredible statement is quoted by Formisano from Philip E. Converse, "The Nature of Belief Systems in Mass Publics," in David E. Apter, *Ideology and Discontent* (New York, 1964), 245. Formisano, *Birth of Mass Political Parties*, 11–12. Cf. Leubke, *Ethnic Voters*, xiv.

11. On this last point, see Foner, *Free Soil, Free Labor, Free Men*, ch. 7.

12. Richard N. Current, *The Lincoln Nobody Knows* (New York, 1958), 58–59.

13. Lee Benson, *Toward the Scientific Study of History* (Philadelphia, 1972), 316–26.

14. See, in general, A. S. Eisenstadt, *Modernization: Protest and Change* (Englewood Cliffs, 1966), and C. E. Black, *The Dynamics of Modernization* (New York, 1966).

15. Raimondo Luraghi, "The Civil War and the Modernization of American Society: Social Structure and Industrial Revolution in the Old South Before and During the War," *Civil War History*, XVIII (Sept. 1972), 242.

16. Also relevant is Barrington Morroe, Jr., *Social Origins of Dictatorship and Democracy* (Boston, 1966), ch. 3. I should note that describing the South as "pre-modern" does not necessarily contradict the findings of Robert Fogel and Stanley Engerman that slavery was a highly profitable investment. Fogel and Engerman, *Time on the Cross: The Economics of American Negro Slavery* (Boston, 1974). George Fredrickson applies the concept of modernization to the Civil War itself, and the question of why the North was victorious, but he explicitly denies its applicability to the question of the causes of the Civil War. Fredrickson, "Blue Over Gray: Sources of Success and Failure in the Civil War," in Fredrickson, ed., *A Nation Divided: Problems and Issues of the Civil War and Reconstruction* (Minneapolis, 1975), 57–80.

17. Robert Kelley, *The Transatlantic Persuasion: The Liberal Democratic Mind in the Age of Gladstone* (New York, 1969).

18. J. R. Pole, *Abraham Lincoln and the American Commitment* (Oxford, 1966), 32; Paul Angle, ed., *Created Equal? The Complete Lincoln-Douglas Debates of 1858* (Chicago, 1958), 18. Cf. Bertram Wyatt-Brown, "Stanley Elkins' Slavery: The Antislavery Interpretation Reexamined," *American Quarterly*, XXV (May 1973), 167.

19. Richard D. Brown, "Modernization and the Modern Personality in Early America, 1600–1865: A Sketch of a Synthesis," *Journal of Interdisciplinary History*, II (Winter 1972), 201–28. E. A. Wrigeley comments on the imprecision of the modernization concept, and how it often seems to be used simply as a synonym for industrialization, in "The Process of Modernization and the Industrial Revolution in England," *Journal of Interdisciplinary History*, III (Autumn 1972), 228, 228n. The general question of the persistence of pre-industrial work habits and ideals in nineteenth-century America is raised in Herbert G. Gutman, "Work, Culture and Society in Industrializing America, 1815–1919," *American Historical Review*, LXXVIII (June 1973), 531–88.

20. Albert Soboul, *The Sans-Culottes*, trans. Remy Inglis Hall (New York, 1972), xv.

21. This point is suggested in J. H. Plumb, "Slavery, Race, and the Poor," *New York Review of Books*, Mar. 13, 1969, 4. David Brion Davis's *The Problem of Slavery in the Age of Revolution* (Ithaca, 1975) re-

lates the growth of anti-slavery in England to changes in attitudes toward labor in a way similar to my argument in the paragraphs below.

22. C. Vann Woodward, *American Counterpoint* (Boston, 1971), 6; Linda Kerber, *Federalists in Dissent* (Ithaca, 1970), 24–44; James M. Banner, *To the Hartford Convention* (New York, 1970), 99–108; Richard J. Buel, Jr., *Securing the Revolution* (Ithaca, 1972), 235.

23. Banner, *To the Hartford Convention*, 108–9; Kerber, *Federalists in Dissent*, 50, 59–63.

24. Rowland Berthoff, *An Unsettled People* (New York, 1971), 182; Stanley Elkins, *Slavery* (Chicago, 1959), ch. 4; Williams, *Contours*, 158. Cf. Fredrickson, *Black Image in the White Mind*, 19–33.

25. The highly competitive, individualistic nature of ante-bellum society also helps to explain the apparent paradox that both racism and anti-slavery thought became more pervasive in the North at the same time. As Stanley Elkins points out, "in a stratified society with strong aristocratic attitudes, there is no need to define the Negro as hopelessly inferior, because the greater portion of society is inferior in varying degrees." In America, by contrast, where freedom implied the ability to compete for advancement, the idea of freeing the slaves inevitably raised the question of social equality. Elkins, in John A. Garraty, *Interpreting American History* (2 vols.: New York, 1970), I, 188–89. Cf. Fredrickson, *Black Image in the White Mind*, 95, and David Brion Davis, "The Emergence of Immediatism in British and American Antislavery Thought," *Mississippi Valley Historical Review* (Sept. 1962), 209–30, one of the many works which relates the new anti-slavery outlook of the 1830s to a faith, engendered by evangelical religion, in the perfectibility of individual men and to a decline in deference to institutions which blocked the path to reform.

26. On notions of "free labor," see Foner, *Free Soil, Free Labor, Free Man*, ch. 1; David Montgomery, *Beyond Equality* (New York, 1965), ch. 1. Cf. the remark by sociologist Wilbert E. Moore; "If one were to attempt a one-word summary of the institutional requirements of economic development, that word would be *mobility*. Property rights, consumer goods, and laborers must be freed from traditional bonds and restraints, from aristocratic traditions, quasi-feudal arrangements, paternalistic and other multi-bonded relations." Moore, "The Social Framework of Economic Development," in Ralph Braibanti and Joseph J. Spengler, eds., *Tradition, Values and Socio-Economic Development* (Durham, 1961), 71.

27. Of course certain northern intellectuals, alienated from the more materialistic aspects of their own culture, turned to the South for the qualities lacking in northern society—"the vestiges of an old-world aristocracy, a promise of stability, and an assurance that gentility . . . could be preserved under republican institutions." William R. Taylor, *Cavalier and Yankee* (New York, 1961), xviii and

passim. I would argue, however, that by the 1840s and 1850s most northerners saw much more to criticize than to admire in southern life.

28. This argument would suggest that the process, described by George Fredrickson, in which ante-bellum radicals abandoned their position as independent critics of American institutions and uncritically identified themselves with their society—which he attributes to the Civil War experience—may have already begun during the 1850s. Fredrickson, *The Inner Civil War* (New York, 1965). John Thomas makes an argument similar to Fredrickson's in "Romantic Reform in America, 1815–1865," *American Quarterly*, XVII (Winter 1965), 656–81. However, Richard O. Curry has criticized both these works, arguing that anti-institutional radical thought persisted after the Civil War. Curry, "The Abolitionists and Reconstruction: A Critical Appraisal," *Journal of Southern History*, XXXIV (Nov. 1968), 527–45.

29. David Rothman, *The Discovery of the Asylum* (Boston, 1971), 107, 129, 214. Two works which deal with the transformation of personality and life styles required by industrial society are Herbert G. Gutman, "Work, Culture, and Society in Industrializing America, 1815–1919," and E. P. Thompson, "Time, Work Discipline and Industrial Capitalism," *Past and Present*, XXXVIII (1967), 58–97.

30. Roy F. Basler, *et al.*, eds., *The Collected Works of Abraham Lincoln* (9 vols.: New Brunswick, 1953–55), I, 108–15; IV, 268. Weld is quoted in Ronald G. Waters, "The Erotic South: Civilization and Sexuality in American Abolitionism," *American Quarterly*, XXV (May 1973), 187. Weld's statement suggests that abolitionists' "anti-institutionalism" may be interpreted as a belief that in the absence of powerful social institutions, "restraints" usually imposed by those institutions would have to be internalized by each individual. Also relevant to the above discussion is George Dennison's argument that the forcible suppression of internal disorder in the North in the 1830s and 1840s set a moral and legal precedent for the northern refusal to allow peaceable secession in 1861. Dennison, " 'The Idea of a Party System': A Critique," *Rocky Mountain Social Science Journal*, IX (Apr. 1972), 38–39n.

31. Foner, *Free Soil, Free Labor, Free Men*, 231–32; Gutman, "Work, Culture and Society," 583; Douglas V. Shaw, "The Making of an Immigrant Community: Ethnic and Cultural Conflict in Jersey City, New Jersey, 1850–1877" (Ph. D. diss., University of Rochester, 1972), 27–40, 75, 119; Formisano, *Birth of Mass Political Parties*, 146–47.

32. This is suggested in James R. Green, "Behavioralism and Class Analysis," 98.

33. This is suggested in David Donald, *Lincoln Reconsidered* (New York, 1956), 19–36, and Clifford S. Griffen, *Their Brothers' Keepers:*

Moral Stewardship in the United States 1800–1865 (New Brunswick, 1960).

34. Richards, *Gentlemen of Property and Standing* (New York, 1970), ch. 5.

35. David Brion Davis, ed., *Ante-Bellum Reform* (New York, 1967), 10. A recent study which attempts to probe this question is Joseph E. Mooney, "Antislavery in Worcester County, Massachusetts: A Case Study" (Ph. D. diss., Clark University, 1971). It is marred by the use of categories like "the common man" as units of social analysis, but its study of signers of an anti-slavery document of 1840 finds a large majority of farmers and artisans (278–79).

36. Brian Harrison, *Drink and the Victorians: The Temperance Question in England, 1815–1872* (Pittsburgh, 1971). The quotation is from page 24.

37. This is suggested in Williams, *Contours,* 280, and in Bernard Mandel, *Labor: Free and Slave* (New York, 1955). Michael Holt shows that in the mid-1850s, Know-Nothing lodge membership came disproportionately from manual workers and skilled artisans. Many of these workers presumably went into the Republican party. Holt, "The Politics of Impatience: The Origins of Know-Nothingism," *Journal of American History,* LX (Sept. 1973), 329–31.

38. William Barney, *The Road to Secession* (New York, 1972); William W. Freehling, "The Editorial Revolution, Virginia, and the Coming of the Civil War: A Review Essay," *Civil War History,* XVI (Mar. 1970), 64–72; Michael P. Johnson, *Toward a Patriarchal Republic: The Secession of Georgia* (Baton Rouge, 1977).

39. Carl Degler concludes that southern dissenters were remarkable largely for their weakness. Degler, *The Other South* (New York, 1974). Cf. Otto Olsen, "Historians and the Extent of Slave Ownership in the Southern United States," *Civil War History,* XVIII (June 1973), 101–16. On the other hand, William Barney suggests that there were severe divisions within the slaveholding class itself. The upper echelons of that class, he argues, became an increasingly closed elite in the 1850s, and younger and lesser planters found the route to upward mobility blocked by the rising price of slaves and concentration of wealth. Secession and slave expansionism, for them, was a route to renewed social mobility. Barney, *The Road to Secession,* 135.

40. [Edmund Ruffin], *Anticipations of the Future* (Richmond, 1860), viii–ix.

41. Fogel and Engerman, *Time on the Cross,* 39–40. My analysis of the situation in the British West Indies is derived from a dissertation in progress at Columbia University by George Tyson. Robert Brent Toplin shows how Brazilian slaveholders actually experienced in the 1880s what southerners may have feared in 1861—the emergence of abolitionism near plantations, slaves running away in large numbers, and the gradual disintegration of

control over the black population. Toplin, "The Spectre of Crisis: Slaveholder Reactions to Abolitionism in the United States and Brazil," *Civil War History*, XVIII (June 1973), 129–38.

42. It is perhaps appropriate to add that this disjunction exists for other periods of American history as well. Writings on the origins of the American Revolution seem to be as devoid of a clear linkage between social and political history as does Civil War historiography. For a speculative attempt to remedy this situation, see Kenneth A. Lockridge, "Social Change and the Meaning of the American Revolution," *Journal of Social History*, VI (Summer 1973), 403–39. Cf. Jack P. Greene, "The Social Origins of the American Revolution: An Evaluation and an Interpretation," *Political Science Quarterly*, LXXXVIII (Mar. 1973), 1–22.

43. Berthoff, *An Unsettled People*, 510; Michael Kammen, "Politics, Science and Society in Colonial America," *Journal of Social History*, III (Fall 1969), 63.

44. The paragraphs which follow are based on my essay, "Politics, Ideology, and the Origins of the American Civil War" [essay III in this collection].

45. Lawrence Stone, *The Causes of the English Revolution 1529–1642* (London, 1972), 10.

46. Luraghi, "Civil War and Modernization," 249. To be fair, Luraghi elsewhere observes that the Civil War "had not so much the task of making free a complete capitalistic structure yet existing, but mainly that of creating the conditions for such a structure to grow" (241).

47. For the South, see Emory Thomas, *The Confederacy as a Revolutionary Experience* (Englewood Cliffs, 1971); for the North, Allan Nevins, *The War for the Union: The Organized War 1863–64* (New York, 1971), and *The War for the Union: From Organized War to Victory, 1864–65* (New York, 1971).

III   POLITICS AND IDEOLOGY

1. Seymour M. Lipset, *The First New Nation* (New York, 1963), 308–11; Frank J. Sorauf, *Political Parties in the American System* (Boston, 1964), 60–65. Distinctions between American political parties, to borrow Marvin Meyers's apt phrase, have usually been along lines of "persuasion," rather than ideology.

2. Donald L. Robinson, *Slavery and the Structure of American Politics 1765–1820* (New York, 1971), 175. See also William N. Chambers and Walter Dean Burham, eds., *The American Party Systems* (New York, 1967), 3–32, 56–89.

3. Sorauf, *Political Parties*, 61.

4. *National Intelligencer*, Oct. 6, 1855.

5. Staughton Lynd, *Class Conflict, Slavery, and the United States Consti-*

tution (Indianapolis, 1967), 161; Robinson, *Slavery and the Structure of Politics*, viii, 244.

6. James M. Banner, *To the Hartford Convention* (New York, 1970), 99–103; Glover Moore, *The Missouri Controversy 1819–1821* (Lexington, Ky., 1953), *passim;* Charles Francis Adams, ed., *Memoirs of John Quincy Adams* (12 vols; Philadelphia, 1874–77), IV, 529; William E. Ames, *A History of the National Intelligencer* (Chapel Hill, N.C., 1972), 121–22.

7. Paul Nagel, "The Election of 1824: Reconsideration Based on Newspaper Opinion," *Journal of Southern History*, XXVI (Aug. 1960), 315–29; Richard H. Brown, "The Missouri Crisis, Slavery, and the Politics of Jacksonianism," *South Atlantic Quarterly*, LXV (Winter 1966), 55–72; Robert V. Remini, *Martin Van Buren and the Making of the Democratic Party* (New York, 1959), 125–32; Richard P. McCormick, *The Second American Party System* (Chapel Hill, 1966), 338–42; Chambers and Burnham, eds., *The American Party Systems*, 21, 97–101.

8. Moore, *Missouri Controversy*, 175; James Young, *The Washington Community* (New York, 1966).

9. Robinson, *Slavery and the Structure of Politics*, 72; Linda K. Kerber, *Federalists in Dissent* (Ithaca, 1970), 24–44; Banner, *To the Hartford Convention*, 104–9; Theophilus Parsons, Jr., "A Mirror of Mens' Minds: The Missouri Compromise and the Development of an Antislavery Ideology" (unpublished seminar paper, Columbia University, 1971); *Congressional Globe*, 31 Congress, 1 Session, Appendix, 1030; 36 Congress, 2 Session, 624. C. Vann Woodward observes that patterns of derogatory sectional imagery existed far earlier than most historians have assumed. Woodward, *American Counterpoint* (Boston, 1971), 6.

10. Banner, *To the Hartford Convention*, 108–9; Kerber, *Federalists in Dissent* 50, 59–63. After the transformation of their party from a national to a regional one, New England Federalists did express their latent anti-southern feelings more openly. Richard Buel, Jr., *Securing the Revolution: Ideology in American Politics, 1789–1815* (Ithaca, 1972), 235.

11. Stanley Elkins, "Slavery and Ideology," in Ann Lane, ed., *The Debate over Slavery* (Urbana, 1971), 376n.; William W. Freehling, *Prelude to Civil War*, (New York, 1966), ch. 9, esp. 333, 358; *Congressional Globe*, 25 Congress, 2 Session, Appendix, 62.

12. Alice Felt Tyler, *Freedom's Ferment* (New York, 1962 ed.), 511; Elkins, "Slavery and Ideology," 374–77; Eric Foner, *Free Soil, Free Labor, Free Men* (New York, 1970), 87–102.

13. Gilbert H. Barnes, *The Anti-Slavery Impulse* (New York, 1964 ed.), 188–90, 195–97; James B. Stewart, *Joshua R. Giddings and the Tactics of Radical Politics* (Cleveland, 1970), ch. 4.

14. Preston King to Gideon Welles, Sept. 16, 1858, Gideon Welles Papers, Library of Congress; Eric Foner, "The Wilmot Proviso

Revisited," *Journal of American History*, LVI (Sept. 1969), 262–70; Chaplain W. Morrison, *Democratic Politics and Sectionalism* (Chapel Hill, 1967), 34–41.

15. Morrison, *Democratic Politics*, 45–51; Eric Foner, "Racial Attitudes of the New York Free Soilers" [essay V in this collection].

16. Avery Craven, *The Coming of the Civil War* (Chicago, 1942), 197; Ronald P. Formisano, *The Birth of Mass Political Parties* (Princeton, 1971), 195, 205–6; Joseph G. Rayback, *Free Soil* (Lexington, 1970), 309; Frederick W. Seward, *Seward at Washington* (2 vols.: New York 1891), I, 71.

17. Foner, *Free Soil, Free Labor, Free Men*, 188; Morrison, *Democratic Politics*, 87–91; Damon Wells, *Stephen Douglas, The Last Years, 1857–1861* (Austin, 1971) 61–67.

18. For the intentional nature of the ambiguities in popular sovereignty, see Robert W. Johannsen, *Stephen A. Douglas* (New York, 1973), 427, 440, 525.

19. Holman Hamilton, *Prologue to Conflict* (Lexington, 1964).

20. Johannsen, *Douglas*, 347, 483. For Webster's efforts to create a national consensus by compromising and suppressing the slavery issue, see Robert F. Dalzell, Jr., *Daniel Webster and the Trial of American Nationalism* (Boston, 1973), *passim*, and Major L. Wilson, "Of Time and the Union: Webster and His Critics in the Crisis of 1850," *Civil War History*, XIV (Dec. 1968), 293–306.

21. Foner, *Free Soil, Free Labor, Free Men*, 194. Of course, on the local level, the Whigs had already been eroding under the impact of such divisive issues as temperance and nativism.

22. Allan Nevins, *Ordeal of the Union* (2 vols.: New York, 1947), II, 107. Cf. Wells, *Douglas*, 64.

23. Paul M. Angle, ed., *Created Equal? The Complete Lincoln-Douglas Debates of 1858* (Chicago, 1958), 5, 17, 18, 35, 70, 202, 303, 332–34, 351. Cf. Harry Jaffa, *Crisis of the House Divided* (Garden City, 1959); Wells, *Douglas*, 110–11.

24. Angle, ed., *Created Equal?*, 22–23, 62–63; Jaffa, *Crisis*, 36. Lincoln declared that the trouble with popular sovereignty was that Douglas "looks upon all this matter of slavery as an exceedingly little thing—this matter of keeping one-sixth of the population of the whole country in a state of oppression and tyranny unequalled in the world." Angle, ed., *Created Equal?*, 35. It is hard to imagine Douglas including the slaves in any way as part of "the population of the whole country."

25. Roy F. Nichols, *The Disruption of American Democracy* (New York, 1948), esp. ch. 15. For Douglas's intentions for the territories and his expectation that popular sovereignty would result in the creation of free states in the West, see Jaffa, *Crisis*, 48; Johannsen, *Douglas*, 276, 279–80, 565; Edward L. and Frederick H. Schapsmeir, "Lincoln and Douglas: Their Versions of the West," *Journal of the West*, VII (Oct. 1968), 546. Lee Benson argues that the en-

trance of free western states into the Union was not a cause of concern for the South, since these new states, like California and Oregon in the 1850s, would likely be Democratic and pro-southern. But the 1850s clearly showed that free, Democratic states could quickly become Republican, and the Lecompton fight demonstrated that free, Democratic states were no longer accept-able to southern leaders, who insisted that Kansas be Democratic *and* slave. Lee Benson, *Toward the Scientific Study of History* (Phila-delphia, 1972), 269.

26. Foner, *Free Soil, Free Labor, Free Men,* esp. chs. 1–2.

27. Glyndon G. Van Deusen, *William Henry Seward* (New York, 1969), ch. 9; Elliot R. Barkan, "The Emergence of a Whig Persuasion: Conservatism, Democratism, and the New York State Whigs," *New York History,* LII (Oct. 1971), 370–86; Seward to James Bowen, Nov. 3, 1844, William Henry Seward Papers, University of Michigan Library; Seward to Weed, Aug. 3, 1846, Thurlow Weed Papers, University of Rochester.

28. Formisano, *Birth of Mass Political Parties,* 329; Foner, *Free Soil, Free Labor, Free Men,* 87–102; Larry Gara, "Slavery and the Slave Power: A Crucial Distinction," *Civil War History,* XV (Mar. 1969), 5–18.

29. Angle, ed., *Created Equal?,* 393. It is futile, in my opinion, to draw too-fine distinctions between various kinds of Republican anti-slavery sentiment, as Lee Benson and Ronald Formisano sometimes have a tendency to do. Though the distinctions be-tween opposition to the slave power, general anti-southernism, and what Formisano calls criticisms of "slavery as an institu-tion," or "antislavery as such" were real ones, these distinc-tions seemed pointless to the South, since even Republicans of the most moderate anti-slavery views advocated policies southerners found unacceptable. More important, the vary-ing degrees and kinds of anti-slavery sentiment fed into and reinforced one another; the Republican ideology, in other words, was much more than the sum of its parts—it must be understood in its totality. See Formisano, *Birth of Mass Political Parties,* 244, 279; Benson, *Toward the Scientific Study,* 295.

30. William W. Freehling, "The Editorial Revolution, Virginia, and the Coming of the Civil War: A Review Essay," *Civil War History,* XVI (Mar. 1970), 68–71.

31. Robert Brent Toplin, "The Specter of Crisis: Slaveholder Reac-tions to Abolitionism in the United States and Brazil," *Civil War History,* XVIII (June 1972), 129–38; John Amasa May and Joan Reynolds Faust, *South Carolina Secedes* (Columbia, 1960), 88.

32. Benjamin F. Wright, ed., *The Federalist* (Cambridge, 1961), 132–34, 357–59. Or, as C. B. MacPherson writes, the American federal theory of politics rests on the assumption "that the politi-

cally important demands of each individual are diverse and are shared with varied and shifting combinations of other individuals, none of which combinations can be expected to be a numerical majority of the electorate." MacPherson, *Democratic Theory: Essays in Retrieval* (Oxford, 1973), 190.

33. William W. Freehling, "Spoilsmen and Interests in the Thought and Career of John C. Calhoun," *Journal of American History*, LII (June 1965), 25–26; Charles M. Wiltse, *John C. Calhoun* (3 vols.; Indianapolis, 1944–51), II, 114, 195, 199, 255, 268–70; III, 416–19, 462–63; May and Faust, *South Carolina Secedes*, 81.

34. David Potter, *The South and the Sectional Conflict* (Baton Rouge, 1968), 44, 58; New York *Tribune*, Apr. 12, 1855.

IV ABOLITIONISM AND THE LABOR MOVEMENT

1. See Harvey Wish, *George Fitzhugh, Propagandist of the Old South* (Baton Rouge, 1943); Richard Hofstadter, *The American Political Tradition* (New York, 1948), ch. 4; Eugene D. Genovese, *The World the Slaveholders Made* (New York, 1969), pt. 2.

2. *Workingman's Advocate* (New York City), Mar. 13, 1830. On artisan radicalism, see Eric Foner, *Tom Paine and Revolutionary America* (New York, 1976).

3. Seth Luther, *Address to the Workingmen of New England* (Boston, 1832), 25; Philip S. Foner, *History of the Labor Movement in the United States* (New York, 1947), I, 272; John R. Commons *et al.*, eds., *A Documentary History of American Industrial Society* (10 vols.: Washington, 1910–11), V, 317; Bernard Mandel, *Labor: Free and Slave* (New York, 1955), 77; Thomas Dublin, "Women, Work and Protest in the Early Lowell Mills," *Labor History*, XVI (Winter 1975), 109–10; Lise Vogel, "Their Own Work: Two Documents from the Nineteenth-Century Labor Movement," *Signs*, I (Spring 1976), 794–800.

4. Walter Hugins, ed., *The Reform Impulse* (New York, 1972), 99–101.

5. Leon Litwack, *North of Slavery* (Chicago, 1961), 160; Joseph G. Rayback, "The American Workingman and the Antislavery Crusade," *Journal of Economic History*, III (1943), 152–63; Lorman Ratner, *Powder Keg* (New York, 1968), 62–67.

6. Alan Dawley, *Class and Community: The Industrial Revolution in Lynn* (Cambridge, 1976), 65; Leonard Richards, *Gentlemen of Property and Standing* (New York, 1970), 140–41; John B. Jentz, "Artisans, Evangelicals, and the City: A Social History of the Labor and Abolitionist Movements in Jacksonian New York" (Ph. D. diss., Graduate Center, City University of New York, 1977), 54–56, 125–35; New York *Daily Sentinel*, Sept. 17, 1831; *Workingman's Advocate*, Oct. 17, 1835; Oct. 1, 1831.

7. *The Liberator,* Jan. 1, 1831.

8. *The Liberator,* Jan. 29, 1831.

9. *The Liberator,* Sept. 5, 1846.

10. Ronald G. Walters, *The Antislavery Appeal* (Baltimore, 1976), 121.

11. Hugins, ed., *The Reform Impulse,* 168. See also Jonathan A. Glickstein, " 'Poverty Is Not Slavery': American Abolitionists and the Competitive Labor Market," *Antislavery Reconsidered: New Perspectives on the Abolitionists,* eds., Lewis Perry and Michael Fellman (Baton Rouge, 1979), 195–218. The italics in the Jay quotation are in the original.

12. George Fredrickson, *The Black Image in the White Mind* (New York, 1971), 32–34; Aileen Kraditor, *Means and Ends in Anerican Abolitionism* (New York, 1969), 244; Gilbert Osofsky, "Abolitionists, Irish Immigrants, and the Dilemmas of Romantic Nationalism," *American Historical Review,* LXXX (Oct. 1975), 908–10.

13. See Gilbert Barnes, *The Anti-Slavery Impulse* (New York, 1933); Anne C. Loveland, "Evangelicism and Immediate Emancipation in American Anti-Slavery Thought," *Journal of Southern History,* XXXII (May 1966), 172–88.

14. Jentz, "Artisans, Evangelicals, and the City," 97, 192–93; *Workingman's Advocate,* Sept. 19, Nov. 21, 1835.

15. *Workingman's Advocate,* Jan. 30, 1830; Lewis Tappan, *Life of Arthur Tappan* (New York, 1870), 329; Bertram Wyatt-Brown, *Lewis Tappan and the Evangelical War Against Slavery* (Cleveland, 1969), 46–47.

16. Williston H. Lofton, "Abolition and Labor," *Journal of Negro History,* XXXIII (July 1948), 249–83; Mandel, *Labor: Free and Slave,* 93.

17. John L. Thomas, "Antislavery and Utopia," in *The Antislavery Vanguard,* ed., Martin B. Duberman (Princeton, 1965), 255–56; *The Liberator,* Aug. 28, 1846; *Life and Times of Frederick Douglass* (New York, 1962), 228.

18. Stephen Oates, *To Purge This Land With Blood: A Biography of John Brown* (New York, 1970), 245–46.

19. Mandel, *Labor: Free and Slave,* 77; *Herald of Freedom* (Concord), June 2, Oct. 6, 1846; Apr. 11, May 2, 1845.

20. *The Liberator,* Sept. 4, 1846; Salem *Ohio Homestead Journal,* cited in *The Liberator,* Apr. 21, 1848.

21. *The Liberator,* Sept. 25, 1846, Mar. 19, 26, Apr. 2, 1847.

22. *The Liberator,* Mar. 26, July 9, Oct. 1, 1847. On this debate, see also Kraditor, *Means and Ends,* 248–50.

23. *The Liberator,* July 9, 1847.

24. David Montgomery, "The Shuttle and the Cross: Weavers and Artisans in the Kensington Riots of 1844," *Journal of Social History,* V (Summer 1972), 411–46.

25. *Working Man's Advocate,* July 6, 1844.

26. Eric Foner, *Free Soil, Free Labor, Free Men: The Ideology of the Republican Party Before the Civil War* (New York, 1970).

27. See Eric Foner, "The Causes of the Civil War: Recent Interpretations and New Directions" [essay II in this collection].

28. David Brion Davis, *The Problem of Slavery in the Age of Revolution* (Ithaca, 1975), 347–61.

29. Davis, *Problem of Slavery,* 364, 373; Dawley, *Class and Community,* 196, 238–39.

30. Michael Fellman, *The Unbounded Frame* (Westport, 1973), 105; Mandel, *Labor: Free and Slave,* 66; Rayback, "American Workingman," 154; Foner, *History of the Labor Movement,* I, 272.

31. See Eric Foner, "Class, Ethnicity, and Radicalism in the Gilded Age: The Land League and Irish-America," [essay VIII in this collection].

32. Barry Goldberg, "Beyond Free Labor" (Ph. D. diss., Columbia University, 1978), provides compelling evidence of the persistence of the idea of "wage slavery" among labor leaders after the Civil War, as a rhetorical device for criticizing the emerging industrial society. Paradoxically, he observes, labor reformers played down the differences between chattel slavery and wage slavery, yet they identified strongly with abolitionism, ignoring that movement's response to the labor reformers of its own time. As late as 1895, the British writer John K. Ingram felt compelled to include an appendix on the "lax" use of the concept of slavery among his contemporaries, especially the term "wage slavery," in his *A History of Slavery and Serfdom* (London, 1895), 263–64.

V   RACIAL ATTITUDES

1. William Chambers, *Things As They Are in America* (London, 1854), 354; Leon F. Litwack, *North of Slavery, The Negro in the Free States, 1790–1860* (Chicago, 1961), especially chs. 1, 3–5; Allan Nevins, *Ordeal of the Union* (2 vols.: New York, 1949), I, 518–20; John C. Hurd, *The Law of Freedom and Bondage in the United States* (2 vols.: Boston, 1862), II, 131, 136, 177, 216–17; William G. Allen, *The American Prejudice Against Colour* (London, 1853), 1; Julian to Convention of Colored Citizens of Illinois, September 17, 1853, George W. Julian Papers, Indiana State Library (italics in original).

2. Charles H. Wesley, "The Participation of Negroes in Anti-Slavery Political Parties," *Journal of Negro History,* XXIX (Jan. 1944), 48; *North Star,* Sept. 1, 1848; Kirk H. Porter and Donald B. Johnson, eds., *National Party Platforms* (Urbana, 1956), 4–9; Norman D. Harris, *History of Negro Servitude in Illinois* (Chicago, 1906), 148; Hartford *Charter Oak,* Oct. 7, 28, 1847; Howard H. Bell, "A Sur-

vey of the Negro Convention Movement, 1830–1861" (Ph. D. diss., Northwestern University, 1953), 75, 82–84.

3. Dixon Ryan Fox, *The Decline of Aristocracy in the Politics of New York* (New York, 1919), 269n.; Dixon Ryan Fox, "The Negro Vote in Old New York," *Political Science Quarterly*, XXXII (June 1917), 252–75.

4. Lee Benson, *The Concept of Jacksonian Democracy* (Princeton, 1961), 320n.; New York *Tribune*, Oct. 4, 1845, Feb. 12, 1846.

5. John R. Hendricks, "The Liberty Party in New York State, 1838–1848" (Ph. D. diss., Fordham, 1959), 152–57; Works Projects Administration, ed., *Calendar of the Gerrit Smith Papers in the Syracuse University Library* (2 vols.: Albany, 1941), I, 239, 244, 260.

6. William Trimble, "The Social Philosophy of the Loco-Foco Democracy," *American Journal of Sociology*, XXVI (May 1921), 713; Frederick Merk, "A Safety Valve Thesis and Texan Annexation," *Mississippi Valley Historical Review*, XLIX (Dec. 1962), 428–36; New York *Morning News*, Mar. 13, 28, Apr. 29, 1846; Robert Gumerove, "The 'New York Morning News,' Organ of the Radical 'Barnburning' Democracy, 1844–1846" (M. A. thesis, Columbia University, 1953), 82–91; Parke Godwin, *Biography of William Cullen Bryant* (2 vols.: New York, 1883), I, 345–46; Litwack, *North of Slavery*, 89; New York *Tribune*, Jan. 12, 1852.

7. C. C. Cambreleng, John Hunter, Thomas Sears, Gouverneur Kemble, Samuel J. Tilden, Arphaxed Loomis, Michael Hoffman, Azel Danforth, William Taylor, Cyrus Kingsley, John A. Kennedy, and James Powers.

8. S. Croswell and R. Sutton, eds., *Debates and Proceedings in the New York State Convention for the Revision of the Constitution* (Albany, 1846), 788–91; cf. 783–85; *Tribune Almanac for the Years 1838 to 1868* (2 vols.: New York, 1868), I, 1847, 43; Boston (semi-weekly) *Republican*, Nov. 16, 1848; *Mr. Greeley's Record on the Questions of Amnesty and Reconstruction* (New York, 1872), 21.

9. Herbert D. A. Donovan, *The Barnburners* (New York, 1925), 92–94; Walter L. Ferree, "New York Democracy; Division and Reunion, 1847–1852" (Ph. D. diss., University of Pennsylvania, 1953), 99.

10. Michael Hoffman to Azariah C. Flagg, Mar. 25, 1845, Azariah C. Flagg Papers, New York Public Library (italics in original); *Proceedings of the Herkimer Mass Convention* (Albany, 1847), 4–8; O. C. Gardiner, *The Great Issue* (New York, 1848), 119.

11. George Rathbun, at Utica Convention: *Proceedings of the Utica Convention* (Albany, 1848), 25. Cf. *The Free Soil Question and Its Importance to the Voters of the Free States* (New York, 1848), 2–7.

12. J. Franklin Jameson, ed., "Correspondence of John C. Calhoun," *Annual Report* of American Historical Association, 1899, II, 1155; *Free Soil Question*, 7; John Bigelow, ed., *Writing and Speeches of Sam-*

uel J. Tilden (2 vols.: New York, 1885), II, 545; *National Era*, Sept. 28, 1848; Boston *Republican*, Aug. 23, 1848; Gardiner, *Great Issue*, 135; *Herkimer Convention*, 28.

13. Morgan Dix, *Memoirs of John Adams Dix* (2 vols.: New York, 1883), II, 114–17; *Congressional Globe*, 30 Congress, 1 Session, Appendix, 866ff.; Simeon B. Jewett to Dix, July 8, 1848, Dix to Thomas Hart Benton, Sept. 9, 1848, John A. Dix Papers, Columbia University Library.

14. Works Projects Administration, eds., *Calendar of the Joshua Reed Giddings Manuscripts in the Library of the Ohio State Archaeological and Historical Society* (Columbus, 1939), 222; *National Era*, July 13, 1848; Letter of Lewis H. Bishop (of Warsaw Historical Society, Warsaw, N.Y.) to author, Mar. 13, 1963; Carter G. Woodson, ed., *The Mind of the Negro As Reflected in Letters Written During the Crisis 1800–1860* (Washington, 1926), 352.

15. Ernest P. Mueller, "Preston King: A Political Biography" (Ph. D. diss., Columbia University, 1957), 335–36, 353; *Congressional Globe*, 29 Congress, 2 Session, 114–15; King to Dix, Nov. 13, 1847, Dix Papers; Thomas M. Marshall, ed., "Diary and Memoranda of William L. Marcy, 1849–1851," *American Historical Review*, XXIV (Apr. 1919), 451.

16. Charles B. Going, *David Wilmot: Free Soiler* (New York, 1942), 174–75n.; Margaret Koshinski, "David Wilmot and Free Soil" (M.A. thesis, Columbia University, 1949), 25; *Congressional Globe*, 29 Congress, 2 Session, Appendix, 317, 30 Congress, 1 Session, Appendix, 1076–79; *Herkimer Convention*, 14.

17. *Congressional Globe*, 31 Congress, 1 Session, Appendix, 943, 30 Congress, 2 Session, 406; Going, *Wilmot*, 338.

18. *Pennsylvania Freeman*, Dec. 7, 1848 (italics in original). In the same editorial, the *Freeman* addressed an eloquent appeal to the entire Free Soil party:

> The colored people . . . are calling for their rights, and contending with long-seated prejudices. We have a right to expect Free Soil men to encourage and assist them; if they will not do this, we ask them in the name of humanity, that they will not feed the popular prejudices against this outcast class.

19. Ralph V. Harlow, *Gerrit Smith* (New York, 1939), 186 (italics in original).

20. Van Buren had settled the dispute with the telling remark, "Is not the vote of Geritt [*sic*] Smith just as weighty as that of [the Barnburner] Judge Martin Grover?" Lucius E. Chittenden, *Personal Reminiscences, 1840–1890* (New York, 1893), 15–16; Oliver Dyer, *Great Senators of the United States* (New York, 1889), 95–96.

21. *Reunion of the Free Soilers of 1848, at Downer Landing, Higham, Massachusetts* (Boston, 1877), 43. Douglass confirmed the incident. *Frederick Douglass' Paper*, Aug. 20, 1852.

22. Oliver Dyer, *Phonographic Report of the Proceedings of the National Free Soil Convention* (New York, 1848), 4, 21; Edward H. Price, "The Election of 1848 in Ohio," *Ohio Archaeological and Historical Quarterly*, XXXVI (1927), 249.

23. The Western Liberty leaders had for some time been striving to broaden their party's platform, to attract anti-slavery men from the Whig and Democratic parties. Joseph G. Raybeck, "The Liberty Party Leaders of Ohio: Exponents of Anti-Slavery Coalition," *Ohio Archaeological and Historical Quarterly*, LVII (Apr. 1947), 165–78.

24. Porter and Johnson, eds. *Party Platforms*, 13–14; Harris, *Negro Servitude*, 167; Lawrence Lader, *The Bold Brahmins* (New York, 1961), 135; Boston *Republican*, Aug. 17, 1848; John Brown to Hale, Aug. 24, 1848, John P. Hale Papers, New Hampshire Historical Society.

25. Dwight Dumond, ed., *Letters of James G. Birney, 1831–1857* (2 vols.: New York, 1938), II, 623.

26. Thomas Van Rensselear to Martin Van Buren, Oct. 16, 1848, in Samuel J. Tilden Papers, New York Public Library; *Pennsylvania Freeman*, Oct. 26, 1848.

27. *North Star*, Sept. 1, 1848. Butler had been Van Buren's Attorney-General. For his views on Negro suffrage, see Butler, "Outline of the Constitutional History of New York," *Collections* of the New York Historical Society, II, Second Series (1848), 62n.

28. *North Star*, Sept. 1, 22, 1848.

29. Bell, "Negro Convention Movement," 106; *North Star*, Nov. 24, 1848, Jan. 12, 1849; (Montpelier, Vt.) *Green Mountain Freeman*, Nov. 11, 1847.

30. Ulrich B. Phillips, ed., "The Correspondence of Robert Toombs, Alexander Stephens, and Howell Cobb," *Annual Report* of American Historical Association, 1911, II, 270.

31. Henry B. Stanton, *Random Recollections* (New York, 1887), 162, 165. That many of the leading Barnburners were motivated in large part by the desire to defeat Cass is beyond question. See Chittenden, *Reminiscences*, 12–14; "Letter of William Allen Butler to George Bancroft," *Proceedings* of Massachusetts Historical Society, LX (Jan. 1927), 118–20; Azariah Flagg to Marcus Morton, June 19, 1848, Gideon Welles to Flagg, Feb. 9, 1848, Flagg Papers, Columbia University Library; John L. O'Sullivan, *Nelson Jarvis Waterbury* (New York, 1880), 11–12. For a different view, see Joseph G. Raybeck, ed., "Martin Van Buren's Desire for Revenge in the Campaign of 1848," *Mississippi Valley Historical Review*, XL (Mar. 1954), 707–16.

32. *National Era*, Nov. 15, 1849.

33. New York *Evening Post*, June 12, July 17, 19, Nov. 24, 1848, Oct. 18, 1850, May 23, July 30, 1851.

34. New York *Evening Post*, Sept. 8, 1851; Margaret Clapp, *Forgotten First Citizen: John Bigelow* (Boston, 1947), 54; John Bigelow, *Ja-*

maica in 1850 (New York, 1851), 160; Hermann Burmeister, *The Black Man* (New York, 1853), 3, 5, 13–15 (reprint from New York *Evening Post*).

35. *Tribune Almanac*, I, 1847, 44, 1849, 49; Edward M. Shepard, *Martin Van Buren*, (Boston, 1888), 427; Boston *Commonwealth*, July 27, 1852.

36. *National Era*, June 15, 1848; Philadelphia *Republic*, Dec. 22, 1848; *North Star*, Dec. 8, 1848. And contrast the Barnburners' opposition to the presence of the free Negro in the territories with the *National Era*'s position: "We are not opposed to the extension of either class of your [the South's] population, provided it be *free*, but to the existence of slavery and the migration of *slaves*." *National Era*, May 3, 1849 (italics in original).

37. Edward Channing, *A History of the United States* (6 vols.: New York, 1912–25), VI, 4; Wilfred E. Binkley, *American Political Parties* (New York, 1954), 186.

38. In virtually every northern state, Negro suffrage was viewed more favorably by the Whigs, and of course the Liberty men, then the Democrats. In states like Ohio and Massachusetts, where the Free Soilers were largely former Whigs and Liberty men, the party fought to extend the social and political rights of free Negroes. Even in these states, however, the party was plagued by the problem of racial prejudice. Emil Olbrich, "The Development of Sentiment on Negro Suffrage to 1860," *Bulletin* of the University of Wisconsin, III (1912); *National Era*, Mar. 18, 1952.

39. *Pennsylvania Freeman*, Feb. 1, 1849.

40. Charles M. Wiltse, *John C. Calhoun* (New York, 1951), 369; Chauncey S. Boucher and Robert P. Brooks, eds., "Correspondence Addressed to John C. Calhoun, 1837–1849," *Annual Report* of American Historical Association, 1929, 389; Jameson, ed., "Correspondence of Calhoun," 1183; Phillips, ed., "Correspondence of Toombs, Stephens, and Cobb," 114; Nevins, *Ordeal of the Union*, I, 255; Frederick W. Seward, *Seward at Washington* (2 vols.: New York, 1891), I, 71.

41. Porter and Johnson, eds., *Party Platforms*, 18–20; New York *Tribune*, Aug. 13, 1852; *National Era*, Aug. 12, 1852.

VI RECONSTRUCTION AND FREE LABOR

1. Howard K. Beale, "On Rewriting Reconstruction History," *American Historical Review*, XLV (July 1940), 807–27; Bernard A. Weisberger, "The Dark and Bloody Ground of Reconstruction Historiography," *Journal of Southern History*, XXV (Nov. 1959), 427–47; Vernon L. Wharton, "Reconstruction," in *Writing Southern History*, eds. Arthur S. Link and Rembert V. Patrick (Baton Rouge, 1965), 295–315; Richard O. Curry, "The Civil War and

Reconstruction, 1861–1877; A Critical Overview of Recent Trends and Interpretations," *Civil War History*, XX (Sept. 1974), 215–28.

2. W. E. B. Du Bois, *Black Reconstruction in America* (New York, 1935); William H. Trescot to Governor James L. Orr, Dec. 13, 1865, South Carolina Governors' Papers, South Carolina Archives.

3. Richard Taylor to Samuel L. M. Barlow, Dec. 13, 1865, Samuel L. M. Barlow Papers, Huntington Library; "Visit to Gowrie and East Hermitage Plantations, March 22, 1867," in Statement of Sales, Gowrie Plantation, Savannah River, Mss. volume, Manigault Family Papers, Southern Historical Collection, University of North Carolina. Taylor, apparently no historian, actually used the date " '99" in his letter, but the meaning seems clear. Manigault had visited China and the Philippines in 1850–51. Louis Manigault, Journal of Travels (typescript), South Caroliniana Library, University of South Carolina.

4. Arney R. Childs, ed., *The Private Journal of Henry William Ravenal 1859–1887* (Columbia, 1947), 269; Eliza F. Andrews, *The War-Time Journal of a Georgia Girl* (New York, 1908), 319; Capt. Isaac A. Rosekrans to James Waters, Oct. 27, 1865, Misc. Records (ser. 2767), Newberne NC Supt., Bureau of Refugees, Freedmen, and Abandoned Lands, Record Group 105, National Archives (hereafter cited as RG 105, N.A.); William A. Graham to David L. Swain, May 11, 1865, William A. Graham Papers, Southern Historical Collection, University of North Carolina; Laura Perry to Grant Perry, Feb. 3, 1869, J. M. Perry Family Papers, Atlanta Historical Society. For general discussion see James L. Roark, *Masters Without Slaves* (New York, 1977), 141–46; Robert P. Brooks, *The Agrarian Revolution in Georgia 1865–1912* (Madison, 1914), 18–26.

5. Sylvia H. Krebs, " 'Will the Freedmen Work?' White Alabamians Adjust to Free Labor," *Alabama Historical Quarterly*, XXXVI (Summer 1974), 151–63; "we the colorde people" to Governor of Mississippi, Dec. 3, 1865, F-41 (1865), Registered Letters Received (ser. 2051), Miss. Asst. Comr., RG 105, N.A.; M. Leland, "Middleton Correspondence, 1861–1865," *South Carolina Historical Magazine*, LXV (1964), 107.

6. Adam Smith, *An Inquiry into the Nature and Causes of the Wealth of Nations* (Modern Library ed.: New York, 1937), 365–66; Howard Temperly, "Capitalism, Slavery and Ideology," *Past and Present*, LXXV (May 1977), 107–9; Eric Foner, *Free Soil, Free Labor, Free Men: The Ideology of the Republican Party Before the Civil War* (New York, 1970).

7. Leon F. Litwack, *Been in the Storm So Long* (New York, 1979), 385. For criticisms of Freedmen's Bureau labor policies, see *ibid.*, 321–26, 384–91, 425; Jonathan M. Wiener, *Social Origins of the New South 1860–1885* (Baton Rouge, 1978), 47–53; William S. McFeely,

Yankee Stepfather: General O. O. Howard and the Freedmen (New Haven, 1979).

8. "Address of Capt. J. E. Bryant to Freedmen's Convention of Georgia, January 13, 1866," Mss. speech, John E. Bryant Papers, Perkins Library, Duke University.

9. Columbia *Daily Phoenix,* June 19, 1865; Augusta *Loyal Georgian,* Jan. 20, 1866.

10. Robert K. Scott to Governor James L. Orr, Dec. 13, 1866, South Carolina Governors' Papers; Kenneth B. White, "Wager Swayne—Racist or Realist?" *Alabama Review,* XXXI (Apr. 1978), 103–6.

11. Lewis C. Chartock, "A History and Analysis of Labor Contracts Administered by the Bureau of Refugees, Freedmen, and Abandoned Lands in Edgefield, Abbeville and Anderson Counties in South Carolina, 1865–1868" (Ph. D. diss., Bryn Mawr College, Graduate School of Social Work and Social Research, 1973), 43; Whitelaw Reid, *After the War* (Cincinnati, 1866), 343; Joseph H. Mahaffey, ed., "Carl Schurz's Letters from the South," *Georgia Historical Quarterly,* XXXV (Sept. 1951), 230–31.

12. *Memorial from the Cotton Planters' Convention, Which Met in Macon, September 6, 1866* (Macon, 1866), 12; Columbia *Daily Phoenix,* July 20, 1865; D. B. McLurin to N. R. Middleton, Sept. 26, 1867, Middleton Papers, Langdon Cheves Collection, South Carolina Historical Scoiety; William E. Highsmith, "Louisiana Landholding During War and Reconstruction," *Louisiana Historical Quarterly,* XXXVIII (Jan. 1955), 44; Raleigh *Semi-Weekly Record,* Aug. 23, 26, 1865.

13. John T. Trowbridge, *A Picture of the Desolated States* (Hartford, 1868), 573; Joyce Appleby, "Ideology and Theory: The Tension Between Political and Economic Liberalism in Seventeenth-Century England," *American Historical Review,* LXXXI (June 1976), 514.

14. *Indiana True Republican* (Richmond, Ind.), Sept. 14, 1865.

15. For a discussion of this point, see Eric Foner, *Tom Paine and Revolutionary America* (New York, 1976), 155–56.

16. New Orleans *Tribune,* Nov. 6, 1865; Ross H. Moore, "Social and Economic Conditions in Mississippi During Reconstruction" (Ph. D. diss., Duke University, 1937), 41; Charles Ramsdell, "Presidential Reconstruction in Texas," *Texas State Historical Association Quarterly,* XI (Apr. 1908), 301; Charles F. Ritter, "The Press in Florida, Louisiana, and South Carolina and the End of Reconstruction 1865–1877: Southern Men with Northern Interests" (Ph. D. diss., Catholic University, 1976), 66–67; Yorkville *Enquirer,* Feb. 14, 1867.

17. For a review and critique of this literature, see Harold D. Woodman, "Sequel to Slavery: The New History Views the Postbellum South," *Journal of Southern History,* XLIII (Nov. 1977), 523–54.

18. *Proceedings of the Annual Convention of the South Carolina Agricultural*

and Mechanical Society (Charleston, 1869), 7. There is a striking discussion of this point in Barbara J. Fields, "The Maryland Way from Slavery to Freedom" (Ph. D. diss., Yale University, 1978), 133–34.

19. Richard Fuke, "Black Marylanders, 1864–1868" (Ph. D. diss., University of Chicago, 1973), 26; Kemp P. Battle to Benjamin S. Hedrick, Jan. 20, 1866, Benjamin S. Hedrick Papers, Perkins Library, Duke University.

20. Fields, "The Maryland Way," 200–203; Will Martin to Governor Benjamin G. Humphreys, Dec. 5, 1865, Mississippi Governors' Papers, Mississippi Department of Archives; Reverend Samuel Agnew Diary, Nov. 3, 1865, Southern Historical Collection, University of North Carolina; Charles Colcock Jones, Jr. to Eva Jones, Nov. 7, 1865, Charles Colcock Jones, Jr. Collection, University of Georgia; Bt. Brig. Gen. Jno. B. Callis to General ?, Dec. 28, 1867, Alabama file, Letters Received by Thomas D. Eliot of House Committee on Freedmen's Affairs (ser. 18), Commissioner, RG 105, N.A.

21. Ulrich B. Phillips, ed., "The Correspondence of Robert Toombs, Alexander H. Stephens, and Howell Cobb," American Historical Association *Annual Report,* 1911, II, 684; Lt. James M. Babcock to Maj. G. D. Reynolds, Nov. 30, 1865, B-8 (1865), Registered Letters Received (ser. 2268), Actg. Asst. Comr. Southern Dist. of Miss., Natchez, RG 105, N.A.

22. Henry Watson, Jr. to Julia Watson, Dec. 16, 1865, Henry Watson, Jr. Papers, Perkins Library, Duke University; Elias H. Deas to daughter, Oct. 20, 1866, Elias H. Deas Papers, South Caroliniana Library, University of South Carolina. Cf. Roger L. Ransom and Richard Sutch, *One Kind of Freedom* (New York, 1977), 44–46.

23. *Nation,* Oct. 5, 1865; Rupert S. Holland, ed., *Letters and Diary of Laura M. Towne* (Cambridge, 1912), 9, 16–20; Elizabeth W. Pearson, ed., *Letters from Port Royal Written at the Time of the Civil War* (Boston, 1906), 181; Edward B. Heyward, undated, incomplete letter, Heyward Family Papers, South Caroliniana Library, University of South Carolina.

24. H. L. Tafft to Lt. Col. H. B. Clitz, Oct. 19, 1865, B-69 (1865), Letters Received (ser. 4109), Dept. of the South, Records of U.S. Army Continental Commands, Part 1, Record Group 393, National Archives; P. Sidney Post to "My dear Sir," Nov. 27, 1867, P. Sidney Post Papers, Knox College, Galesburg, Ill.; Willie Lee Rose, *Rehearsal for Reconstruction: The Port Royal Experiment* (Indianapolis, 1964), 37–38, 50, 128, 217–18, 301; Pearson, ed., *Letters,* 275.

25. Willard Range, *A Century of Georgia Agriculture, 1850–1950* (Athens, 1954), 7–8; H. C. Nixon, *Lower Piedmont Country* (New York, 1946), 10; Rose, *Rehearsal for Reconstruction,* 303, 382.

26. T. J. Woofter, Jr., *Black Yeomanry: Life on St. Helena Island* (New

York, 1930), 45, 117, 136–37, 140–45; Contract, Dec. 11, 1872, Albert A. Batchelor Papers, Department of Archives and Manuscripts, Louisiana State University; Brooks, *Agrarian Revolution*, 60. Cf. Ronald Davis, "Good and Faithful Labor: A Study in the Origins, Development, and Economics of Southern Sharecropping" (Ph. D. diss., University of Missouri, 1974), 123, which reports that in the Natchez District in 1880, 85 per cent of renters grew corn, while only 50 per cent of sharecroppers did.

27. Joe B. Wilkins, Jr., "Window on Freedom: The South's Response to the Emancipation of the Slaves in the British West Indies, 1833–1861" (Ph. D. diss., University of South Carolina, 1977); Lewis M. Ayres to D. H. Jacques, Dec. 26, 1865, Lewis M. Ayres Papers, South Caroliniana Library, University of South Carolina; John H. Moore, ed., *The Juhl Letters to the 'Charleston Courier'* (Athens, 1974), 69–70.

28. C. Vann Woodward, "The Price of Freedom," in *What Was Freedom's Price?*, ed., David L. Sansing (Jackson, 1978), 98–106; Pete Daniel, "The Metamorphosis of Slavery, 1865–1900," *Journal of American History*, LXVI (June 1979), 88–99; Gwendolyn M. Hall, *Social Control in Slave Plantation Societies* (Baltimore, 1971), 120–22; Philip Curtin, *The Two Jamaicas* (Cambridge, 1955), 104–9; Vernon Burton, "Race and Reconstruction: Edgefield County, South Carolina," *Journal of Social History*, XII (Fall 1978), 36.

29. Edmund S. Morgan, *American Slavery, American Freedom* (New York, 1975); Louisville *Democrat* in Columbia *Daily Phoenix*, Aug. 3, 1866; James L. Owens, "The Negro in Georgia During Reconstruction 1864–1872" (Ph. D. diss., University of Georgia, 1975), 63; Selma *Southern Argus*, Feb. 24, June 23, 1870; Michael S. Wayne, "Ante-Bellum Planters in the Post-Bellum South: The Natchez District, 1860–1880" (Ph. D. diss., Yale University, 1979), 86.

30. William Ivy Hair, *Bourbonism and Agrarian Protest: Louisiana Politics 1877–1900* (Baton Rouge, 1969), 46, Cf. *Rural Carolinian*, I (Oct. 1869), 52: "Land is the one thing that we have in abundance."

31. Robert A. Gilmour, "The Other Emancipation: Studies in the Society and Economy of Alabama Whites During Reconstruction" (Ph. D. diss., Johns Hopkins University, 1972), 119; Sam Nostlethwaite to James A. Gillespie, Mar. 14, 1869, James A. Gillespie Papers, Department of Archives and Manuscripts, Louisiana State University.

32. See Pearson, ed., *Letters*, 147.

33. Robert W. Fogel and Stanley L. Engerman, *Time on the Cross* (2 vols: Boston, 1974); Eugene D. Genovese, *The Political Economy of Slavery* (New York, 1965); Barrington Moore, Jr., *Social Origins of Dictatorship and Democracy* (Boston, 1966), 121.

34. Grady McWhiney, "The Revolution in Nineteenth-Century Alabama Agriculture," *Alabama Review*, XXXI (Jan. 1978), 3–32. See also Nixon, *Lower Piedmont*, 54–56, and the excellent discussion in

Stephen H. Hahn, "The Roots of Southern Populism: Yeoman Farmers and the Transformation of Georgia's Upper Piedmont, 1850–1890" (Ph. D. diss., Yale University, 1979).

35. Gordon B. McKinney, *Southern Mountain Republicans 1865–1900* (Chapel Hill, 1978); Otto H. Olsen, "Reconsidering the Scalawags," *Civil War History*, XII (Dec. 1966), 304–20; William C. Harris, "A Reconsideration of the Mississippi Scalawag," *Journal of Mississippi History*, XXXII (Feb. 1970), 3–42.

36. Gilmour, "The Other Emancipation," 63–68, 114, 130–44; Frank J. Huffman, "Old South, New South: Continuity and Change in a Georgia County, 1850–1880" (Ph. D. diss., Yale University, 1974), 71, 222; Joe Gray Taylor, *Louisiana Reconstructed 1863–1877* (Baton Rouge, 1974), 382; *Annual Message of Gov. J. L. Alcorn to the Mississippi Legislature, Session of 1871* (Jackson, 1871), 28; Gavin Wright, *The Political Economy of the Cotton South* (New York, 1978), 164.

37. William D. Cotton, "Appalachian North Carolina: A Political Study, 1860–1899" (Ph. D. diss., University of North Carolina, 1954), 51; John H. Cain to Governor Rufus Bullock, May 10, 1870, Rufus Bullock Papers, Georgia Department of Archives and History; T. W. Alexander *et al.* to Herschel V. Johnson, Feb. 11, 1868, Herschel V. Johnson Papers, Perkins Library, Duke University. Cf. Kenneth E. St. Clair, "Debtor Relief in North Carolina During Reconstruction," *North Carolina Historical Review*, XVIII (July 1941), 215–35.

38. Carol K. R. Bleser, *The Promised Land* (Columbia, 1970); William C. Harris, *The Day of the Carpetbagger: Republican Reconstruction in Mississippi* (Baton Rouge, 1979), 507.

39. William C. Carson *et al.* to General George G. Meade, Jan. 1868, C55 (1868), Letters Received (ser. 5783), Third Military District, Record Group 393, National Archives; Harold D. Woodman, "Post-Civil War Southern Agriculture and the Law," *Agricultural History*, LIII (Jan. 1979), 21; Peter Kolchin, *First Freedom* (Westport, 1972), 45; Joel Williamson, *After Slavery* (Chapel Hill, 1965), 148–59; Jackson *Weekly Mississippi Pilot*, Aug. 29, 1870, Jan. 23, 1875; R. H. Woody, "The Labor and Immigration Problems of South Carolina During Reconstruction," *Mississippi Valley Historical Review*, XVIII (Sept. 1931), 200; *Rural Carolinian*, III (Mar. 1872), 335.

40. Thomas Holt, *Black Over White* (Urbana, 1977), 152–53; Burton, "Race and Reconstruction," 38–39; Ralph I. Middleton to Henry A. Middleton, Aug. 24, 1869, Middleton Papers, Langdon Cheves Collection; W. H. Robert to Governor Daniel H. Chamberlain, Dec. 9, 1874, South Carolina Governor's Papers.

41. James W. Garner, *Reconstruction in Mississippi* (New York, 1901), 307–8; Selma *Southern Argus*, Feb. 3, 1870; Range, *Century of Georgia Agriculture*, 73; Frances Butler Leigh, *Ten Years on a Georgia Plantation Since the War* (London, 1883), 131–32. Cf. M. W.

Hungerford to Governor Rufus Bullock, Dec. 6, 1868, Georgia Governors' Papers, Georgia Department of Archives and History, for an instance of a white justice of the peace ruling for a black in a dispute concerning the division of a crop.

42. Beale, "Rewriting Reconstruction History," 827; Hiram Cassidy to Oscar J. Stuart, Aug. 23, 1871, Oscar J. Stuart Papers, Mississippi Department of Archives; A Statement of Dr. Bratton's Case (London, Ont., 1872), 8; James C. Mohr, ed., Radical Republicans in the North (Baltimore, 1976), xiv.

43. Charleston Daily Republican, July 28, 1870; The Republican Platform! (broadside, Savannah, 1873), Bryant Papers.

44. Eric Foner, "Thaddeus Stevens, Confiscation, and Reconstruction" [essay VII in this collection]; Edmund L. Drago, "Black Georgia During Reconstruction" (Ph. D. diss., University of California, Berkeley, 1975), 133–44; Charles Vincent, Black Legislators in Louisiana During Reconstruction (Baton Rouge, 1976), 98–101; Charleston Daily Republican, Nov. 30, 1869, Feb. 17, 1871; W. H. Robert to Governor Daniel H. Chamberlain, Dec. 9, 1874, South Carolina Governors' Papers.

45. Wiener, Social Origins; Kenneth G. Greenberg, "The Civil War and the Redistribution of Land: Adams County, Mississippi, 1860–1870," Agricultural History, XXV (Apr. 1978), 292–307; A. Jane Townes, "The Effect of Emancipation on Large Landholdings, Nelson and Goochland Counties, Virginia," Journal of Southern History, XLV (Aug. 1979), 403–12.

46. Rural Carolinian, II (Jan. 1871), 195, III (Jan. 1872), 173; Selma Southern Argus, Feb. 17, 1870. Cf. Jeffrey M. Paige, Agrarian Revolution (New York, 1975), 17.

47. Rural Carolinian, II (July 1871), 573; Southern Field and Factory, I (Mar. 1871), 116; Kolchin, First Freedom, 47; Selma Southern Argus, Feb. 17, 1870; Brooks, Agrarian Revolution, 52–54 (but see Drago, "Black Georgia," 246–56, challenging Brooks's contention); Savannah Morning News, Jan. 30, 1869; J. Carlyle Sitterson, Sugar Country (Lexington, 1953), 243–44; Harris, Day of the Carpetbagger, 277; Frank B. Conner to Lemuel P. Conner, Feb. 3, 1867, Lemuel P. Conner Family Papers, Department of Archives and Manuscripts, Louisiana State University; Charleston News and Courier, July 8, 1873.

48. Wiener, Social Origins, 71; Ralph I. Middleton to Henry A. Middleton, Feb. 8, 1870, May 2, 1872, Middleton Papers, Langdon Cheves Collection; Rural Carolinian, II (Mar. 1871), 324, III (Feb. 1872), 229.

49. Selma Southern Argus, Feb. 3, 1870; Rural Carolinian, I (Nov. 1869), 71: Yorkville Enquirer, Apr. 2, 1868; Frank B. Conner to Lemuel P. Conner, May 16, 1867, Lemuel P. Conner Family Papers; George W. Hagins to Henry Watson, Jr., Sept. 8, 1867, Henry Watson, Jr. Papers.

50. W. R. Jones to Governor William H. Smith, Aug. 9, 1870, Alabama Governors' Papers, Alabama Department of Archives and History; Affidavit of Eli Barnes, Nov. 20, 1869, Georgia Governors' Papers; P. C. Cudd to Governor Robert K. Scott, May 17, 1867, South Carolina Governors' Papers. Cf. J. C. A. Stagg, "The Problem of Klan Violence: The South Carolina Up-Country, 1868–1871," *Journal of American Studies*, VIII (1974), 303–18.

51. Harris, *Day of the Carpetbagger*, 482; Wayne, "Natchez District," 288; Nellie Morton to Rev. Gustavus D. Pike, Apr. 7, 1871, American Missionary Association Archives, Amistad Research Center, Dillard University.

52. *Proceedings of the Tax-Payers' Convention of South Carolina* (Charleston, 1874), 12–13, 51.

53. J. G. deRoulhac Hamilton, ed., *The Correspondence of Jonathan Worth* (2 vols.: Raleigh, 1909), II, 1155–56, 1185, 1217–18; Elizabeth McPherson, ed., "Letters from North Carolina to Andrew Johnson," *North Carolina Historical Review*, XXIX (Jan. 1952), 110–11.

54. S. S. Ashley to Bro. Woodworth, Jan. 1, 1869 (dated 1868), American Missionary Association Archives; Daniel E. Huger Smith *et al.*, eds., *Mason Smith Family Letters 1860–1868* (Columbia, 1950), 236; Rev. Samuel Agnew Diary, Nov. 3, 1865. Ironically, this new, truncated definition of freedom as simply self-ownership had already been promoted by certain abolitionists before the Civil War. See Eric Foner, "Abolitionism and the Labor Movement in Antebellum America" [essay III in this collection].

55. *Address of the Democratic White Voters of Charleston to the Colored Voters of Charleston, The Seaboard, and of the State Generally* (Charleston, 1868), 3–4; Mrs. C. M. Cheves to Henry A. Middleton, Aug. 26, 1868, Middleton Papers, Langdon Cheves Collection; "Letter of William Henry Trescot on Reconstruction in South Carolina, 1867," *American Historical Review*, XV (Apr. 1910), 574–82; Sarah Woolfolk Wiggins, *The Scalawag in Alabama Politics, 1865–1881* (University, Ala., 1977), 34; Savannah *Morning News*, Aug. 19, 1873.

56. C. Vann Woodward, *The Strange Career of Jim Crow* (New York, 1955); Savannah *Advertiser and Republican*, Aug. 17, 1873; Beaufort *Tribune*, May 10, 1877.

57. Alrutheus A. Taylor, *The Negro in South Carolina During the Reconstruction* (Washington, 1924), 263–64; Frenise A. Logan, *The Negro in North Carolina 1876–1894* (Chapel Hill, 1964), 49–50; William W. Rogers, *The One-Gallused Rebellion* (Baton Rouge, 1970), 28; William Cohen, "Negro Involuntary Servitude in the South, 1865–1940: A Preliminary Analysis," *Journal of Southern History*, XLII (Feb. 1976), 34–35; Woodman, "Post Civil War Southern Agriculture," 319–37; *Address to the Voters of North Carolina* (Raleigh, 1875).

58. Powhaten Lockett to Joseph Wheeler, Jan. 1, 1876, Joseph Wheeler Papers, Alabama Department of Archives and History; William Eaton to David S. Reid, Sept. 20, 1875, David S. Reid Papers, North Carolina Department of Archives; E. Merton Coulter, *Negro Legislators in Georgia During the Reconstruction Period* (Athens, 1968), 143–70 (an account strongly biased against Campbell); *Sufferings of the Rev. T. G. Campbell and His Family, in Georgia* (Washington, 1877); New York *Commercial and Financial Chronicle*, in *Appleton's Annual Cyclopedia*, n. s., II (1877), 231.

59. New York *Times*, Apr. 26, 1875; Robbins Little to John E. Bryant, July 10, 1875, Bryant Papers.

60. Mohr, *Radical Republicans*, xv; A. W. Spies to Governor James L. Orr, Nov. 30, 1866, South Carolina Governors' Papers; New York *Commercial and Financial Chronicle*, Jan. 18, 1868; Robbins Little to John E. Bryant, July 10, 1875, Bryant Papers. Cf. the classic analysis by William D. Hesseltine, "Economic Factors in the Abandonment of Reconstruction," *Mississippi Valley Historical Review*, XXII (1935), 191–210.

61. See David Montgomery, *Beyond Equality* (New York, 1967); Alfred D. Chandler, *The Visible Hand: The Managerial Revolution in American Business* (Cambridge, 1977); John G. Sproat, *"The Best Men"* (New York, 1968). Relevant to the breakup of the Radical coalition is Ellen DuBois, *Feminism and Suffrage* (Ithaca, 1978).

62. Morgan, *American Slavery, American Freedom;* Charleston *News and Courier*, July 28, 1877. Herbert G. Gutman, *Work, Culture, and Society in Industrializing America* (New York, 1976), suggests the centrality of the problem of labor discipline in the North in these years.

VII THADDEUS STEVENS

1. "The American Constitution and the Impeachment of the President," *Blackwood's Edinburgh Magazine*, CIII (June 1868), 717; Springfield *Weekly Republican*, Aug. 15, 1868. Young Georges Clemenceau, reporting American events for a Paris newspaper, was much taken with Stevens, describing him as the "Robespierre" of one of the "most radical revolutions known to history." Clemenceau, *American Reconstruction 1865–1870*, ed. Fernand Baldensperger (New York, 1928), 77, 79, 165, 227.

2. For descriptions of Stevens's personality, see George Fort Milton, *The Age of Hate* (New York, 1930), 263–64; J. W. Binckley, "The Leader of the House," *The Galaxy*, I (July 1866), 494; *The Reminiscences of Carl Schurz* (3 vols.: New York, 1907–8), III, 213–14. Ms biographical sketch, probably by Edward McPherson, Thaddeus Stevens Papers, Library of Congress. For his pre-war political career, see Richard N. Current, *Old Thad Stevens: A Story of Am-*

bition (Madison, 1942), chs. 2–9; Fawn Brodie, *Thaddeus Stevens, Scourge of the South* (New York, 1959), chs. 4–12.

3. Roy F. Basler *et al.*, eds., *The Collected Works of Abraham Lincoln* (9 vols.: New Brunswick, 1953–55), V, 49; J. A. Woodburn, "The Attitude of Thaddeus Stevens Toward the Conduct of the Civil War," *American Historical Review*, XII (Apr. 1907), 567–68; *Congressional Globe*, 37 Congress, 1 Session, 414; 3 Session, 239; 38 Congress, 1 Session, 316; 2 Session, 126; Alexander K. McClure, *Abraham Lincoln and Men of War-Times* (Philadelphia, 1892), 265.

4. William A. Dunning, *Reconstruction, Political and Economic, 1865–1877* (New York, 1907), 64; Justin S. Morrill, "Notable Letters from My Political Friends," *The Forum*, XXIV (1897–98), 141; James G. Blaine, *Memorial Address on the Life and Character of James Abram Garfield* (Washington, 1882), 10–11; W. R. Brock, *An American Crisis* (London, 1963), 62–68, *Congressional Globe*, 37 Congress, 2 Session, 2054.

5. Brooks M. Kelley, "Simon Cameron and the Senatorial Nomination of 1867," *Pennsylvania Magazine of History and Biography*, LXXXVII (Oct. 1963), 366–67, 388–89; Boston *Advertiser*, Aug. 13, 1868; David Donald, *The Politics of Reconstruction, 1863–1867* (Baton Rouge, 1965), 81; Eric L. McKitrick, *Andrew Johnson and Reconstruction* (Chicago, 1960), 260–68, and *passim*.

6. Cincinnati *Commercial*, Jan. 1, 1866; *Congressional Globe*, 39 Congress, 1 Session, 2544; Woodburn, "Stevens and the Conduct of the War," 571–72; Lancaster *Express*, Sept. 8, 1865. Cf. the assessments of Stevens's leadership in New York *Tribune*, Dec. 19, 1865; New York *Evening Post*, Apr. 3, 1866; *Nation*, Jan. 24, 1867.

7. McKitrick, *Andrew Jackson and Reconstruction*, 268; Charles R. Williams ed., *Diary and Letters of Rutherford Burchard Hayes*, (5 vols.: Columbus, 1922–26), III, 9.

8. Walter L. Fleming, " 'Forty Acres and a Mule,' " *North American Review*, CLXXXIII (May 1906), 721–37; T. Harry Williams, *Lincoln and the Radicals* (Madison, 1941), 26–27; James G. Randall, *Constitutional Problems Under Lincoln*, rev. ed. (Urbana, 1964), 276–80; Leonard P. Curry, *Blueprint for Modern America* (Nashville, 1968), 85, 95–99; *Congressional Globe*, 37 Congress, 2 Session, 3400.

9. *Congressional Globe*, 38 Congress, 1 Session, 19, 519; 2 Session, 1025–26; LaWanda Cox, "The Promise of Land for the Freedmen," *Mississippi Valley Historical Review*, XLV (Dec. 1958), 413–19, 431–35; Patrick W. Riddleberger, "George Washington Julian: Abolitionist Land Reformer," *Agricultural History*, XXIX (July 1955), 109–10; Fleming, " 'Forty Acres,' " 722–25; Randall, *Constitutional Problems*, 284–86, 316–17.

10. Eric Foner, *Free Soil, Free Labor, Free Men: The Ideology of the Republican Party Before the Civil War* (New York, 1970).

11. *Congressional Globe*, 39 Congress, 1 Session, 536.

12. George S. Merriam, *The Life and Times of Samuel Bowles,* (2 vols.: New York, 1885), II, 125; Benjamin B. Kendrick, *The Journal of the Joint Committee of Fifteen on Reconstruction* (New York, 1914), 92–105; *Congressional Globe,* 39 Congress, 1 Session, 2460, 2544.

13. *Congressional Globe,* 39 Congress, 1 Session, 2459; 40 Congress, 1 Session, 205; Benjamin W. Arnett, ed., *Duplicate Copy of the Souvenir from the Afro-American League of Tennessee to Hon. James M. Ashley of Ohio* (Philadelphia, 1894), 407–8; Riddleberger, "Julian," 108–114; Benjamin F. Butler, *Butler's Book* (Boston, 1892), 908–9, 961; *National Anti-Slavery Standard,* Nov. 17, 1866. For Sumner's complex views on the relative importance of land and the suffrage, see David Donald, *Charles Sumner and the Rights of Man* (New York, 1970), 119–20, 201; Edward L. Pierce, *Memoir and Letters of Charles Sumner,* (4 vols.: Boston, 1877–93), IV, 76, 229, 247–60; *The Works of Charles Sumner* (10 vols.: Boston, 1870–83), IV, 275; X, 220–25; XIII, 320–21.

14. *Congressional Globe,* 31 Congress, 1 Session, Appendix, 141–43; 40 Congress, 1 Session, 205. A self-made man himself, Stevens once described his social ideals as those of "the honest farmer, mechanic or laborer," as opposed to both the aristocrat and the "vagabond, the idle and dissipated." The prosperous yeomen of Lancaster County, Pennsylvania, were the bedrock of his political strength. Stevens assumed that black yeoman farmers would act pretty much as white farmers did. He did not view the freedmen, just emerging from slavery, as members of a distinct culture who might react in unpredictable ways to economic stimuli. Where blacks were allowed the choice, there were already signs of a reluctance to cultivate the "slave crop" cotton for the market, and a tendency to retreat into self-sufficiency. Black farmers might, in other words, have turned out to be quite different from the market-oriented farmers of the North idealized by Stevens. *Proceedings and Debates of the Convention of the Commonwealth of Pennsylvania, to Propose Amendments to the Constitution . . .* (14 vols.: Philadelphia, 1837–38), III, 167; Lancaster *Express,* Feb. 7, 1866; Joel Williamson, *After Slavery* (Chapel Hill, 1965), 44; Willie Lee Rose, *Rehearsal for Reconstruction* (Indianapolis, 1964), 82, 170, 226.

15. *Congressional Globe,* 39 Congress, 2 Session, 1317; *Reconstruction: Speech of the Hon. Thaddeus Stevens, Delivered in the City of Lancaster, September 7, 1865* (Lancaster, 1865), 2–5; *National Anti-Slavery Standard,* June 15, 1867.

16. Joseph Schafer, ed., *Intimate Letters of Carl Schurz, 1841–1869* (Madison, 1928), 341; William B. Hesseltine, "Economic Factors in the Abandonment of Reconstruction," *Mississippi Valley Historical Review,* XXII (Sept. 1935), 191–210; Philadelphia *Public Ledger,* Jan. 23, 1866; Cincinnati *Gazette,* Dec. 2, 1865; New York *Times,* Aug. 18, Nov. 2, 14, Dec. 18, 1865; Jan. 4, 15, 17, Sept. 2, 1866. Cf. Thomas Wagstaff, "Call Your Old Master—'Master': Southern

Political Leaders and Negro Labor During Presidential Recon- struction," *Labor History*, X (Summer 1969), 323–45.

17. Earle D. Ross, "Horace Greeley and the South," *South Atlantic Quarterly*, XVI (Oct. 1917), 333–34; New York *Tribune*, Sept. 12, 29, Oct. 11, 1865; *Nation*, Nov. 8, 1866; William D. Kelley, *Speeches, Addresses and Letters on Industrial and Financial Questions* (Philadelphia, 1872), 182–83; Robert Sharkey, *Money, Class, and Party* (Baltimore, 1959), 165–66.

18. *Congressional Globe*, 38 Congress, 1 Session, 1187–88, 2251. When Stevens pressed the confiscation issue in 1867, his proposal in- cluded a prohibition of the sale of lands in plots exceeding 500 acres, an attempt to prevent the engrossment of large tracts of land by northern speculators. *Congressional Globe*, 40 Congress, 1 Session, 203.

19. *Congressional Globe*, 39 Congress, 1 Session, 3240–41, 3687–88, 2 Session, 985; New York *Tribune*, Mar. 23, 1867; John J. McCarthy, "Reconstruction Legislation and Voting Alignments in the House of Representatives, 1863–1869" (Ph. D. diss., Yale University, 1970), 263.

20. J. Williamson to Thomas A. Jenckes, Feb. 16, 1866, Thomas A. Jenckes Papers, Library of Congress. For views of Stevens as an agent of northern capitalists, see Current, *Stevens*, and Williams, *Lincoln and the Radicals*. Of course, as Sharkey shows in *Money, Class and Party*, northern capitalists were hardly unanimous on po- litical and economical questions.

21. *Reconstruction—Lancaster Speech;* J. W. McClurg to Stevens, Sept. 27, 1865; Joseph Bailey to Stevens, Sept. 22, 1865, Stevens Pa- pers; *Congressional Globe*, 39 Congress, 1 Session, 104; 39 Con- gress, 1 Session, House Executive Document No. 99; New York *Times*, May 5, 1866.

22. *Congressional Globe*, 39 Congress, 1 Session, 655, 658, 748, 1966; William S. McFeely, *Yankee Stepfather, General O. O. Howard and the Freedmen* (New Haven, 1968), 213–20, 226–29; Christie Farnham Pope, "Southern Homesteads for Negroes," *Agricultural History*, XLIV (Apr. 1970), 202–5; Warren Hofnagle, "The Southern Homestead Act: Its Origins and Operation," *Historian*, XXXII (Aug. 1970), 615–29.

23. McFeely, *Yankee Stepfather*, 229–31; New York *Herald*, Feb. 8, 1866; *Congressional Globe*, 37 Congress, 2 Session, 243.

24. *Nation*, Feb. 21, 1867.

25. New York *Times*, Feb. 2, 1866.

26. *Congressional Globe*, 40 Congress, 1 Session, 49, 203; Springfield *Weekly Republican*, Mar. 23, 1867; New York *Times*, Mar. 13, June 7, 12, 1867; *Sumner Works*, XI, 124–29; *National Anti-Slavery Stan- dard*, June 15, 22, 1867; James M. McPherson, *The Struggle for Equality* (Princeton, 1964), 411; Chicago *Tribune*, July 18, 1867; Philadelphia *Press*, Mar. 21, May 8, 1867; Boston *Advertiser*, Apr.

27, 1867; Philadelphia *North American and United States Gazette*, Mar. 14, 16, May 1, 27, 1867.

27. New York *Times*, May 29, June 2, 1867. See New York *Herald*, May 2, 1866, attributing Steven's confiscation proposals to his desire for compensation for the burning of his iron works.

28. Cincinnati *Commercial*, July 25, 1867; *Nation*, Mar. 21, May 9, 16, 1867; New York *Times*, Feb. 19, Mar. 10, Apr. 10, June 27, 1867. Cf. Springfield *Weekly Republican*, Apr. 27, June 15, 1867.

29. New York *Times*, July 9, 1867. Cf. Boston *Advertiser*, June 13, 1867; "The Agrarians—Division of Property," *De Bow's Review*, n.s., IV (Dec. 1867), 586-88.

30. *Nation*, June 27, 1867; Philadelphia *Press*, May 3, 16, 1867; Cincinnati *Commercial*, Apr. 15, June 5, 1867; E. L. Godkin, "The Labor Crisis," *North American Review*, CV (July 1867), 199. In New York, the month of May witnessed strikes involving railroad workers, masons, hod carriers, stablemen, printers, carpenters, and shoemakers. New York *Tribune*, May 13, 14, 16, 18, 1867.

31. William F. Zornow, " 'Bluff Ben' Wade in Lawrence, Kansas: The Issue of Class Conflict," *Ohio Historical Quarterly*, XLV (Jan. 1956), 44-52; New York *Times*, June 12, 20, July 1, 1867; Felice A. Bonadio, *North of Reconstruction: Ohio Politics, 1865-1870* (New York, 1970), 148-49.

32. Springfield *Weekly Republican*, Mar. 18, 1867; New York *Tribune*, Mar. 21, 23, 1867; New York *Times*, June 10, 1867. Cf. Cincinnati *Commercial*, Apr. 12, 1867; Springfield *Weekly Republican*, Apr. 27, 1867; New York *Times*, Apr. 30, May 13, 20, June 13, Aug. 21, 1867.

33. Philadelphia *North American and United States Gazette*, July 1, 1867; J. H. Rea to Stevens, Jan. 9, 1866; Henry W. McVay to Stevens, Mar. 1, 1867; P. H. Whitehurst to Stevens, Mar. 22, 1867, Stevens Papers; William Birthright to John Broomall, July 14, 1867, John Broomall Papers, Historical Society of Pennsylvania; Raleigh *Standard*, cited in New York *Times*, Apr. 10, 1867; Philadelphia *Press*, cited in New York *Times*, May 30, 1867; Boston *Advertiser*, June 25, 1867; Washington *Daily Morning Chronicle*, Dec. 13, 1867.

34. Boston *Advertiser*, June 13, 1867; New York *Times*, Apr. 8, 19, May, 2, 18, 30, June 12, 1867; New York *Tribune*, Apr. 20, 24, 1867; Hamilton J. Eckenrode, *The Political History of Virginia During the Reconstruction* (Baltimore, 1904), 67; Alrutheus A. Taylor, *The Negro in the Reconstruction of Virginia* (Washington, 1926), 209-12.

35. New York *Tribune*, Apr. 25, May 6, 17, 27, June 10, 1867; New York *Times*, Apr. 24, 1867; Chicago *Tribune*, July 17, 1867; Jack P. Maddex, *The Virginia Conservatives, 1867-1879* (Chapel Hill, 1970), 53.

36. New York *Times*, Apr. 28, May 24, 29, June 22, 1867; New York *Herald*, July 8, 1867; New York *Tribune*, May 23, 1867; Boston *Advertiser*, May 25, 1867.

37. New York *Tribune,* Mar. 26, Apr. 30, 1867; New York *Times,* June 22, July 31, Sept. 9, 19, 27, 1867; *Nation,* Aug. 8, 1867; J. G. de Roulhac Hamilton, *Reconstruction in North Carolina* (New York, 1914), 245–47.

38. Ellis P. Oberholtzer, *Jay Cooke, Financier of the Civil War,* (2 vols.: Philadelphia, 1907), II, 28; Sharkey, *Money, Class, and Party,* 95, 119; Mary L. Hinsdale, ed., *Garfield-Hinsdale Letters* (Ann Arbor, 1949), 112. Cf. Springfield *Weekly Republican,* Oct. 26, 1867; *Harper's Weekly,* Oct. 26, 1867; Philadelphia *North American and United States Gazette,* Oct. 11, 1867; Michael Les Benedict, "The Rout of Radicalism: Republicans and the Election of 1867," *Civil War History,* XVIII (Dec. 1972), 334–44.

39. New York *Tribune,* Aug. 14, 1868; *Independent,* Aug. 27, 1868; Brock, *American Crisis,* 282; Philadelphia *Press,* Aug. 12, 1868; George F. Hoar, *Autobiography of Seventy Years,* (2 vols.: New York, 1903), I, 239. Shortly before his death, Stevens predicted that in the future southern whites would bar black voting by adopting property qualifications "applicable to all classes alike, which would reach down to just about the black line," and he condemned the emerging sharecropping and crop lien systems, *Congressional Globe,* 40 Congress, 2 Session, 108, 1966, 2214.

40. In *Beyond Equality* (New York, 1967), an important contribution to the historiography of Reconstruction, David Montgomery has argued that radical Republicanism broke up in the late 1860s under the impact of forces outside Reconstruction, particularly the emergence of a class-conscious labor movement whose demands challenged the radicals' vision of a harmonious social order founded on equality before the law. Montgomery, however, ignores the fact that all the challenges he cites, from the danger of class legislation to the radicals' inability to move beyond "equality before the law," were present in an issue at the core of Reconstruction—confiscation. Cf. W. E. B. Du Bois, *Black Reconstruction* (New York, 1935), a frustrating, flawed, but monumental study which deserves careful reading by anyone interested in Reconstruction. Chapter 14 discusses the decline of radicalism.

VIII THE LAND LEAGUE AND IRISH-AMERICA

1. *Irish World* (New York City), Feb. 16, 23, 1884; *United Irishman* (New York City), Feb. 16, 1884; Charles F. Horner, *The Life of James Redpath and the Development of the Modern Lyceum* (New York, 1926), 297–99.

2. Arnold Schrier, *Ireland and the American Emigration 1850–1900* (Minneapolis, 1958), 4–8, 160; Oliver MacDonagh, "The Irish Famine Emigration to the United States," *Perspectives in American History,* X (1976), 357–446; Stanley Aronowitz, *False Promises* (New York, 1973), 146; Robert Ernst, *Immigrant Life in New York City*

1825–1863 (New York, 1949), 69–71; Oscar Handlin, *Boston's Immigrants* (New York, 1968 ed.), 216–217; *10th Census,* 1880, I, 465, 752–55, 865, 892.

3. Philip H. Bagenal, *Parnellism Unveiled* (Dublin, 1880), 2; David Doyle, "The Irish and American Labor 1880–1929," *Saothar: Journal of the Irish History Society,* I (1975), 42–53; David Doyle, *Irish Americans, Native Rights, and National Empires* (New York, 1976), ch. 2; David Montgomery, *Beyond Equality* (New York, 1966), 36; Daniel J. Walkowitz, "Statistics and the Writing of Working Class Culture: A Statistical Portrait of the Iron Workers in Troy, New York, 1860–1880," *Labor History,* XV (1974), 422, 439; Ira Rosenwaike, *Population History of New York City* (Syracuse, 1972), 71–73; Stephan Thernstrom, *Poverty and Progress* (New York, 1969 ed.), 110; Bruce Laurie, Theodore Herschberg, and George Alter, "Immigrants and Industry: The Philadelphia Experience, 1850–1880," *Journal of Social History,* IX (1975), 235–43.

4. Victor A. Walsh, "Class, Culture, and Nationalism: The Irish Catholics of Pittsburgh, 1870–1883" (unpublished seminar paper, University of Pittsburgh, 1976), 3–6, 53–76; Thernstrom, *Poverty and Progress,* 155–60, 177, 184; *10th Census,* I, 715–43; Douglas V. Shaw, "The Making of an Immigrant City: Ethnic and Cultural Conflict in Jersey City, New Jersey, 1850–1877" (Ph. D. diss., University of Rochester, 1972), 170; Dennis J. Clark, *The Irish in Philadelphia* (Philadelphia, 1973), 129, 136–37, 166.

5. *Freedman's Journal* (Dublin), Mar. 27, 1880; Philip H. Bagenal, *The American Irish and Their Influence on Irish Politics* (London, 1882), 126.

6. William D'Arcy, *The Fenian Movement in the United States* (Washington, 1947); Sir F. Bruce to Earl of Clarendon, Dec. 4, 1865, Clarendon Deposit, Bodleian Library, Oxford; John Devoy, *Recollections of an Irish Rebel* (New York, 1929), 26–30; L. M. Cullen, *Life in Ireland* (London, 1968), 146–51; E. M. Archibald to Earl of Derby, Feb. 9, 1877, F.O. 5/1599/55, Public Record Office, London; New York *Sunday Democrat,* June 11, 1876.

7. D'Arcy, *Fenian Movement,* 26–27, 102, 151; Marcus Bourke, *John O'Leary* (Tralee, 1967), 151; E. M. Archibald to Earl of Derby, Feb. 16, 1876, F.O. 5/1556/5; "Constitution of the V.C., 1877," F.O. 5/1706/12, Public Record Office; *The Land League* (New York City), Feb. 5, 1881.

8. T. W. Moody, "The New Departure in Irish Politics, 1878–9," in H. A. Cronne *et al.,* eds., *Essays in British and Irish History in Honour of James Eadre Todd* (London, 1949), 303–33; John Devoy, *The Land of Eire* (New York, 1882), 41–43; William O. Brien and Desmond Ryan, eds., *Devoy's Post-Bag 1871–1928* (2 vols.: London, 1948–53), I, 340–47.

9. New York *Gaelic-American,* Sept. 8, 1906; Barbara L. Solow, *The Land Question and the Irish Economy, 1870–1903* (Cambridge, 1971),

114–17, 122–27; Cormac Ó Gráda, "Post-Famine Adjustment: Essays in Nineteenth-Century Irish Economic History" (Ph. D. diss., Columbia University, 1973), 24–26, 44; Bernard Becker, *Disturbed Ireland* (London, 1881), 85–86; E. Cant-Wall, *Ireland Under the Land Act* (London, 1883), 153; Samuel Clark, "The Political Mobilization of Irish Farmers," *Canadian Review of Sociology and Anthropology*, XII (1975), 484; T. Wemyss Reid, *Life of the Right Honourable William Edward Forster* (2 vols.: London, 1880), II, 294–95.

10. R. Barry O'Brien, *The Life of Charles Stewart Parnell* (2 vols.: London, 1898), I, 204; *Freeman's Journal*, Mar. 27, 1880; Barbara M. Solomon, *Ancestors and Immigrants* (Cambridge, 1956), 55; James J. Greene, "American Catholics and the Irish Land League, 1879–1882," *Catholic Historical Review*, XXXV (1949), 19–42; *Speech Delivered by Michael Davitt in Defence of the Land League* (London, 1890), 105.

11. *United Ireland* (Dublin), Aug. 13, 1881; *Irish Nation* (New York City), Nov. 13, 1881; *Irish World*, Oct. 2, 1880.

12. E. M. Archibald to Foreign Secretary, May 14, 1880, F.O. 282/21/171, Public Record Office; Circular, Mar. 30, 1880, Terrence V. Powderly Papers, Catholic University of America; *The Land League*, Feb. 5, 1881; Michael F. Funchion, "Chicago's Irish Nationalists, 1881–1890" (Ph. D. diss., Loyola University of Chicago, 1973), 75–80.

13. James P. Rodechko, "Patrick Ford and His Search for America: A Case Study of Irish-American Journalism, 1870–1913" (Ph. D. diss., University of Connecticut, 1967); Rodechko, "An Irish-American Journalist and Catholicism: Patrick Ford and the Irish World," *Church History*, XLIX (1970), 524–40.

14. William O'Brien, *Recollections* (New York, 1905), 274; *Irish World*, Feb. 9, 1878; *Freeman's Journal*, Apr. 3, 1882; Samuel Gompers, *Seventy Years of Life and Labor* (2 vols.: New York, 1925), I, 80–82; II, 31–32; John M. Davis to Powderly, Apr. 26, 1880, Powderly Papers.

15. *Irish World*, Jan. 19, May 4, 25, June 15, 1878; May 29, 1879; Apr. 10, 1880; Jan. 29, July 30, Aug. 6, 1881; Mar. 4, 1882; Thomas N. Brown, *Irish-American Nationalism 1870–1890* (Philadelphia, 1966), 31.

16. The legacy of the abolitionist movement was far broader than indicated in James McPherson, *The Abolitionist Legacy* (Princeton, 1976).

17. Patrick Ford, "The Irish Vote in the Pending Presidential Election," *North American Review*, CXLVII (1888), 187; *Irish World*, Apr. 6, 1878; Jan. 15, 1881.

18. *Irish World*, Feb. 23, Apr. 27, May 4, 1878; Sept. 27, Nov. 15, Dec. 29, 1879; Feb. 21, Oct. 2, 16, Nov. 13, 20, 1880.

19. *Irish World*, Feb. 2, May 4, July 13, 20, 1878; Sept. 27, 1879; Oct.

9, 1880; Michael A. Gordon, "Studies in Irish and Irish-American Thought and Behavior in Gilded Age New York City" (Ph. D. diss., University of Rochester, 1977), 434; New York *Herald*, Oct. 10, 1879; Brown, *Irish-American Nationalism*, 50.

20. *Irish World*, Mar. 2, 1878; Jan. 17, Oct. 16, 1880; Jan 28, 1882; Oct. 16, 1886; New York *Gaelic-American*, June 23, 1906.

21. *Irish World*, July 19, Aug. 30, 1879; May 22, Oct. 2, 1880.

22. Bagenal, *American Irish*, 180; *Freeman's Journal*, Aug. 15, 1881; *Irish World*, Oct. 9, Nov. 13, 1880; James S. Donnelly, Jr., *The Land and the People of Nineteenth-Century Cork* (London, 1975), 248–49; O'Brien, *Recollections*, 273.

23. *Irish World*, Aug. 2, Nov. 8, 1879; Jan. 3, Mar. 6, May 8, 1880; Jan. 29, 1881; Feb. 25, 1882; Aug. 4, 1883; U.S. Senate, Committee on Education and Labor, *Report of the Committee of the Senate Upon Capital and Labor* (3 vols.: Washington, 1885), I, 843.

24. *Freeman's Journal*, Apr. 3, 1882; Robert F. Walsh, "The Boston Pilot: A Newspaper for the Irish Immigrant, 1829–1908" (Ph. D. diss., Boston University, 1968); New York *Gaelic-American*, June 23, 1906; William L. Joyce, "Editors and Ethnicity: A History of the Irish-American Press, 1848–1883" (Ph. D. diss., University of Michigan, 1974), 5, 161; Francis G. McManamin, "John Boyle O'Reilly, Social Reform Editor," *Mid-America*, XLIII (1961), 36–54; Devoy, *Recollections*, 152, 159.

25. Katherine E. Conway, "John Boyle O'Reilly," *The Catholic World*, LIII (1891), 211–16; James B. Cullen, *The Story of the Irish in Boston* (Boston, 1893), 310–13; Boston *Pilot*, June 28, 1879; Aug. 14, 1880; Brown, *Irish-American Nationalism*, 53–54; Joyce, "Editors and Ethnicity," 157–58, 187–88.

26. Arthur Mann, *Yankee Reformers in the Urban Age* (Cambridge, 1954), 27–39, 50; *Irish World*, Mar. 25, 1882.

27. F. S. L. Lyons, *Charles Stewart Parnell* (New York, 1977), 98; *The Irishman* (Dublin), May 1, 1880; Oct. 4, 1879.

28. Funchion, "Chicago," 126; O'Brien and Ryan, eds., *Devoy's Post-Bag*, I, 517, 520; *United Irishman*, Apr. 16, 23, 30, May 14, 1881; Mar. 18, 1882.

29. *Freeman's Journal*, Dec. 27, 1878; Thomas N. Brown, "The Origins and Character of Irish-American Nationalism," *Review of Politics*, XVIII (1956), 351–52; O'Brien and Ryan, eds., *Devoy's Post-Bag*, I, 10; II, 106; Devoy, *Recollections*, 25; *Irish Nation*, Mar. 11, June 24, 1882.

30. Gustavus Myers, *The History of Tammany Hall* (2nd ed., New York, 1917), 251–52; J. Fairfax McLaughlin, *The Life and Times of John Kelly, Tribune of the People* (New York, 1885); Alexander B. Callow, Jr., *The Tweed Ring* (New York, 1966), 62–75; Gordon, "Studies in Irish-American Thought," 387–88; Melvyn Dubofsky, *When Workers Organize* (Amherst, 1968), 21; New York *Times*, June 8, 1879.

31. *Irish World*, Oct. 25, 1879; Nathan Glazer and Daniel P. Moyni-

han, *Beyond the Melting Pot* (Cambridge, 1963), 229; Alfred Connable and Edward Silberfarb, *Tigers of Tammany* (New York, 1967), 188, 192; William V. Shannon, *The American Irish* (New York, 1966), 72–73; Matthew P. Breen, *Thirty Years of New York Politics* (New York, 1899), 623; New York *Star*, Mar. 3, 30, Apr. 1, May 9, 11, Nov. 15, 1880.

32. New York *Star*, Mar. 6, 1880; *Liberty* (New York City), Dec. 24, 1881; Joseph Denieffe, *A Personal Narrative of the Irish Revolutionary Brotherhood* (Shannon, 1969), 28.

33. *Irish Nation*, June 10, 1882; Michael Davitt, *The Fall of Feudalism in Ireland* (London and New York, 1904), 652–57; Eric Strauss, *Irish Nationalism and British Democracy* (New York, 1951), 173; Conor Cruise O'Brien, *Parnell and His Party* (Oxford, 1957), 59–74; *Irish World*, May 4, 1878; Feb. 22, 1879; Nov. 20, Dec. 18, 1880; Feb. 19, Apr. 23, 1881. On the issue of agricultural laborers, see Philip H. Bagenal, " 'Uncle Pat's Cabin,' " *The Nineteenth Century*, XII (1882), 925–38; Charlotte G. O'Brien, "The Irish 'Poor Man,' " *The Nineteenth Century*, VIII (1880), 876–87.

34. Donnelly, *Cork*, 4–7, 119, 130–31; Clark, "Political Mobilization," 494–95; T. Desmond Williams, ed., *Secret Societies in Ireland* (Dublin, 1973), 34. On the social base of the League, see also Sam Clark, "The Social Composition of the Land League," *Irish Historical Studies*, XVII (1971), 447–69; and for a convincing analysis of the relationship between famine and the development of capitalist agriculture, Claude Meillassoux, "Development or Exploitation: Is the Sahel Famine Good Business?," *Review of African Political Economy*, I (1974), 27–33.

35. Davitt, *Fall of Feudalism*, 257; *Speech by Davitt*, 106; Funchion, "Chicago," 129–32; Cullen, *Irish in Boston*, 331–33.

36. New York *Irish-American*, Jan. 28, 1882; *The Irishman*, Sept. 18, 1880; James J. Roche, *Life of John Boyle O'Reilly* (New York, 1891), 207–12; Boston *Pilot*, Nov. 5, Dec. 17, 1881; John Finerty to Patrick Collins, Nov. 9, 1881, Special Irish Collection, Boston College.

37. *Irish Nation*, Dec. 17, 1881; Feb. 25, Mar. 4, 11, 1882.

38. Joyce, "Editors and Ethnicity," 6–7; New York *Irish-American*, Aug. 23, 1879; Jan. 10, June 12, 1880; *Irish World*, Apr. 16, Dec. 3, 1881.

39. *Irish World*, Oct. 14, 1882; *Second Annual Convention of the Irish National Land League of the United States* (Buffalo, 1882), 19–20.

40. *Irish World*, Oct. 23, 1880; Apr. 16, 1881. The Irish Nationalist leader T. P. O'Connor believed that "a dollar sent through the *Irish World* is a significant endorsement of the principles enunciated by the *Irish World*." C.O. 904/15/1, Public Record Office.

41. New York *Times*, June 24, 1881; *Irish World*, Jan. 15, May 21, July 30, Aug. 27, 1881; Oct. 7, Nov. 11, 1882.

42. *Irish World*, May 29, Dec. 11, 1880; Jan. 15, Apr. 16, May 5, 1881;

Boston *Pilot,* Feb. 5, 1881; Walsh, "Class, Culture and Nationalism," 127–36.

43. Funchion, "Chicago," 20, 55–56, 83–87; Clark, *Irish in Philadelphia,* 101, 171–72.

44. Wayne G. Broehl, Jr., *The Molly Maguires* (Cambridge, 1964), 97–98, 208; Clifton K. Yearley, Jr., *Enterprise and Anthracite* (Baltimore, 1961), 172–75, 215; Robert V. Bruce, *1877: Year of Violence* (Indianapolis, 1959), 294–95; John R. Commons *et al., History of Labor in the United States* (2 vols.: New York, 1918), II, 189–91.

45. Ralph J. Ricker, *The Greenback-Labor Movement in Pennsylvania* (Bellefonte, Pa., 1966), 39–43, 64, 73; Hendrick B. Wright to Powderly, Mar. 11, 1881, Powderly Papers; Jonathan Garlock, "A Structural Analysis of the Knights of Labor" (Ph. D. diss., University of Rochester, 1974), 65–79; Victor R. Greene, *The Slavic Community on Strike* (South Bend, 1968), 81, 87; Terence V. Powderly, *Thirty Years of Labor, 1859–1889* (New York, 1967 ed.), 102–4.

46. *Irish World,* Nov. 6, 1880; Jan. 22, 29, Apr. 9, May 28, 1881.

47. *Irish World,* July 24, Oct. 9, 1880; Apr. 16, 1881; Broehl, *Molly Maguires,* 83, 361.

48. Vincent J. Falzone, "Terrence V. Powderly: Mayor and Labor Leader, 1849–1893" (Ph. D. diss., University of Maryland, 1970); O'Brien and Ryan, eds., *Devoy's Post-Bag,* II, 60; Patrick Collins to Powderly, May 10, 1880, Powderly Papers; Buffalo *Daily Courier,* Jan. 14, 1881; *Irish World,* Mar. 5, 1881; Apr. 29, 1882; Powderly, *Thirty Years,* 184.

49. Henry J. Browne, *The Catholic Church and the Knights of Labor* (Washington, 1949), 55–63, 229; Peter Ward to Powderly, May 10, 1881; W. J. Hudson to Powderly, May 13, 1881, Powderly Papers; Terence V. Powderly, *The Path I Trod,* ed., Harry J. Carman *et al.* (New York, 1940), 179.

50. Herbert G. Gutman, *Work, Culture, and Society in Industrializing America* (New York, 1976), 244, 256–57; George E. McNeill, ed., *The Labor Movement* (Boston and New York, 1887), 221–29; *Thirteenth Annual Report of the Bureau of Statistics of Labor* (Boston, 1882), 195–415; Philip T. Silva, Jr., "The Position of Workers in a Textile Community: Fall River in the Early 1880's," *Labor History,* XVI(1975), 230–48; *Irish World,* Dec. 4, 1880; Sept. 24, 1881; Paul Buhle, "The Knights of Labor in Rhode Island," *Radical History Review,* XVII (Spring 1978), 40–48.

51. Rodman Paul, *Mining Frontiers of the Far West* (New York, 1963), 69, 76–80, 128; Richard E. Lingenfelter, *The Hardrock Miners* (Berkeley, 1974), 131–56; Brown, *Irish-American Nationalism,* 169; Vernon H. Jensen, *Heritage of Conflict* (Ithaca, 1950), 17–21.

52. Lingenfelter, *Hardrock Miners,* 166; Melvyn Dubofsky, *We Shall Be All* (New York, 1969), 19–22; Neil L. Shumsky, "San Francisco's Workingmen Respond to the Modern City," *California Historical*

Quarterly, LV (1976), 51–52; *Irish World,* Oct. 16, 1880; *Freeman's Journal,* Nov. 22, 1880.

53. Michael A. Gordon, "The Labor Boycott in New York City, 1880–1886," *Labor History,* XVI (1975), 184–229; *Liberty,* Dec. 24, 1881; Mathew Maguire *et al.,* to Henry George, Apr. 17, 1881, Henry George Papers, New York Public Library; *Irish World,* May 6, 1882; New York *Star,* Aug. 24, 1880; Apr. 4, 1881.

54. New York *Star,* Dec. 17, 1880; Jan. 18, Feb. 8, 11, 25, Mar. 7, 12, Aug. 31, Sept. 2, 4, Oct. 4, 9, 1881; New York *Tribune,* Jan. 5, 1882; Leonard Dinnerstein, "The Impact of Tammany Hall on State and National Politics in the Eighteen-Eighties," *New York History,* XLII (1961), 242–44.

55. *Irish World,* Feb. 11, Oct. 28, 1882; United Irishman, Feb. 18, 1882; Gordon, "Labor Boycott," 196–98; U.S. Senate, *Report of the Committee on Capital and Labor,* 805, 840; Peter A. Speek, *The Single Tax and the Labor Movement* (Madison, 1915), 24; New York *Star,* Jan. 31, 1882.

56. *John Swinton's Paper* (New York City), Feb. 28, 1886; *Irish World,* Jan. 1, 1881; May 6, Sept. 16, 1882; Gordon, "Studies in Irish-American Thought," 541–47; Douglas V. Shaw, "Labor, Irish Nationalism and Anti-Monopoly: Jersey City in 1882" (paper delivered at annual meeting, American Historical Association, 1974), 10–14.

57. Handlin, *Boston's Immigrants,* 126–42; Jay P. Dolan, *The Immigrant Church* (Baltimore, 1975), 122–27; Gilbert Osofsky, "Abolitionists, Irish Immigrants, and the Dilemma of Romantic Nationalism," *American Historical Review,* LXXX (1975), 889–912; Lydia Maria Child to Charles Sumner, July 4, 1870, Charles Sumner Papers, Harvard University.

58. Osofsky, "Abolitionists and Immigrants," 896–97; MacDonagh, "The Irish Famine Emigration," 384–86; Ernst, *Immigrant Life,* 100–101; Montgomery, *Beyond Equality,* 126–34.

59. Joseph Lee, *The Modernization of Irish Society 1848–1918* (Dublin, 1973), 65, 72, 93–95; *Freeman's Journal,* Dec. 15, 1879; Aug. 15, 1881; Norman O. Palmer, *The Irish Land League Crisis* (New Haven, 1940), 150; Dublin *Evening Mail,* Feb. 2, 1880.

60. Irving H. Bartlett, *Wendell Phillips, Brahmin Radical* (Boston, 1961), 381; *Freeman's Journal,* Dec. 17, 1879; *Irish World,* Dec. 13, 1879; Apr. 10, 1880.

61. Horner, *Redpath,* 7–12, 254–56; James Redpath, *Talks About Ireland* (New York, 1881), 31–32; *Irish World,* Apr. 17, June 5, 12, 1880; James Redpath to Patrick Collins, May 8, 1881, Special Irish Collection; *Freeman's Journal,* Aug. 18, 1880; July 27, Oct. 6, 1881; *Proceedings at a Farewell Dinner given by the Land League of New York to James Redpath* (New York, 1881), 12–13.

62. Report of the Metropolitan Police, as Regards the Irish National

Land League, Aug. 10, 1880, Carton 9, Irish Land League Police Reports, State Paper Office, Dublin Castle; *The Land League: Socialism in Ireland* (Dublin, 1880), 14; *Freeman's Journal*, Sept. 13, 1880; Devoy, *Land of Eire*, 87.

63. John G. Sproat, *"The Best Men"* (New York, 1968); New York *Tribune*, Nov. 22, 1879; Nov. 25, 1880; [Lysander Spooner], *Revolution* (New York, 1880); O'Brien and Ryan, eds., *Devoy's Post-Bag*, I, 509; *Freeman's Journal*, Jan. 30, 1880; Sept. 26, 1881.

64. *Freeman's Journal*, Sept. 19, 1881; New York *Star*, Aug. 1, 1880; Buffalo *Daily Courier*, Jan. 14, 1881; *Irish World*, Mar. 5, 1881.

65. Cork *Examiner*, Oct. 4, 1882; Henry George, *Progress and Poverty* (4th ed., New York, 1884), 270, 305; *The Times* (London), Sept. 6, 1882; *Freeman's Journal*, June 12, 1882; Stuart Bruchey, "Twice Forgotten Man: Henry George," *American Journal of Economics and Sociology*, XXXI (1972), 113–38.

66. *Irish World*, Oct. 28, 1882; J. A. Hobson, "The Influence of Henry George in England," *The Fortnightly Review*, n.s., LXII (1897), 837; Henry George, Jr., ed., *Complete Works of Henry George* (10 vols.: New York, 1906–11), III, 82.

67. Charles A. Barker, *Henry George* (New York, 1955), 320–55; U.S. Senate, *Report of the Committee on Capital and Labor*, I, 244; *Irish World*, May 1, Dec. 11, 1880; Jan. 22, 1881; Jan. 6, 1883; Henry George to Patrick Ford, Nov. 9, 1881, Letterbook, George Papers, George, Jr., ed., *Complete Works*, III, 8–12, 73–74, 107–8.

68. George, *Progress and Poverty*, 496; George, Jr., ed., *Complete Works*, III, 96; George R. Geiger, *The Philosophy of Henry George* (New York, 1933), 336–37; Henry F. May, *Protestant Churches and Industrial America* (New York, 1949), 154; Gutman, *Work, Culture, and Society*, 79–118.

69. Mann, *Yankee Reformers*, 24–25; Aaron I. Abell, *American Catholicism and Social Action* (Garden City, 1950), 27–29, 47–51; Dolan, *Immigrant Church*, 121–22.

70. Rodechko, "An Irish-American Journalist," 526–27; *Irish World*, Apr. 5, 1879; Nov. 13, 1880; Gordon, "Studies in Irish-American Thought," 93–94.

71. Sylvester L. Malone, *Dr. Edward McGlynn* (New York, 1918); Geiger, *Philosophy of George*, 344–46; Dolan, *Immigrant Church*, 66; New York *Sun*, Apr. 30, 1870.

72. Circular, Mar. 30, 1880, Powderly Papers; New York *Sun*, July 6, 1882; *Irish World*, July 15, Aug. 12, Sept. 2, 1882.

73. Greene, "American Catholics," 25–26; William B. Faherty, "The Clergyman and Labor Progress: Cornelius O'Leary and the Knights of Labor," *Labor History*, XI (1970), 175–89; Brenda K. Shelton, *Reformers in Search of Yesterday* (Albany, 1976), 31, 53, 161; Robert D. Cross, *The Emergence of Liberal Catholicism in America* (Cambridge, 1958); John T. Ellis, *The Life of James Cardinal Gibbons* (2 vols.: Milwaukee, 1952).

74. *Irish World,* Jan. 29, 1881.

75. Michael Davitt, *The Land League Proposal* (Glasgow, 1882); Michael Davitt, *Leaves From a Prison Diary* (2 vols.: London, 1885), II, 93, 99.

76. Charles E. Reeves, "Davitt's American Tour of 1882," *Quarterly Journal of Speech,* LIV (1968), 357–62; O'Brien and Ryan, eds., *Devoy's Post-Bag,* II, 121; New York *Irish-American,* June 17, 1882; Boston *Pilot,* cited in *Irish Nation,* June 17, 1882; Boston *Pilot,* July 1, 1882; New York *Star,* June 10, 18, 1882.

77. *Irish Nation,* June 10, 17, 1882; *Irish World,* Jan. 7, June 24, July 15, Sept. 2, 1882; George, Jr., ed., *Complete Works,* X, 384–87; *United Irishman,* Sept. 16, 1882.

78. T. W. Moody, "Michael Davitt, 1846–1906: A Survey and Appreciation," *Studies,* XXXV (1946), 437; Devoy, *Land of Eire,* 91; *Freeman's Journal,* May 31, Aug. 22, Oct. 9, 1882.

79. Algar L. Thorold, *The Life of Henry Labouchere* (London, 1913), 234; F. Sheehy-Skeffington, *Michael Davitt* (London, 1967 ed.), 18–23; T. W. Moody, "Michael Davitt and the British Labour Movement," *Transactions, Royal Historical Society,* 5 ser., III (1953), 56–58; *Speech of Michael Davitt,* 30; Lyons, *Parnell,* 232.

80. E. Eldon Barry, *Nationalisation in British Politics* (London, 1965), 17–40, 57–60; John Saville, "Henry George and the British Labour Movement," *Science and Society,* XXIV (1960), 321–33; Clive J. Dewey, "The Rehabilitation of the Peasant Proprietor in Nineteenth Century Economic Thought," *History of Political Economy,* VI (1974), 17–47; Joy McAskill, "The Treatment of 'Land' in English Social and Political Theory 1840–1885" (B. Litt thesis, Oxford University, 1959), 50–75, 156–76, 241–43; H. J. Perkin, "Land Reform and Class Conflict in Victorian Britain," in J. Butt and I. F. Clarke, eds., *The Victorians and Social Protest* (London, 1973), 191–93; *Reynolds's Newspaper* (London), June 22, 1879.

81. *Irish World,* July 1, 1882; New York *Irish-American,* July 15, 1882; *Irish Nation,* June 3, July 8, 1882.

82. Brown, *Irish-American Nationalism,* 159–66; unidentified newspaper clipping, Apr. 1883, F.O. 5/1861/187, Public Record Office; *Irish World,* Oct. 12, 1882.

83. For example, John A. Garraty's fine survey of the Gilded Age, *The New Commonwealth* (New York, 1968), contains no mention of the Land League and, more important, its chapter on social thought completely ignores the ferment within the Catholic Church during this period.

84. Brown, *Irish-American Nationalism,* 24, 41, 46; Alexander Sullivan, "The American Republic and the Irish National League of America," *American Catholic Quarterly Review,* IX (1884), 43–44.

85. Thomas N. Brown, quoted in Glazer and Moynihan, *Beyond the Melting Pot,* 241; Shannon, *American Irish,* 134–36; Henry George to Terence V. Powderly, Apr. 19, 1883, Powderly Papers.

86. *Irish World,* July 9, 1881.
87. Buffalo *Daily Courier,* Jan. 14, 1881. A too-little known discussion of the complex interplay of nationalism and class consciousness is contained in Ber Borochov, *Nationalism and the Class Struggle* (New York, 1937).
88. Moody, "Davitt and British Labour," 53–76; Solow, *Land Question,* 189–94; Karl Marx and Frederick Engels, *Ireland and the Irish Question* (New York, 1972), 284, 292–93.
89. Perkin, in Butt and Clarke, eds., *Victorians,* 179–83, 208–13; R. C. K. Ensor, "Some Political and Economic Interactions in Later Victorian England," *Transactions, Royal Historical Society,* 4 ser., XXXI (1949), 25–26; Barry, *Nationalisation,* 64–67, 138–41; James Hunter, "The Gaelic Connection: The Highlands, Ireland and Nationalism, 1873–1922," *Scottish Historical Review,* LIV (1975), 180–85; Paul R. Thompson, *Socialists, Liberals, and Labour* (London, 1967), 113; James D. Young, "Changing Images of American Democracy and the Scottish Labour Movement," *International Review of Social History,* XVIII, pt. 1 (1973), 78–81; John Rae, "Social Philosophy," *Contemporary Review,* XLV (1884), 295; Patrick Ford to William O'Brien, Mar. 11, 1903, William O'Brien Papers, National Library of Ireland.
90. Gordon, "Studies in Irish-American Thought," xxi, 335; Commons, *Labor Movement,* II, 453; New York *Sun,* Sept. 19, 1886; *John Swinton's Paper,* Sept. 19, 1886; Stephen Bell, *Rebel, Priest, and Prophet: A Biography of Dr. Edward McGlynn* (New York, 1937).
91. Garlock, "Knights of Labor," 6; Cross, *Liberal Catholicism,* 26–27; Charles Leinenweber, "Socialists in the Streets: The New York City Socialist Party in Working Class Neighborhoods, 1908–1918," *Science and Society,* XLI (1977), 161.
92. Aronowitz, *False Promises,* 146–49, 156; Philip Taylor, *The Distant Magnet* (New York, 1971), 197; Henry Merwin, "The Irish in American Life," *Atlantic Monthly,* LXXVII (1896), 293; Doyle, *Irish Americans;* David Montgomery, "The Irish and the American Labor Movement" (unpublished essay, 1976).
93. Leinenweber, "Socialists in the Streets," 164; Dubofsky, *We Shall Be All,* 24, 68; Doyle, *Irish Americans;* John D. Buenker, *Urban Liberalism and Progressive Reform* (New York, 1973), 30–45, 204–5; John A. Ryan, *Social Doctrine in Action* (New York, 1941), 8–9.

Acknowledgments

Numerous friends and colleagues generously offered their advice and criticism when the essays collected in this volume were originally published. I reiterate my appreciation, first expressed where the pieces originally appeared. I do wish, however, to take this opportunity to thank certain individuals for their invaluable contributions: Ira Berlin and Leslie Rowland for their unfailing generosity in sharing materials and ideas from the Freedmen and Southern Society Project, Fred Siegel for his ongoing intellectual stimulation and encouragement, and Lynn Garafola for a very special comradeship.

The dedication to James P. Shenton, in whose classes I first studied the many complex issues posed by the American Civil War, is a recognition of two decades of loyal friendship.

E.F.

Index

Abolitionism, 10, 11, 36-76, 78, 151; class determinants of, 26-27, 42, 61; emergence of, 22-26, 31-32, 36-44; in England, 74-76; evangelical, 65-66, 71-74; interpretation of, 16; Irish-Americans and, 180, 182, 183, 195; labor and, 24, 27-28, 58-76; *see also* Anti-slavery movement
Acton, Lord, 36
Adams, John, 53
Adams, John Quincy, 37, 42
Aiken, D. Wyatt, 118, 119
Alabama, 107-8, 111-13, 115, 120, 123, 124, 146
Alcorn, James L., 113
American Anti-Slavery Society, 90, 142, 181
American Federation of Labor, 199
American Land League, *see* Irish-American Land League
American National League, 194, 195
American Revolution, 8, 10, 16, 53, 58
Ancient Order of Hibernians, 150
Andrew, John, 133
Annales school of historiography, 6-7
Anti-abolitionism, 66, 75, 76

Anti-Catholicism, 153
Anti-slavery movement, 43-44, 72-76, 100; abolitionism replaced by, 72; Free-Soilism and, 43, 44, 72-73, 79-93; *see also* Abolitionism
Anti-Slavery Society, 90, 142, 181
Appleby, Joyce, 104
Arkansas, 107
Artisan societies, 74
Ashley, James, 134, 139
Ashley, S. S., 121, 122
Atkinson, Edward, 109, 116, 148

Baltimore (Md.), 126
Banks, Nathaniel P., 137
Banner, James, 39-40
Barnburners, 80-84, 86, 88-93
Battle, Kemp P., 106
Beale, Howard K., 115-16
Beardian view of Civil War, 31
Bellamy, Edward, 75
Benson, Lee, 19
Berthoff, Rowland, 23, 30
Bigelow, John, 90
Bird, Francis W., 86, 183
Birney, James G., 83, 87

Black Codes, 104, 114, 118, 123
Blaine, James G., 129, 148
Blanc, Louis, 160
Bleeding Kansas, 49-50
Blissert, Robert, 178, 179, 191, 193
Boorstin, Daniel, 8
Boston (Mass.), 91, 170, 171
Boston *Advertiser* (newspaper), 146-47
Boston *Pilot* (newspaper), 162-63, 168, 170, 171
Botts, John Minor, 146
Boyce, Ed, 199-200
Boycotting, 182
Bray, John F., 158
Brazil, 30
Brennan, Thomas, 163
Brisbane, Albert, 63
Brown, John, 68
Brown, Richard, 21
Brown, Thomas N., 194-95
Brownson, Orestes, 60
Bryant, John E., 101, 124-25
Bryant, William Cullen, 80, 90
Butler, Benjamin F., 86, 88, 134, 142, 145

Calhoun, John C., 41-43, 52, 57, 93
California, 90, 171
California Workingmen's party, 165
Cambreleng, C. C., 81, 89
Cameron, Simon, 130
Campbell, Tunis G., 115, 124
Carey, Henry, 100
Cass, Lewis, 44, 89, 91
Catholic Church, 180, 194; labor and, 162-63, 186-89, 198; Land League and, 157, 174-75, 187-89, 199; Tammany Hall and, 165, 183
Catholics, 17, 26, 27; *see also* Irish-Americans
Central Labor Union, 179, 188, 191, 198
Chamberlain, Daniel H., 115
Chartists, 158, 193
Chase, Salmon P., 86
Chicago (Ill.), 169-71
Chicago *Western Citizen* (newspaper), 87
Child, Lydia Maria, 179-80
Chinese, 111
Choate, Rufus, 36
Cincinnati (O.), 61

Cincinnati *Commercial* (newspaper), 143
Civil War, American: causes of, 15-53; economic results of, 112, 113; heritage of, 11-12; historiography and, 3-4, 6, 9, 12, 15-16; "modernization" thesis and, 19-23, 25, 32; "new political historians" on, 17-19
Clan na Gael, 150, 154, 163, 164, 173
Class, social: of abolitionists, 26-27; in ante-bellum North, 21-22; ethnicity and, 25-26, 195-96; historiography and, 6, 9, 10, 12, 17, 18; Irish-Americans and, 195-96, *and see* Labor movement, Irish-Americans and; in post-bellum South, 111, 114; slavery and, for abolitionists, 65; "wage slavery" and, 60
Class conflict, Reconstruction and, 114, 118, 120, 122-25
Clay, Henry, 43, 45
Cobb, Howell, 107
Coffin handbill, 59-60
Colfax, Schuyler, 147
Collins, John A., 67-68
Collins, Patrick, 167, 169
Colonization Society, 90
Colorado, 171, 176
Communist, The (periodical), 67-68
Confiscation, 131-49
Congress, U.S.: confiscation and, 131-32, 138-44, 146-47; slavery and, 36-48, 83; *see also* House of Representatives, U.S.; Senate, U.S.
Conner, James, 122
"Consensus" school of historians, 4, 6, 11
Constitution, U.S., 47, 53; Fourteenth Amendment to, 140; three-fifths clause of, 22, 37, 41
Constitutional Conventions: Federal, 36; New York State, 79, 80, 82
Cooke, Henry, 148
Cotton production, Reconstruction and, 108-9
Cromwell, Oliver, 193
Cronin, Patrick, 188
Curtin, Andrew, 130

Dallas, George Mifflin, 44
Davis, David Brion, 22, 27, 74, 76

Davitt, Michael, 155, 156, 166, 176-77, 181, 182, 188-94, 197
Dawley, Alan, 61, 74-76
Debtor relief, 113-14
Declaration of Independence, 47
Deism, 65, 73
Democratic party, 19, 20, 44, 79; Free-Soil movement and, 79-84, 86, 88-93; Irish-Americans and, 163-65, 177-78, 199; "pre-modern" constituency of, 26; during Reconstruction, 113-14, 121; Wilmot Proviso and, 43, 81, 83-85
Democratic-Republicans, 79
Devoy, John, 155, 156, 160, 164, 166-68, 191, 193
Devyr, Thomas, 69-70, 158
District of Columbia, 85, 86
Dix, John A., 83, 88, 89
Donald, David, 15
Douglas, Stephen A., 21, 31, 45-48, 51
Douglass, Frederick, 49, 68, 86, 88
Dred Scott decision, 47, 49-50
Du Bois, W. E. B., 98, 120
Dunning, William, 97-98

Egan, Patrick, 163
Elkins, Stanley, 16, 23
Engerman, Stanley, 29-30, 112
England, 197-98; abolitionism in, 74-76; Land League and, 192-94
Enlightenment, 65, 66
Ethnicity, 17, 18; class and, 25-26; see also Race
Ethnocultural approach to history, 17, 20, 25; see also "New political history"
Evangelicism, 65-66, 71, 72, 186
Evans, George Henry, 61-62, 66, 69-70, 73

Fall River (Mass.), 171, 175-76
Farrell, Thomas, 187
Federalist papers, 52
Federalists, slavery and, 22-23, 37, 39-40
Fencing laws, 112, 117
Fenian Brotherhood, 153-57, 160, 162-64, 180, 181, 197
Fessenden, William P., 142, 147

Finerty, John, 167
First International, 178
FitzGerald, Frances, 7
Fitzhugh, George, 40, 57, 61
Flagg, Azariah C., 81
Fogel, Robert W., 29-30, 112
Ford, Patrick, 157-63, 166-70, 176, 177, 183, 185, 187, 190, 191, 194, 198-200
Formisano, Ronald, 26
Forster, William, 155
Franklin, Benjamin, 39
Free Democracy, 92; see also Free-Soil movement
Free labor ideology, 10, 24, 49, 57-58, 76; post-bellum South and, 98-112, 126
Free-Soil movement, 43, 44, 72-73, 78-93
Freedmen: free labor and, 98-112, 121-22, 136, 137; land ownership by, 108-9, 111-12, 119-22, 131-49
Freedmen's Bureau, 101-3, 107, 132, 138-40
Freehling, William, 51

Gag Rule, 41, 50
Garrison, William Lloyd, 16, 27-28, 39, 42, 62-63, 68, 70-72, 76, 88, 157, 159, 162, 182
Gates, Seth M., 42, 83
Genovese, Eugene D., 20, 112
George, Henry, 160, 184-86, 189-91, 193-95, 197-99
Georgia, 99, 102, 104, 107, 108, 113-15, 120, 123, 124; 1868 Constitution of, 113-14
Gibbons, James Cardinal (archbishop of Baltimore), 189
Giddings, Joshua, 42, 85
Gilmour, Richard (bishop of Cleveland), 187
Gladstone, William Ewart, 166, 190
Gompers, Samuel, 158
Gowan, Franklin B., 172
Grace, William R., 153
Grant, Ulysses S., 149
Great Famine, Irish, 151, 153, 166, 180
Greeley, Horace, 24, 69-70, 75, 79-81, 136-37, 147

Greenback-Labor party, 159, 165, 172, 173
Guyana, 110

Haiti, 61, 110
Hale, John P., 81, 87
Hardie, James Keir, 197
Harrison, Brian, 27
Hartz, Louis, 8
Healy, T. M., 162
Herald of Freedom (periodical), 68-69
Heyward, Edward B., 108
Hill, Benjamin H., 123
Hobsbawm, E. J., 6
Hoffman, Michael, 81
Hofstadter, Richard, 8, 9, 11
House of Representatives, U.S., 156; Thaddeus Stevens and, 129-31, 138; *see also* Congress, U.S.
Howard, General O. O., 101, 105, 138
Hunkers, 80, 81, 89, 91
Hunnicutt, James, 146
Hyndman, H. M., 197

Ideology, 8, 9; anti-slavery, *see* Abolitionism *and* Anti-slavery movement; party system and, 34-53; republican, 10, 58-59, 64, 122, 184; Republican party, 26, 47-53, 73, 76, 148, 149; sectional, growth of, 31-33
Illinois, 77-78, 171
Indiana, 77-78
Iowa, 77-78, 93
Ireland: nineteenth-century nationalism in, 153-56, 160, 163, 166-68; *see also* Irish-Americans
Irish-American Land League, 76, 151, 156-57, 160-200
Irish-Americans, 25-26, 65, 105, 150-200
Irish Democratic Labor Federation, 197
Irish Land League (in Ireland), 155, 166-67, 181-82, 184, 191-94; *see also* Irish-American Land League
Irish Nation (newspaper), 164
Irish National Convention (1881), 165-66

Irish World, The (newspaper), 157-62, 165-76, 184, 185, 195, 196, 200
Irishman, The (Dublin newspaper), 163
Izard, Allen S., 122

Jackson, Andrew, 38, 39, 51
Jacksonian democracy, 24, 31, 39, 79, 172
Jacksonian labor movement, 158
Jamaica, 110
Jay, William, 64, 70, 71
Jefferson, Thomas, 40
Jeffersonian democracy, 40, 41, 121
Jentz, John, 61, 63
Jersey City (N.J.), 179, 185
Johannsen, Robert, 45
Johnson, Andrew, 121, 138
Julian, George W., 78, 121, 132, 134, 137, 139

Kearney, Denis, 176-77
Kelley, Robert, 20
Kelley, William D. ("Pig Iron"), 137, 139, 147
Kelly, "Honest John," 165, 177-78
"Kilmainham Treaty," 190
King, Preston, 81, 83-84, 89
Knights of Labor, 76, 172-74, 186, 189, 194, 195, 198, 199
Kossuth, Lewis, 156
Ku Klux Klan, 119-20

Labor Leagues, Irish, 192
Labor movement, 10, 126-27; abolitionism and, 24, 27-28, 58-76; Irish-Americans and, 157-59, 171-80, 184-89, 191, 195-200; *see also* Trade unions
Labor party (Britain), 197
Land Act, Gladstone's, 166
Land League, *see* Irish-American Land League; Irish Land League
Land ownership by freedmen, 108-9, 111-12, 119-22, 131-49
Laplace, Marquis Pierre Simon, 19
Leadville (Co.), 171, 176
Leavitt, Joshua, 87
Lecompton Constitution, 48
Liberal party (Britain), 20, 190, 197

Liberator, The (newspaper), 62, 67, 69-72, 157

Liberty party, 42, 44, 78; Free Soilers and, 79, 83, 85-88, 93

Lincoln, Abraham, 19, 21-22, 25, 28, 29n, 32, 33, 46-47, 73-74, 100, 129, 148; confiscation and, 131, 132; significance of election of, 50-53

Lincoln-Douglas debates, 46-48

Lipset, Seymour M., 34

Locke, David R., 183

Locke, John, 192

Loco-focos, 80

Louisiana, 111, 137

Lowell (Mass.) strike, 59-60

Luraghi, Raimondo, 20, 32

Luther, Seth, 59

Lynn (Mass.), 61, 74-75

McCaffrey, James, 156

McCloskey, John Cardinal, 165, 187

McCormick, Richard, 38

McDonnell, J. P., 158

McFeely, William, 140

McGlynn, Edward, 187-89, 191, 193, 198, 200

McLaughlin, William, 180

McNeill, George, 178, 186

McWhiney, Grady, 112

Madison, James, 36, 52

Maguire, P. J., 178

Manigault, Louis, 98-99

Mann, Arthur, 163

Marcy, William L., 84

Marx, Karl, 197

Marxism, 58; historiography and, 6-8

Maryland, 106

Massachusetts, 171, 175-76

Middleton, Ralph I., 119

Middleton family, 100

Mill, John Stuart, 192

Mississippi, 107, 111, 113-16, 118, 122

Missouri, 113, 171

Missouri debates, 37-39, 41, 43, 45

Modernization thesis, 7, 19-23, 25, 32

Molly Maguire trials, 170

Monroe, James, 37

Montgomery, David, 180

Moore, Barrington, Jr., 112

Morgan, Edmund, 126

Morrill, Justin, 129

Morris, Thomas, 78

Napoleon Bonaparte, 19

Nation, The (periodical), 136, 140-41, 143

National Era (newspaper), 89-92

National Intelligencer (newspaper), 37

National Labor Union, 76

National League (Ireland), 194

Nativism, 18, 19, 26, 65, 153, 179-80, 194

Nebraska bill, 45

Nevins, Allan, 46

New Departure, Irish-nationalist, 155

New England, 59, 67, 175; Federalists in, 22-23, 37, 39-40

New Hampshire, 59, 68-69

New Jersey, 171

New Mexico, 90

"New political history," 7, 9, 17-19

"New social history," 5-6, 9

New York City, 59; abolitionism in, 61, 66; anti-abolitionist riot of 1834 in, 66; Irish in, 151, 153, 154, 156, 158, 164-66, 168-70, 177-79, 187-88, 194, 198

New York *Daily Sentinel* (newspaper), 61

New York *Evening Post* (newspaper), 80, 90-91

New York *Herald* (newspaper), 140

New York *Irish-American* (newspaper), 168, 190, 193

New York *Morning News* (newspaper), 80

New York *Star* (newspaper), 165, 177-79

New York State, 171; Democrats of, and Free-Soil movement, 79-84, 86, 88-93; Free-Soil movement in, 78-93; Whigs in, 48-49

New York *Sun* (newspaper), 188

New York Times (newspaper), 124-25, 141, 143-45, 169

New York *Tribune* (newspaper), 53, 79, 136, 182, 183

Newark Land League, 186

No-Rent Manifesto, 166, 178, 191

North Carolina, 99, 106, 113, 121, 124, 146

Northwest Ordinance, 83-84

O'Brien, William, 161

O'Connell, Daniel, 157, 160, 180, 183

O'Kelly, James J., 190
O'Leary, Cornelius, 188
Oregon, 77-78
O'Reilly, John Boyle, 162-63, 167, 168
Orr, James L., 102, 125
Osofsky, Gilbert, 65
Otis, Harrison Gray, 39, 40
Owen, Robert, 61, 66, 67

Paine, Thomas, 10, 19, 58, 61, 158, 192
Parnell, Charles Stewart, 153, 155-57,
    161, 164-66, 192, 194
Pennsylvania, 84-85, 92, 129, 130, 136,
    137, 168-75, 189
Pennsylvania Freeman, The (newspaper),
    85, 92
Philadelphia (Penn.), 59, 92, 170
Philadelphia North American (news-
    paper), 142
Philadelphia Press (newspaper), 145,
    148
Philbrick, Edward, 109, 116
Phillips, Wendell, 39, 69, 72, 134, 135,
    142, 150-51, 162, 181, 195
Pietist-ritualist distinction, 17, 26
Pittsburgh (Penn.), 169
Plantation system: advent of free labor
    and, 98-112, 118-19, 136; confis-
    cation issue and, 131-49
Pocock, J. G. A., 10
Pole, J. R., 21
Polk, James Knox, 84
Port Royal experiment, 109
Potter, David, 16, 53
Powderly, Terence V., 173-75, 196,
    198
Prejudice, racial, see Racism
Presidency, institution of, 7, 35, 37, 38,
    51
Progress and Poverty (George), 184-85
Protestantism, 17, 19, 26, 65-66; re-
    form tradition of, Irish-Americans
    and, 150-51, 156, 179-87
Proudhon, Pierre Joseph, 158
Providence (R.I.), 175

Quincy, Edmund, 71

Race, 9, 10, 12, 16
Racism: of abolitionists, 16; Free-Soil

movement and, 78-93; Irish-
    Americans and, 159; Liberty party
    and, 78; northern, 77-78
Railroad strikes, 126-27, 172
Raleigh Standard (newspaper), 145
Reading Railroad, 172
Reconstruction, 12, 70, 97-127; socio-
    economic ramifications of, 112-27;
    Thaddeus Stevens and, 129-49;
    transition from slave to free labor
    during, 98-112, 121-22; see also
    Confiscation
Reconstruction Act (1867), 141
Redeemers, 123-24
Redpath, James, 150, 181-83, 198
Reform tradition, Protestant, 150-51,
    156, 179-87
Reid, Whitelaw, 103
Religious belief, 17, 18, 26; see also
    Catholics; Protestantism
Republican party, 165, 178; aboli-
    tionism and, 24, 28, 49-52, 73;
    confiscation issue and, 131-49; in
    1850s, 20, 76; Federalists and, 37,
    39-40; ideology of, 26, 47-53, 73,
    76, 148, 149; labor and, 73-74; in
    post-bellum South, 113-17, 119-21,
    123, 145-47; Protestantism and, 19;
    radical wing of, 115-17, 125, 131,
    133, 148, and see Stevens, Thaddeus
Republicanism, 10, 58-59, 64, 122, 184
Rhode Island, 171, 175
Richards, Leonard, 27, 31, 61
Ritchie, Thomas, 38
Rockdale (Penn.), 6
Rogers, Nathaniel P., 68
Rose, Willie Lee, 108-9
Rossa, Jeremiah O'Donovan, 163-64
Rothman, David, 25
Ruffin, Edmund, 29
Ryan, John A., 200

St. Lawrence County (N.Y.), 80-81, 83
Scalawags, 113
Schurz, Carl, 103, 136
Scott, Robert K., 102, 103
Sea Island conflicts, 108-9, 116
Secession, 28, 51-53; Lincoln on, 25
Second Great Awakening, 65
Selma Southern Argus (newspaper),
    110-11, 118

Senate, U.S., 142; *see also* Congress, U.S.

Seward, William H., 29n, 40, 44, 48-49, 93

Shannon, William, 195

Sharecropping, 119, 120, 123, 148

Sherman, William Tecumseh, 132, 139

Sickles, Daniel E., 121

Silbey, Joel, 18

Siney, John, 171-72, 180

Skaneateles (N.Y.), community, 67

Skidmore, Thomas, 59

Slade, William, 42

Slave Power, 26, 41-43, 48-50, 78, 92

Slave trade, 36

Slavery: Civil War causation and, 3-4, 11, 15-22, 28-30, 35-53; Congress and, 36-48, 83; Constitution and, 36-37, 47; expansion of, 50-51, 78; Federalists and, 22-23, 37, 39-40, 79; Southern defense of, 31-33, 40-41; *see also* Abolitionism; Antislavery movement

Smith, Adam, 100, 104-5, 107

Smith, E. Pershine, 100

Smith, Gerrit, 85, 87-89

Smith, James M., 123

Soboul, Albert, 22

Social Democratic Federation (Britain), 197

Social history, 5-9

Socialist party, 199

Sorauf, Frank, 36

South America, emancipation in, 110

South Carolina: 1869 Labor Convention of, 117; Reconstruction in, 98, 99, 108, 114-20, 122, 146; secession convention of, 51-53

Southern Homestead Act (1866), 111, 139-40

Spence, Thomas, 160, 192

Spooner, Lysander, 183

Standard Oil Company, 178

Stevens, Thaddeus, 39, 121, 128-49

Stone, Lawrence J., 31

Suffrage, black, 121-24, 133-34, 140, 145

Sullivan, Alexander, 194-95

Sumner, Charles, 134, 142

Swayne, Wager, 102-3

Swepson, George, 113

Tammany Hall, 164-66, 177, 178, 183, 198, 199

Tappan, Arthur, 39, 65-66

Tappan, Lewis, 39, 65-66

Taylor, Richard, 98

Tax-Payers Conventions, 120, 121

Temperance, 18-20, 24, 27

Tenant Leagues, 177

Tennessee, 113

Texas, 118; annexation of, 42-44, 80; 1866 Constitutional Convention of, 105

Tilden, Samuel J., 80, 81, 89

Toledo *Blade* (newspaper), 183

Toombs, Robert. A., 130

Tories, 20, 192, 194

Towne, Laura, 108-9

Trade unions, 24, 76, 126; Irish-Americans and, 171-79, 191, 195, 198-200; *see also* Labor movement *and specific unions*

Trescot, William H., 98, 122-23

Trevelyan, G. M., 7-8

Trumbull, Lyman, 138-39

Turner, Frederick Jackson, 6

Turner, Nat, 40, 61

Tweed, William Marcy ("Boss"), 165

Tyler, John, 42

Union League, 146

Unions, *see* Trade unions

Utica (N.Y.), 61

Vagrancy laws, 104, 115, 118

Van Buren, John, 81, 84, 89

Van Buren, Martin, 38, 43-44, 82, 86-89, 91, 93

Virginia, 37, 51, 146, 147

Virginia City (Nev.), 176

Voice of Industry (newspaper), 60

Voltaire, 19

Wade, Ben, 144

"Wage slavery," 59-61, 64, 70, 71, 76

Wallace, Anthony, 6

Walsh, Lawrence, 168, 170

Ward, Samuel R., 88, 93

Washington *Daily Morning Chronicle* (newspaper), 146

Webster, Daniel, 45
Weld, Theodore, 16, 25, 28
West, William, 62, 70
West Indies, 110, 111
West Virginia, 113
Western Federation of Miners, 199-200
Whigs, 36, 38, 44, 45, 49, 68, 79, 81, 83, 87, 93, 113, 127
Whittier, John Greenleaf, 162
Williams, Archbishop John Joseph, 162
Williams, William Appleman, 23
Wilmot, David, 84-85, 92
Wilmot, Proviso, 43, 81, 83-85

Wilson, Henry, 417
Wolfe Tone Club of Washington, 150
Woodward, C. Vann, 22, 123
Workingman's Advocate (newspaper), 59, 61
Workingman's party, 61
Workingmen's Benevolent Association, 171-72
Worth, Jonathan, 121
Wright, Hendrick B., 172
Wyndham Land Act (1903), 197

Young, James, 38-39

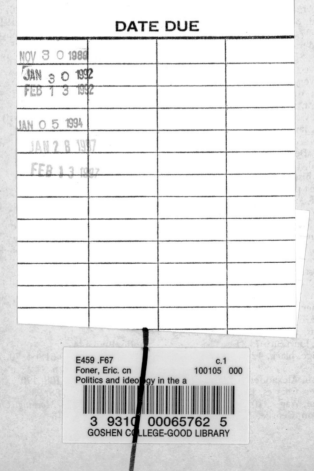